CONVULSING BODIES

CONVULSING BODIES

RELIGION AND RESISTANCE IN FOUCAULT

MARK D. JORDAN

STANFORD UNIVERSITY PRESS

STANFORD, CALIFORNIA

Stanford University Press
Stanford, California

© 2015 Mark D. Jordan. All rights reserved.

An earlier version of some portions of Chapter 4 appeared as "Foucault's Ironies and the Important Earnestness of Theory," *Foucault Studies*, no. 14 (September 2012): 7–19.

Printed in the United States of America on acid-free, archival-quality paper

Library of Congress Cataloging-in-Publication Data

Jordan, Mark D., author.
 Convulsing bodies : religion and resistance in Foucault / Mark D. Jordan.
   pages cm
 Includes bibliographical references and index.
 ISBN 978-0-8047-8902-8 (cloth : alk. paper) —
 ISBN 978-0-8047-9276-9 (pbk. : alk. paper)
 1. Foucault, Michel, 1926-1984—Religion. 2. Human body (Philosophy) I. Title.
 B2430.F724J67 2014
 194—dc23

 ISBN 0-8047-9280-6 (electronic)

Typeset by Bruce Lundquist in 10/14 Palatino

CONTENTS

Introduction:
Embodied Reading, *or* The Masked Philosopher   1

1   Hunter of the Sacred   13

2   The Dismembered Assassin and the
Well-Scrubbed Delinquents   41

3   The Buffoon-King and the Possessed Nuns   63

4   Chatting Genitals   93

5   The Sobbing Matron and the Loquacious Monk   119

6   The Artist of Pleasures   143

7   The Violated Mother and the Naked Philosopher   169

Conclusion:
Embodied Writing, *or* Among the Mourners   193

Acknowledgments   201

Notes   203

Bibliography   229

Index   239

CONVULSING BODIES

EMBODIED READING, *OR* THE MASKED PHILOSOPHER

READING TAKES TIME. Its passing often leaves traces—in marginal scribbles, in typed outlines, in proud commentaries on collected works. Some traces are evidently grander than others. Some even pretend to be analytic geometries within spheres of pure thought. For all that, they are still traces of a body's time spent.

Reading, no matter how cumulative, occupies different times. I began to read books by Foucault more than thirty-five years ago. I started to record this reading on a warm Cambridge Saturday in June 2011. I finished recording about two years later in San Francisco. The traces would have been different if I had recorded them over another interval.

A reader moves through texts in segments of bodily life. Reading falls among other episodes—accomplishments, boredoms, traumas. It calls on other readings already done or set aside. Before starting through Foucault this time, I had studied more of Nietzsche, Bataille, Klossowski, Blanchot—whom I have come to count as Foucault's teachers of writing. I took up novels that Foucault cited or that he professed in conversation to admire. I listened to music that taught him form, including music by one of his lovers. But I followed as well my own associations to Henry James, Guy Davenport after Fourier, Marguerite Yourcenar on Piranesi.

Before writing down this record of a reading, I "came out" as a gay man, fell away from Christian community, and returned to it. I spent most sunsets of a July watching fog over Kite Hill in San Francisco. I held men as they died from the "complications" of the unnamable virus that killed Foucault. I lived beyond the age at which he died.

Which of these moments determined how I read him now? Which kind of story best tells my life as a reader or Foucault's as a writer? Does context for his writing consist of academic appointments, conferences, copulations, bitter losses, half-remembered dreams, or impressions of fugitive sunlight? I couldn't say. I suspect that the demand to choose already distracts attention from reading—already supplants its record with something more like a fan's collection of souvenirs.

■

Some scholars, like some fans, end by substituting relics of a fetishized life for the work. Perhaps they were first impassioned by the work or by rumors of it. Then it slipped out of reach. Their fandom demanded more reliable contact. So they began slighting the work to seize tokens of its maker. For old-school Hollywood fans, these were autographs and photo spreads. Scholarly fans of this species prefer journalistic interviews, dedicated blogs, tales of conference sightings, and thick biographies—properly "theorized."

I can't join their passionate collecting. I know that some biographical reports help reading; that interviews or occasional pieces can illuminate more elaborate works; that archived papers do yield secrets worth knowing. I envy some friends their mastery of the Foucault archives and their queer love for his life, a love fully alert to the abuses of biography and his distaste for it.[1] But I keep remembering a story by Henry James, "The Death of the Lion."

In it, an occasional journalist—an academic manqué—arrives to do a feature on a novelist whom he admires. Charmed by the man's innocent privacy, he abandons the assignment in order to pen an earnest appreciation of the latest novel. (You can predict his harried editor's reaction.) Just then the novelist is catapulted into unexpected fame. The reformed journalist's abiding admiration impels him to become a sort of protector. When a young woman clutching a borrowed autograph book shows up to lay eyes on the new celebrity, this volunteer gatekeeper persuades her that truer fandom would refuse any meeting in order to attach itself more intimately to the work. "When you encounter a genius as fine as this idol of ours," he pleads with her, "let him off the dreary duty of being a personality as well. Know him only by what's best in him, and spare him for the same sweet sake. . . . He's badgered, bothered, overwhelmed, on the pretext of being applauded."[2] The woman agrees. As befits a romantic comedy wrapped around an authorial tragedy, she marries the journalist-become-protector after the novelist is indeed badgered to a premature death.

James's plea for closeting authors is, of course, the reproach of one fandom against another. Some fandom supplements words with tokens of bodies and representations of their circumstances. Other fandom wants the author's body for its words. Fans fight over the kinds of bodily contacts. The protective couple also raises up the novelist as an "idol." Since their idolatry attaches to his texts, they fight together to safeguard his energy for producing them or, once that battle is lost, to preserve what he has written. They are not interested in joining him at a country house so as to brag of it afterward. They do not want breezy accounts of his "surroundings," "his study, his literary sanctum, the little things he has about, or other domestic objects or features."[3] They want his texts. They spend years searching for one, his last, which was casually mislaid by a fan of the other sort.

When it comes to Foucault, I am that young woman. I skimmed the biographies, examined some photographs, heard or watched a few recordings, but I got little satisfaction from them. So I have put down my autograph book. My pleasure in Foucault's body comes from reading what it wrote. I am lured not by his bodily life but by whatever lured him to write endlessly about the bodily production of our words for bodies.

■

You may already suspect me of setting a trap. First I insist on the particular time of reading and the physical traces it leaves behind. Then I reject as lesser fandom the pursuit of biographical stories and material relics.

This is not a trap so much as a riddle—one of the most persistent in Foucault. He sees, as much as any literary fan, that writing comes out of a living body. He exerts himself to write about bodies. But he also sees the dangers of most writing about embodied lives. The forms of power under which many of us now live count on capturing bodies in approved records, not least by training bodies to speak themselves though set scripts. Thoroughly modern power, as Foucault describes it, is a literature of reduction. Even older powers, like influential codes of religious ethics, express an extraordinary compositional wish to prescribe life in detail and then to describe it for the sake of judgment at the scale of an eternal fate. How to write embodied life responsibly, how to have bio-graphy that is not the shorthand of power? That is a question Foucault pursued over decades by writing. The force of the question is lost whenever *his* biography is treated as self-evident.

I go further. If we have heard academic chat about Foucault, we have probably heard that he taught the "death of the author." How often do we also hear the self-contradiction in that claim? Or how often do readers of Foucault let the texts assigned to his name float free of the control of the author function they have projected for him?[4] My reader's fandom is so severe that I can almost dispense with the fiction of a continuing author in order to attach myself to particular works. "The admiration devoted to an author, even if it holds nothing back, is regularly compatible with a complete indifference to the announcement of the publication of a new book by him."[5]

That is the chill in James's story: the young couple's devotion to their author is, of course, not to him at all. They need his bodily person only for what it writes. If they mourn him, they regret especially that there will be no more of his books—though, really, who can be sure that further volumes coming from that body would have been as reliably pleasurable?

■

Unlike James's beleaguered novelist, Foucault knew how to play to his fans and to play with them. He performed—atrocious pun—many fan dances for them. Though it would be more precise (and less atrocious) to say that he fashioned ephemeral masks through which to elude his academic fans—especially when they set out to tag him for their collections of cultured specimens.

There is no better example of Foucault's fan play than one of his inversions of the celebrity interview. In its edition of April 6–7, 1980, *Le monde—dimanche* published as part of a long-running series an interview by Christian Delacampagne. Few casual readers could have known that it was an interview of Foucault, since he declined to name himself. The interview was published under the title "The Masked Philosopher." Indeed, Foucault's association with the interview became widely known only after his death, when it was reprinted under his name in an anthology of the newspaper series.[6]

Foucault labored long over his responses. He helped the interviewer rephrase the questions. So he played hard with his fans—with their notion of the celebrity interview, of course, but also with their expectations for reporting thought. Some might want to see Foucault's insistence on anonymity as a second-order vanity, a contrivance for luring more attention. But the image of the "masked philosopher" has Nietzsche's considerable authority behind it: the interview is a philosophic tableau, not a trick of narcissism.[7] Since Foucault's insistence on anonymity should still be respected, I will refer to the interview subject only (or emblematically) as the Philosopher.[8]

The interview begins with a question about the choice for masking, understood as anonymity rather than embellishment or enticement. The Philosopher replies with an anecdote meant to expose the fixation on academic celebrity. As the Philosopher tells it, some (presumably European) psychologists arrive at an African village to perform an experiment. They screen a film about three characters, then ask the local viewers to recount it. But—so the anecdote goes—the villagers are interested only in the play of shadow and light through the trees. This is apparently not a filmed record of shadow and light but the shadow and light cast by the projected film onto the landscape nearby. Not a represented light in the film but the unintended effects of the film's projection.

The Philosopher draws the contrast: "With us, characters [*personnages*] fix the law of perception. Our eyes prefer to be carried to the figures that go and come, arise and disappear." The Philosopher turns this far-reaching explanation into a caution about how some fandom forsakes writings in favor of publicized characters. "Why did I suggest to you that we use anonymity? From nostalgia for the time when, being quite unknown, what I said had some chance of being heard. The surface of contact had no ripple with the eventual [*éventuel*] reader. The effects of the book might splash up in unexpected places and trace shapes that I had never thought of."[9]

"With us, characters fix the law of perception." This tells how "we" see stories—stories about texts and authors, but also stories about what is called intellectual or institutional history. Appreciate, then, the disruption caused by anonymity. For a Philosopher to appear as anonymous—or to refuse appearance behind the mask of anonymity—deprives the reader not only of this character's name but of its place on authoritative maps or its role in established plots. Anonymity refuses the comforts of theoretical system or social typecasting. If an author has no name, she or he or they have no dossier, no ID card, no assigned rank in the hierarchy of sciences, no predetermined "subject position."[10] An anonymous author cannot be a satisfying target for most fandom, cannot be always known in advance.

The Philosopher's deliberate frustration of the fan's passion means to direct passionate attachment to textual effects. You should desire contact, the masked voice implies, not with the sensational life or fetishized body of the author but with the surface of the text—a surface best pictured as liquid, mobile, trembling with ripples. A text supplies not the solid grip of a hand on a celebrated body but the fugitive caress of shimmering surface—another Nietzschean image.[11]

The anonymous speaker in this anti-interview imagines a relationship between a text and a reader-to-come, a relationship that is a contingent event of meeting. The "eventual reader" is the reader who encounters the text as an event yet to arrive. (The writer named Michel Foucault sometimes describes this encounter as an embodiment: a book is a tiny event that leads at once to an infinite game of repetitions or doublings or impalpable incarnations.)[12] From that scene of meeting, surprising effects may follow—so long as they are not precluded by discounting in advance what a text may say or do.

Imagine an authorship that forswears fame in order to attend only to the transient effects of its textual surfaces. That strives only to register ripples on a skittish surface.[13] That strives to *be* ripples, undoing its own propensity to become a closed object. Imagine writing that is more interested in the play of its light and shadow than in plots and personages—or that uses its own plots and personages to project light into unfamiliar landscapes, on unintended readers. Imagine above all a writing that doesn't secure its unity or its relations to bodies by appealing to the *personnage* of the Author.

■

The interviewer (the other mask) presses again on the choice of anonymity. Does it mean to condemn contemporary philosophers' hunger for publicity? Not at all, the Philosopher answers. The problem is not new. If the unmasked faces of philosophers now appear in the media (at least in France), they used to appear, crowned with laurels, as hallway busts in preparatory schools. The problem arises not from the conditions of contemporary media but from misleading assumptions about authorship. "Really I'm very touched by a letter that Kant wrote when he was already quite old: he was hurrying, he says, . . . to finish one of his books for the Leipzig Fair. I repeat this to show that it doesn't have any importance. Publicity or no publicity, fair or no fair, the book is something else." The Philosopher is not concerned with publicity—or profitable publishing—but with an address to the reader: "the eventual reader, the only character here who interests me." The voice from behind the mask professes no interest in the interviewer, the marketer, or the consumer who demands clichés pinned to a recognizable name. But then, it seems, the Philosopher also has no interest in the author—not in old Kant, after all, except sentimentally. Nor any interest in self—in the nameless speaker being interviewed as an author. Her or his or their only declared interest is in the event of reading, especially reading that becomes writing.[14]

The Philosopher's allusions to Nietzsche marks this transition. He cannot speak without quoting and so transmuting text. His reading prepares for his writing.

■

Nietzsche associates masks with representations of divinity. *Beyond Good and Evil* begins by observing that every great teaching must inscribe itself with a frightening grimace, often called "religion." The book ends by showing that only gods do not need masks. They rely on their golden nakedness for concealment.[15] If the mask is an instrument of anonymity, it is also an implement for theater and ritual. The Masked Philosopher speaks at once as dramatic actor and high priest—as two kinds of actor. The mask itself, like a text, has a kind of immortality. It is the frozen figure of the author who doesn't die.

■

Behind the mask of this interview sits Foucault—or, rather, "Foucault." That is the name attached to a man whom I have not known except as an author. It is the name of an author who has mattered to me because of my passion for particular texts. He is my projection in at least two ways. I have doubtless fashioned my image of him out of my desires, fears, and discoveries. But I have also endowed him with the unity of my episodes of reading. "Foucault" is the name of my companion (and adversary) on transits through some texts that share, among other things, the circumstance of having that name imprinted on their title page. I use that name as a cipher for the projected source of my textual passions.

I'm drawn to this Foucault's repeated contacts with religion and especially with Christianity. Those contacts are a central part of my textual attraction. But I have no plans to claim Foucault for religion, much less for Christianity—whatever exactly it means to talk without specification of "religion" or even "Christianity." For me, there is no formulable essence of religion, no clear way of separating its words from the rest of human speech. (The claim that religion can be neatly bounded is a corollary of atheism, while the denial of God's existence can be the highest pitch of theology.) Nor am I satisfied with simple judgments about who belongs inside Christianity and who doesn't. (According to old versions of Christianity, such judgments are impossible for human beings and pretending to them is sinful.) I don't mean to (re)baptize Foucault. As a passionate reader of his texts, I insist only that others not skip over what he writes about gods and their devotees.

■

A reader looking for religion in Foucault may indeed look to explicit treatments of Christianity. A first reading of Foucault's major works from the 1970s and 1980s will discover that Christianity appears in them both frequently and prominently. But Foucault also engages with the religious elsewhere in his writing, especially when he tries to register bodies that elude or excite speech by resisting it. Even his explicit discussions of Christianity are much less concerned to present or correct some narrative history than they are to examine it as an insistent example of speech with power over bodies. So if Foucault is interested in details of Christian doctrine, law, and ritual, he attends most to the forces that move through Christian speech and then after it. He appreciates Christianity as a succession of forms of power, but even more as a library of genres for speech and the figures they project.

Taught by Nietzsche, Foucault takes up Christianity as a rhetorical provocation. He responds to it in various ways. Sometimes he is a sympathetic exegete and unlikely defender. Then he is a formal analyst or structural engineer. He will notice the appropriation of Christianity's rhetorical forms by its angriest critics; he will let his own texts imitate the Christian speeches he describes. He is a gifted mimic of Christian voices. He will say at one moment that the form of his language is "profoundly anti-Christian," then proceed to testify at length to a double "conversion" that enabled him to write or else declare that his daily writing practice is both absolution and benediction.[16] None of these responses makes him a tacit Christian. Their combination does suggest that he has unusual sensibilities for religious rhetoric and that he is never unaware of the effects on bodies of the religious texts he reads.

Readers underestimate the importance of religious topics when they look only for what Foucault says about religion. "Religion" is not a category that Foucault relies on for his most important writing. He often just assumes its usual meanings. He neither projects a fixed essence behind the term nor uses it with a single valuation. For him, Christianity is a religion or a series of religions.[17] So are the ancient civic cults and mysteries. But so too, by analogy, is modern psychiatry. Foucault's thinking about what we ordinarily call "religion" moves through other notions: most frequently ritual but also ceremony or liturgy, doctrine or dogma, myth or scripture. None of these terms is separated from the supposedly secular. Foucault's inquiry presupposes that religion arises from and issues in fields of forces inseparable from the rest of human history. What distinguishes it is not some rigid connection with an already separate realm of special entities. Religion is distinguished instead by how it arranges languages and practices—teachings and rituals—to control this world and the bodies very much in it.

Even so, Foucault does not entirely absorb gods and their rites into the everyday. Some elements typically called "religious" persist in his writing as boundary markers for moments of unexpected fracture and unlikely transformation. He sometimes uses the more potent notion of "the divine" or "the sacred [*le sacré*]." The latter term has a significant history in various modern debates but also in recent writers whom Foucault engages. In some of them, notably Durkheim, the sacred is definitionally (if ambivalently) opposed to the profane. In others of these writers, notably Dumézil, it is wrapped from the first around articulations of social sovereignty. Foucault is interested in some religions because of their salience in the genealogy of contemporary forms of power, but he is also drawn to human bodies that delimit power by scrambling language when they speak about the sacred or to it. Bodies are shaped by religious powers, and bodies use religious discourses or practices to resist powers. In the fugitive gaps between controlling words and bodies convulsed by pain or ecstasy, Foucault discovers moments of resistance.

Religious speeches and rituals have in Foucault an unusual intimacy with bodily speech—speeches about bodies, speeches uttered by bodies. When he approaches the joint (tendon, membrane) at which speech enters into skin or issues from it, he often reverts to religious terms or examples, to ritual analogies or instances. He does so especially when there is a question of what cannot be spoken. Religion tries to regulate how bodies sound. That sound—Foucault wants above all to hear that sound, in the moment when it refuses to become speech.

■

Here I aim to record my latest, my last fandom as a reader of Foucault texts. I don't want to replace them with paraphrase, much less to make a scrapbook in which I copy out passages next to commentary from the quarterlies or pictures clipped from magazines. I record my reading only of some texts—not all that bear the name "Foucault" but many of them. (Readers whose encounter with Foucault began and ended with *The Order of Things* or *The Archeology of Knowledge* may be surprised at how rarely these two appear.) I take the texts I do read mostly in chronological order, only to simplify the exposition of cross-references and to appreciate some variations. I attend to the texts as distinct compositions, according to their various forms. For my fandom, the objects of liveliest interest are works, not theses or theories. Academic vices being as strong as they are, I repeat in a louder voice: This is *not* a comprehensive or systematic survey of the development of Foucault's ideas on religion.[18] I wish only to stand in front of a selection of Foucault's texts, pointing here and there in admiration. I want to bring some of his characters back onstage in their garish masks. I want to applaud Foucault among them—the old busker.

This is my Foucault reading diary. Beginning in June 2011 from a celebrity interview that was not a celebrity interview, with a masked man who died exactly twenty-seven years before, whose works still wait on events to assume bodies.

CHAPTER 1

HUNTER OF THE SACRED

THE BOOK THAT BEGAN TO TRANSFORM Michel Foucault into "Foucault" is about the sounds of missing bodies. On its surface, the *History of Madness* (rather, *Folly and Unreason*) tells a story about the rise of the modern category of insanity and its institution (in the chilling singular).[1] Two events "signal" the underlying historical change with "a singular clarity." The first is the founding of the "General Hospital" (1657) and the "great confinement" of the poor. The second is the freeing of chained inmates at one unit of that hospital, the Bicêtre, in 1794.[2] Foucault will restage these apparently opposed tableaux, a confinement and a (supposed) liberation, into a single plot: the coalescing of "a great, immobile structure" of new power. But his first famous book wants even more to tell the exclusion of the "mad" from the earshot of "reasonable" people. Reason usually prefers not to see the antics of the insane, but it likes even less to hear their disconcerting speech—to consider it *as* speech. Or to remember that madness used to be accounted a divine visitation.

In the years immediately after publishing *History of Madness*, Foucault wrote a number of texts that are typically lumped together as literary. Indeed, much of his work from the 1960s is ascribed to a "literary period," as to a phase or a temporary "illusion."[3] It is not always clear whether the reference is to Foucault's style, the objects of his interest, or his professional identity. "Literary" does clearly mean to distinguish this writing from what comes after it. Foucault is supposed to have moved on to something more satisfying—at least for some readers with other identifications.

I don't share the relief at Foucault's near escape from literature. For me, the essays from the 1960s carry forward the most interesting efforts of *History of Madness*, the passages in which Foucault strains to represent bodily speech that refuses the superintendence of Reason. But his essays after the thick dissertation-book do more than that. (He is an author who can do several things at once.) In the essays, as in the book, Foucault pursues the connection of madness to the modern category of literature.[4] He also explores the border supposed to divide literature from philosophy. He sets and then studies a canon of authors who move back and forth across it. He tracks their pursuit of "the sacred" as it retreats beyond the edge of language or reason, through the empty space left by the flight of European gods or God. The study of the canon and the pursuit of the sacred are intimately connected. Throughout *History of Madness*, Foucault returns to a list of writers or artists whose passions place them outside reasonable language or thought. The canon includes Hölderlin, Nerval, Van Gogh, Nietzsche, and Artaud. Foucault associates these figures with the collapse of speech in a coincidence of cosmic opposites, but also with forgotten ceremonies, acts of blasphemy, and strange apostleship.[5]

After publishing *History of Madness*, Foucault doesn't write directly about the figures of this mad canon. He does treat three figures that he regularly names together: Georges Bataille, Pierre Klossowski, Maurice Blanchot. Years later, in a public conversation, one of his longtime readers will say to Foucault that these three are like a "magic constellation" glittering over his works. If timidity prevents him from acknowledging the extent of his debt to them, Foucault will reply, it also holds him back from inscribing his own work "under the sign, under the epigraph of their names as one protects oneself by some divinity."[6] His relationship to the three is ambivalent in the way a creative debt must be. Through them lies what Foucault accounts a greater debt, to Nietzsche. Two of the three—Bataille and Klossowski—are famous readers of Nietzsche. Another acquaintance remembers Foucault a decade earlier saying that he wouldn't dream of writing on Nietzsche because he admired him too much. Writing about these three is a way to overcome that anxiety too.[7]

Foucault writes about three predecessors in order to discharge debts while finding his own compositional form. His essays are experiments in a kind of formal study that is neither dominant nor submissive, neither a reduction nor a transcription. Understanding the experiments requires attention to their details. So I choose just the main appreciations that Foucault wrote about his three predecessors during the 1960s.[8] The first, on Bataille, was published in *Critique*. The journal had been founded in 1946 by Bataille himself—one of a series of publishing projects. Foucault joined its editorial board in 1962. His essay, "Preface to Transgression," appeared the very next year in a volume dedicated to Bataille's memory. The second study, of Pierre Klossowski, was published during 1964 in the *Nouvelle revue française*, that organ of modern French letters. The final piece, on Blanchot, came out in a 1966 issue of *Critique*. I read these three experiments in form against the desires Foucault declares at the start of *History of Madness*.

LISTENING FOR LOST VOICES

The original preface to *History of Madness* opens with two quotations. They are not set off as epigraphs. They fall within Foucault's text, and they appear without precise citation. One comes from Pascal; the other, from Dostoyevsky. The quotations are supposed to be familiar: "this other text from Dostoyevsky," Foucault says, as if he were pointing to it in a commonplace book or picking up an index card from a shared table. Foucault takes from Pascal the notion of a turn or trick of madness that is entangled with reason; from Dostoyevsky, the image of futile confinement. Foucault writes: "One must make the history of this other turn of madness—of this other turn by which men, in the gesture of sovereign reason that encloses their neighbor, communicate with and recognize each other through the merciless language of non-madness."[9]

To do the history, Foucault must describe a moment before the distinction between Reason and Madness is safely settled within "the reign of truth" and then reinforced by "the lyricism of protestation." Foucault wants to enter into "this zero degree of the history madness" when it is still "undifferentiated experience." He wants to narrate, from its first moments, the progress of this other turn, which ends by partitioning Reason and Madness into two separate spaces, rendering them "deaf to every exchange."[10] The turn is both a ruse and a feat. By it a sovereign power speaks more articulately over the concealment of what it opposes. The madman is enclosed so that other neighbors may communicate in order to pronounce one another perfectly reasonable.

Writing this history, Foucault longs to recover a rustic dawn-language that once registered a dialogue between Reason and Madness or, rather, their confused inseparability. Foucault strains to imagine that lost language, its "imperfect words, without fixed syntax, slightly stammering." Failing that, he at least refuses to ratify the victory of that other language, the psychiatric monologue, over an enforced silence of the mad. "I have not wanted to make the history of this [clinical] language; rather the archeology of this silence."[11]

The history of the lost language in which Reason and Madness might accomplish an awkward exchange cannot be written as standard history. It can only be an episodic account of cultural "limits," of the cultural processes for marking what must be kept outside. The (modern European) culture that results is defined by its exclusions, by "this hollowed emptiness, this white space." Here culture makes "essential choices": "it makes the division [*partage*] that gives it the face of its positivity."[12] Foucault will bring the reader back to that word *partage*, but he already links it here with a face—or a figure, a mask, a personification.

What is this madness that must be excluded (tragically) in order to constitute our culture, the modern West? It is nothing else, Foucault replies at once, than "*the absence of oeuvre.*" Foucault will say more elsewhere about this controversial phrase, but here he speaks of the exclusion from reason's history of any writing by the mad. They are excluded because history silences whatever doesn't fit within its sequels. "History is only possible on the basis of an absence of history, in the middle of this great space of murmurs."[13] This space is at once the possibility of increasingly articulate history and its occluded origin: "last residue, sterile beach of words, sand traversed and immediately forgotten, not preserving, in its passivity, anything but the empty imprint of the removed figures." (Foucault favors this image of the erased beach on which words and figures were once incised. He will use it in a few years at the melodramatic conclusion of his second famous book.) "The fullness of history is not possible except in the space, at once empty and peopled, of all the words without language that give understanding to the one who lends an ear to the deaf noise from beneath history, the stubborn murmur of language that speaks *by itself*."[14]

A refusal to hear this language goes along with the refusal to treat certain kinds of gestures or acts as a work or to allow certain figures to take a place in history. "One must offer the ear, bend down to the muttering of the world, try to perceive so many images that have never been poetry." Bend down, like a hunter, to hear sound vibrating through earth. Of course, the task implied by the metaphor is doubly impossible: it would require the reconstitution of what has been reduced to dry dust; it would forget that this mumbling exists—for itself, for others—only through the separation imposed by reason. Foucault cannot experience unconfined madness. He can only study what holds it captive. Doing so, he always seeks the original exclusion, the separation of reason's language or history's bright promises from "this murmur of somber insects."[15]

A little later in the preface, Foucault explains that he has gone directly to the surviving archives because he wants to hear not the psychiatric versions of an official truth but "these words, these texts that come from underneath language. . . . And perhaps to my eyes the most important part of this work is the place that I have left to the very text of the archives."[16] Note again what is singular and what plural: the *text* of the archives, as if a single scroll of words had been cut up and scattered among registries, records offices, libraries. But note as well the ideal of transcription, of writing again already written voices at their dictation. Voices, not bodies: the archive is not a morgue or mausoleum. It holds words about bodies, not the bodies themselves. But the tongues behind those words draw Foucault.

To present these voices requires a language that will not betray or silence whatever archives can still speak. Foucault must write the text "in a language without support," a language that puts itself into play. This "simple problem of elocution" (an irony) is his chief compositional challenge: to find a language neutral enough to lure the exiled words of madness while still registering the scientific judgments by which they are excluded. Foucault's text wants to take on some of the function of the dawn-language of lost exchange. So it follows a single rule, proposed in the testimony of a poet, René Char: "I withdraw from things the illusion that they produce to preserve themselves from us, and I leave them the part that they concede to us."[17] This is like lifting a mask to permit deeper masking—or else recognizing the paradox in authoring the record of an authorless murmur. In later colloquia and interviews, in the endless back and forth of academic quarreling, Foucault will say a number of other things about how and why he wrote *History of Madness*. Yet here, in the original preface, he quotes a poetic rule from Char. A reader can reject Foucault's refusal to justify his method or even to describe it properly, but a careful reader won't simply ignore this poetic rule while inserting another method on Foucault's behalf.

Foucault supplies the citation to Char in a footnote. The rule comes from a short prose piece, "Suzerain," which recounts a friendship through which the speaker sought the language for a crepuscular past, like the dim dawn before the separation of Reason from Madness. For a time, the piercing friendship evoked by Char guarded itself with silence as it crossed seascapes beneath words. But the sentence that Foucault quotes falls in a paragraph that ends in disenchanted solitude. The sentence is not an abstract precept of method; it is the stage of a journey that extends beyond the end of Char's short text. There is more: this is not the first hint at Char in the preface nor the first time Foucault has used Char to authorize a book.[18]

The last paragraph of the original preface to *History of Madness* is an unattributed quotation. It exhorts "pathos-companions"—companions of and in a curious suffering—to cultivate the "legitimate strangeness" that will allow them to hear the "new mystery" that sings in their bones. This is also a quotation from Char. It comes from "Partage formel," "Formal Partition" (on the clumsiest translation), which is a program in aphorisms.[19]

"Formal Partition": Char's title permits Foucault a significant pun. He uses *partage* throughout the preface to describe the division between Reason and Madness. He and Char both play on the word's doubleness. Like the English "share," *partage* means a division within a whole, a separation that supposes a prior unity. In Char, the *partage* is formal. So too in Foucault: Reason divides for the sake of form itself, in order to make forms. It also divides by forming—by enclosing, constructing, instituting. A formal division is the original condition for Reason's singular voice.

Char writes a poetic manifesto—or, rather, given his estrangement from the surrealists, an antimanifesto. Its numbered fragments propose a hermetic teaching on the sources, powers, and prospects for poetry. Poetry is taken to be self-evidently synonymous with truth. So it is not surprising that Char twice invokes Heraclitus, figure of the pre-Socratic fusion of wisdom and enigmatic utterance. With Heraclitus, Char's language recalls at many points the language of revelation or ritual. There are initiates, lustrations, creators skimming over deeps, miracles, transcendent essences, and the execution of heretics. Indeed, the poet is inhabited by "powerful and fantastic gods" who give law and demand exegesis. All of this echoes in Foucault. The action that Foucault performs in bending down to hear the murmurs is a direct response to a command in Char: "The poet recommends: 'Bend down, bend down further.'"[20] To the page of poetry. To the archival document not yet recognized as poetry. To the murmurs of the silenced mad. To the echoes of retreating gods.

Many readers, most famously Jacques Derrida, have found Foucault's original preface to *History of Madness* unconvincing.[21] Foucault himself wrote a new preface for the retitled edition of the book a decade later, devouring his authorship.[22] I cling to the original preface for several reasons. To me, it is both moving and beautiful. It testifies to desires that Foucault never renounces. It is also the overture to Foucault's writing on the hunt for something sacred.

ON BATAILLE: TRANSGRESSIVE SEEKING

When I turn from Foucault's first famous book to the essays on his trio of predecessors, I don't follow a single itinerary. If madness makes its turns (according to Pascal), Foucault makes his. The three essays are not points on a single line. They may not even suggest the circumference of a circle. They are distinct stylistic responses to the sacred, so they pose separate challenges to Foucault's own writing.

Foucault's memorial to Bataille is a palimpsest of a predecessor's terminologies, genres, structures, and erotic plots. Foucault often writes by intimate mimesis, merging his voice with another's.[23] Here he rehearses Bataille's technical terms as if they were his own. Sometimes he italicizes them: *interior, sovereign, inner experience, extreme of the possible, comic operation,* even *meditation.* At other times he arranges the terms in clarifying patterns: sacrifice, ecstasy, and communication appear as modes of a single cultural operation. But Foucault also pretends that Bataille's words are so familiar that they can be quoted without citation, as if from memory. The essay's original version contains no footnotes. So, from beginning to end, Foucault speaks about Bataille's central preoccupation, experience, without quotation marks and in a variety of contexts: the experience of sexuality, of transgression, of contestation; sovereign experiences, experiences essential to a culture, experience that has lost language. These phrases are not quotations. They are reenactments or, better, performed variations.

Foucault revivifies Bataille's images and symbols. He quotes passages that speak of the immense and silent sky; of crushing, endless night, pierced sometimes by a cry or a laugh, by stellar apparitions and ghostly lights, or by nothing. Foucault's readers overhear Bataille narrate stupor and drunkenness, describe copulating bodies that become earth, evoke the desperate heart and the monstrous eye.[24] Foucault fuses these images with his own imagination of power. In this memorial preface, he represents Bataille chiefly through spaces: the empty space of thin limits; the cultural space in which "we" act and speak; the space in which the sacred plays, appears, vanishes. The reader hears at once a representation of Bataille and a reiteration of the guiding image of exclusion from Foucault's *History of Madness.* The verbal echoes between the preface to transgression and the original preface to *History of Madness* are so strong that Foucault seems to swallow Bataille into his recent book—or else to inscribe his completed book within the corpus (the written body) of Bataille.

Foucault's imitation of Bataille moves up from terms and images to other textual elements. The essay's genre is indebted to Bataille's habit of composing prefaces to his own works. For *Madame Edwarda,* Bataille drafted multiple prefaces, finally settling on one that distinguished him from "Pierre Angélique," the novel's pseudonymous author and protagonist. For *L'Abbé C,* Bataille supplied an unsigned narrative preface that explains the finding of the manuscript for the rest of the book.[25] And so on. Foucault locates these prefatory devices among Bataille's strategies for scattering his authorial subject. They go along with other techniques that put distance between thinking and writing—techniques like the alternation of fiction and reflection, the twisting of compositional time, or deliberate oppositions between speech and speaker. So too Foucault's "Preface" means not so much to provide easy access as to prepare for the effect of Bataille's writing. Foucault doesn't summarize the meaning of texts; he studies their evocation of an experience. His essay is, after all, a "Preface to Transgression." For "us"—for Bataille, Foucault, their readers—transgression "prescribes not only the sole manner of finding the sacred in its immediate content but of recomposing it in its empty form, in its absence thus rendered brilliant."[26] This is a preface to hunting the sacred through writing its absence.

The structure of Foucault's essay resembles Bataille's fragmentary discursiveness in *Inner Experience* more than his own schemas. If Foucault often composes in dense outlines, this essay retraces the "detours and returns" that it discovers in Bataille's corpus, walks the "labyrinth" that it finds there. The essay has a deliberately circular structure, both topically and narratively.[27] It is divided topically into five sections, each of which views Bataille's transgression from a different angle. Each section ends by pointing to the one that follows, so that the reader is directed to gaze both at the central tableau and at the circuit that delimits it.

Section 1

"Our" contemporary discourse about sexuality is directly linked to the proclamation of the death of God. That Absence opens the empty space in which sexuality becomes a thin limit. It is the limit for conscience or consciousness, since sexuality is the meaning of the *un*conscious; for law, since incest is the only universal prohibition; for language, since desire and its consummation fall into silence. Bataille reveals not only the intrinsic connection between our speech about sexuality and our proclamation of the death of God but the very meaning of our having killed God. Indeed, Bataille means by eroticism "an experience of sexuality that in itself links the surpassing of the limit to the death of God." Beneath both the new language of sexuality and the old Western languages of God there stands the "singular experience": transgression. We do not yet have the language for it. In Bataille's writing, Foucault adds in a final couplet, we have only "the charred stump, the promising cinder."[28] (This is a coded reference to a particular ritual, as will soon become clear.)

Section 2

Limit and transgression imply one another. They are united necessarily in the violent instant of the crossing. Foucault situates Bataille's thought of transgression after Western philosophy's long preoccupation with contradiction. He connects it to Blanchot's notion of contestation: both gesture toward an experience that puts everything in question, but not by mere denial. Transgression is "the solar reverse of satanic negation; it has a part linked to the divine [le divin], or rather it opens, from the limit that indicates the sacred [le sacré], the space where the divine can happen." Western philosophy has led to this point and turned away from it—until Nietzsche, whose narratives gesture toward this language-after-contradiction, beyond dialectic. Philosophy's return to discursive language after Nietzsche refuses what he accomplished. Only the writers of extreme language—Bataille, Blanchot, Klossowski—now show transgression, and mostly through what we call the "erotic." Erotic philosophy takes different forms: against Sade's splicing together of philosophic disquisitions with erotic recitatives, Bataille displays the subject's failure to speak—shows the subject "stretched out on the sand of what it cannot any more say."[29] This speechlessness is condensed in Bataille's famous image of the reversed eye, the eye turned upward or inward by orgasmic ecstasy or death. (Already the limit of speech is linked to convulsion.)

Section 3

Foucault locates the failure of language within another story about Western philosophy. The transit beyond dialectical language is the moment at the end of an epoch—or before it, at the dawn of Greek thinking. Or it is the (repeated?) moment of Zarathustra's arrival.[30] Bataille writes into the void left by the murder of God, in the growing desert of nihilism, but also on the Nietzschean geography peopled by Zarathustra, his shadow, his monkey, a braying donkey, the over-man, Dionysus, Christ. After Nietzsche's collapse on the streets of Turin, uttering a madman's cries, this geography can seem only a place for suffering. The void opened by God's Absence, enacted by the ritual of empty transgression, is the disruptive possibility of the mad philosopher. It requires the further sacrifice of the philosophic speaker. Bataille's writing performs the philosopher's spectacular execution, his *supplice*. His very writing of his experience is inevitably a *supplice*. (What is often decried as the density of Foucault's writing in this essay might be better conceived as the convulsions of discursive language in the moment of its sacrifice.)

Section 4

Foucault describes Bataille's language as boulders, cliff faces, but also as a circle that points back to itself, folds over itself. His language is an eye: a globe of night circling a void that cups both light and emptiness. For Bataille, the eye acts in a transgressive instant. It can be plucked out or turned inside, where it finds not a superior inwardness, not a deeper night, but its prior engagement with death. Foucault quotes a scene from *Bleu du ciel*: as the narrator and Dorothée copulate among tombstones on All Souls, funerary candles are stars; earth is heaven. The plucked or reversed eye is language at the moment when it erupts: "laughter, tears, eyes turned up in ecstasy, the mute and bulging horror of sacrifice."[31] (The revolving eye is the condition of Bataille's writing— and the shape of Foucault's essay: the eye is a labyrinth that convulses inside the second labyrinth of the skull.)

Section 5

"We" have recently discovered gestures that consummate and consume by expense, excess, limit, transgression. The "sky of unreality" under which Sade placed sexuality, its doubled relation to transgression, indicates the impossibility of describing it in dialectical terms. Indeed, sexuality's arrival announces the need for a language beyond contradiction.

> Sexuality is not decisive for our culture except as spoken and in the measure that it is spoken. It is not our language that has been, for at least two centuries, eroticized; it is our sexuality that since Sade and the death of God has been absorbed into the universe of language, denatured by it, placed by it in that emptiness where it establishes its sovereignty and where it ceaselessly poses, as Law, limits that it transgresses.[32]

In the linguistic consequences of that absorption, we encounter both the absence of God and our death. Foucault calls on a passage from

Leiris to liken the space of this encounter in Bataille's writing to "the white beach" of a bullring. He ends with the famous scene at Seville's bullring from *Story of the Eye.*

Foucault's memorial for Bataille is a circle both thematically and metaphorically. It begins and ends with the emptied space in which sex is denatured and absorbed into (circling, failing) language. A circular structure and circular metaphors are entirely appropriate for a work that praises and repeats Bataille's interest in Nietzsche's Zarathustra, prophet of the eternal return. But the structure is also narratively circular so far as it stages a single episode of erotic transgression. Its first and last quotations from Bataille record erotic suspension, then consummation.

The first quotation is from an episode in *L'Abbé C* where the priest, Robert, kneels down before Éponine to recite a penitential psalm. When she wakes from reverie to notice him, she is almost bowled over by laughter, turning to fall against a balustrade. The wind lifts her coat to expose her bare ass—the first thing the priest sees as he raises his eyes heavenward. A transgressive gaze, but also a suspension of erotic action: in this excerpt, he only gazes.

Foucault ends by quoting the scene in which the matador's eye, gored out, becomes by analogy the bull's testicle that Simone inserts beneath her dress. The sky overhead liquefies. The moment brings back the memory of an earlier partner (and victim), but it also completes the suspended touch: "It seemed to me, in that ungraspable instant, to touch her."[33] The "it" is at least the matador's eye, the matador himself, the bull's horn, and perhaps the narrator. There are many allusions here—not least to Nietzsche's *Zarathustra.* That rewriting of the Gospels ends with a scene in which Zarathustra, blinded by a sky turned to doves, reaches out to touch his companion-lion's fur—before he descends the mountain (again) as the Sun. But Foucault's last quotation from Bataille, which displaces his voice by way of conclusion, also consummates the erotic action suspended in the first quotation. The line of the erotic limit is crossed so that it can be crossed again.

■

For Foucault, Bataille's writing recognizes a relocation of the sacred. The recognition occurs not in a theory but in a text that leads to embodied practice while girdling it with necessary silence. Saying this much, Foucault's memorial recalls a project in which the names of Bataille and Klossowski were originally—and ritually—linked. In July 1937, the third issue of the magazine *Acéphale* (Headless) published a short declaration about "sacred sociology." The list of signatories for the declaration differed from the editors and contributors to the magazine, but Bataille and Klossowski appeared on both. Religion was central to *Acéphale*, which carried the subtitle *Religion, Sociology, Philosophy*. Its emblem, drawn repeatedly by André Masson, was a naked, headless man whose entrails were exposed; whose genitals were covered by a skull; who held in one hand flames like a "sacred heart," in the other a sacrificial knife.[34] Inside the front cover, there was a motto in boldfaced capital letters: "We are fiercely religious."

The dramatic declarations and illustrations were gestures against fascist political movements, which the editors saw as false religions. Above the declaration "we are fiercely religious," an aphorism from Kierkegaard: "What has the face of politics and imagines itself to be politics will be unmasked one day as a religious movement." Fascism is the extreme of monocephalic society, in which the single head is a pinnacle of absolute authority represented as divine.[35] Fascism attempts to contain God within the military camp of a single nation. It scavenges older religious traditions, Christian and pagan, to make a church of its nationalized racism.

How to fight the concealed religious energy of fascism? By taking back its supposed sources, such as Nietzsche. By unmasking it as decayed monotheism. But most of all by setting up a counter-community in which religious energies could be deployed against it. The magazine was linked to a secret ritual community that sometimes met by a lightning-scarred oak tree in the forest of Marly—Foucault's "blasted stump."[36] Fantasies swirl still around these transgressive rites, which flirted (so they say) with human sacrifice. Of course, every Christian Eucharist recalls a human sacrifice. Whatever did or didn't happen in the forest rituals, some participants there knew Christianity in its radical implications.

All of this frames that announcement of a more public community in the issue of *Acéphale* for July 1937: "Note about the Founding of a College of Sociology." It begins by regretting how little agreed progress has been made in the study of "social structures." Researchers haven't sufficiently modified their presuppositions and methods in view of their own discoveries. In particular, they have failed to reflect on the resistance that any disclosures of social functioning must encounter. The representations that animate society are necessarily "contagious and *activist*." Exposing them provokes resistance. For the study of social structures to proceed more seriously, it must develop "a moral community" stronger than ordinary scholarly networks, more adept at handling the "virulent character" of social representations. This moral community doesn't demand unanimity of motive from those who want to join. Its sufficient basis is a "preoccupation" with the "more precise knowledge of the essential aspects of social existence." The name for this knowledge is *"sacred sociology*, so far as it implies the study of social existence in all those manifestations in which there comes to light the active presence of the sacred."[37]

The College of Sociology did not convene for long. The founders were split by theoretical disagreements and fits of pique. Still the project of the college can be traced into many later writings of both the founders and their readers. Writing about Bataille and Klossowski on the sacred, Foucault negotiates his own membership in the invisible College. He also measures his distance from it. The imitation of Bataille is a required apprenticeship. Foucault will go on to write otherwise. But it is important for him to remain an alumnus of the long ago College.

ON KLOSSOWSKI: THE PROSE OF DIVINE FLESH

Klossowski may be the College of Sociology's most elusive raconteur. His relation with Bataille was richly ambivalent, and it became more so in the telling. Always evasive about his own itinerary, for philosophical reasons as much as anything, he gave obscure or misleading answers in later interviews. Much earlier, he published and then suppressed a recollection of the religious project of *Acéphale* and the College.[38] This much is clear: The years of Klossowski's closest collaboration with Bataille were also the years leading up to his most intense involvement with ecclesiastical institutions. In the winter of 1939, Klossowski left Paris for Lyon on what would become a pilgrimage through various Roman Catholic religious communities—the Benedictines of Hautecombe, the Dominicans at La Lesse near Chambéry, a community of lay students attached to the Dominicans at Saint-Maximin, two diocesan seminaries, a short stay with the Franciscans.[39] By 1944, he was involved with a Protestant ministry to war refugees and then converted to Lutheranism. In the next year, nostalgic for Catholicism, he abjured that conversion.

Foucault may have known Klossowski's religious biography poorly or in contradictory versions. He is more interested in Klossowski's writing than in any summary of the life. A year after publishing "Preface to Transgression," Foucault made public a similar appreciation of Klossowski. "The Prose of Actaeon" so resembles "Preface to Transgression" that it can seem a simple continuation, the second panel of a diptych (or, with the piece on Blanchot, a triptych). "The Prose of Actaeon" is indeed a continuation, but it allows Foucault to configure the relations of language, divinity, and bodies otherwise than when reading Bataille—opening different possibilities for his own writing. If Foucault pursues the same questions in these two appreciations, he does not write them in the same way. His study of Klossowski is less tightly structured. It proceeds discursively, by association. Its language, while attuned to Klossowski's, also turns away from it. Foucault does not now attempt, as with Bataille, to mimic the narrative arc of the novels. It is as if he hesitates to follow Klossowski's experiments in language even while applauding them. Or perhaps he cannot follow.

"The Prose of Actaeon"—the title must be explained at the end—surveys Klossowski's corpus, from philosophical expositions (not unlike Foucault's own essay) through numerous novels. Foucault deciphers the corpus with the help of *The Bath of Diana*, a short work of idiosyncratic genre. In it, Klossowski restages Ovid's version of the myth in which the hunter Actaeon stumbles upon the goddess Diana bathing in the woods. For his transgression, Actaeon is turned into a stag, with the taunt that he should now speak what he has seen of unclothed divinity. Unable to shape words, Actaeon runs from the goddess's grotto only to be mauled by his own hunting dogs.

On some pages, Klossowski explicates this myth with scholarly devices. On others, he restages it, inventing thoughts and speeches, most especially for the Demon who is imagined as the necessary intermediary for the goddess's incarnation and Actaeon's startled vision.

Klossowski enriches the myth until it carries every doubt about the experience of an embodied divine. Long before Actaeon is changed in a way that makes it impossible for him to speak the divine flesh he has glimpsed, Klossowski's reader has stumbled into the labyrinth of mirrors that encircles the divine body. Foucault knows this, of course, so presents the short work as much more than an antiquarian exegesis. Klossowski wants to recover a way of representing the relation of divinity to sexed human bodies—a way known to the ancients but also to some schools of Christian theology.

Klossowski's writing revives a long-lost experience that was silenced by official Christianity and modern philosophy since Descartes. In it, God and the Devil are not safe opposites but confusing twins. Klossowski finds the confusion in Greco-Roman mythology and in certain discarded forms of Christianity, such as early modern demonology.[40] Retrieving this experience, Klossowski anticipates its fuller return in "our" cultural future. Fastening on return, Foucault applies to Klossowski Nietzsche's formula for announcing Zarathustra: "*Incipit* Klossowski, as Zarathustra."[41] Foucault means at least to associate Klossowski's book with Nietzsche's prophecies of the return of old gods after the demise of the God that has monopolized two European millennia. The divine-that-comes may prefer to speak its first lessons with the voice of a Demon. Foucault quotes at length Klossowski's translation of a passage from *Gay Science* in which the eternal return is proposed as a demonic test of one's love for life.[42] The barely recalled experience of some divine beyond binaries, of a mirror-god, promises the love of life in a body without eschatological stipulations.

Foucault begins again: Klossowski rejects philosophical dialectic to enter a middle space, a mirror space, in which a divinity can appear that is neither God nor Satan, a divinity not bound by a dialectical Either/Or. In place of the binary, Klossowski presents a simulacrum. Foucault does his best to explain this necessarily elusive notion. He provides a sort of lexicon: the simulacrum is a "vain image," a "representation," a "lie that leads to taking one sign for another," a "sign of the presence of a divinity," the "simultaneous arrival of the Same and the Other." It is at once "simulacrum, similitude, simultaneity, simulation, and dissimulation."[43] A simulacrum is not the opposite of divine appearance. It is the ambiguous condition for any divine representation among human bodies—or for the interaction of human bodies with each other in desire.

Foucault steps back to approach along another path. He distinguishes a linguistic understanding of sign from a religious one (where "linguistic" means semiotic and "religious," Christian). The linguistic sign designates a meaning or a thing by its position in the play of other signs. In the religious domain, some signs have another function: they say what they mean only through their relation to a privileged original. They become the transitory double of the one Original. Every tree in Christian scriptures points forward or backward to the Cross. The event of the Cross changes the meaning of trees in every other passage. The forbidden tree in the Garden of Eden, occasion for humankind's fall, "has become one day what it always was," the Tree of Redemption.[44] This kind of religious sign is at once prophetic and ironic; it points to an origin that has not yet been revealed while already refracting it into the present. On Foucault's reading, Klossowski recovers this structure of religious sign from repressed depths of Christian experience, but also from Nietzsche's staging of Dionysus in relation to Christ—from Christian theology's never-completed contest with Greco-Roman religious narrative.[45] Klossowski then applies the sign structure to human beings; he treats them as (pagan) epiphanies. Human bodies become semaphores of gods, "simulacra much more dizzying than the painted faces of divinities."[46] Bodies are absorbed into signs.

Foucault describes the rules for characters in Klossowski's novels, but he is more interested in using them to characterize "our" cultural space, the desert we inhabit since the disappearance of Christian theology. "We" are no longer either Catholics who scrutinize signs or Calvinists who refuse to trust them while submitting to divine sovereignty. On this empty, silent sand, we no longer possess either theology or myth. Yet Klossowski tries still to speak, through our linguistic poverty, recognizing his own language as simulacrum.[47] He is like Actaeon at the myth's end: he struggles to say what he has glimpsed of the goddess Diana even as his face is pulled into the muzzle of a speechless stag. Klossowski's writing is the prose of Actaeon, disturbing our abandoned silence with garbled reports of divinity. It recalls the lost languages of ancient myth and heretical theology, the lost spaces in which Christians were enchanted by their demons or pagans stumbled upon their naked gods. The spaces are not completely closed. They have re-treated into the region of language we call "literature," the only (virtual) space left for saying such things.

Foucault's choice to read Klossowski's whole corpus through a short work on Diana and Actaeon puts all the weight on his relation to it. The relation is hardly simple. I notice three features in Klossowski that do not appear in Foucault's appreciation.[48] The first is the retelling of pagan religion through the technical categories of Christian theology. The second is Diana's sex. The third is the theatrical variation of voice in Klossowski's book: on some pages it is more a script for a tableau than an essay, an obvious reminder of its own staging.[49] The three points of divergence between Foucault's account and Klossowski's book of myth suggest resistance to Klossowski's manner of writing. They mark Foucault's decision (or fate) to write otherwise.

First, the *persistence of Christian categories* in Klossowski. Foucault repeats Klossowski's critique of simple-minded appeals to Christian conversion. When Claudel and Du Bos urge Gide to convert, Gide is right to refuse them in order to remain faithful to the God of ruses.[50] Of course, it is one thing to refuse the ordinary criteria of Christian membership and another to free oneself from the hold of Christianity on language or imagination. Klossowski retains a theologian's technical vocabulary after abandoning Christian communities. Gide's refusal of conversion—or Klossowski's jumbling of Christian memberships—or Foucault's abstention from the truth of Christianity doesn't undo Christian languages. The mere rejection of Christianity doesn't restore the religious languages or imaginaries eclipsed by it.

Foucault will later scruple over this cultural situation across two volumes of *History of Sexuality* as he tries to find language for sexuality before Christianity. He seems not so scrupulous here—or not so attentive to Klossowski's mixed language. If Klossowski revives a lost experience, he does so in terms rendered technical by Christianity. For example, he begins the meditation on Actaeon and Diana by speaking of the imagination of vanished people (what Foucault calls the lost experience), but he quickly enough turns to the traces of their dead languages in our living ones, the fragments of their images in our imaginings. What Klossowski offers is not so much the experience of pagan devotees and some heterodox Christians but the reconception of pagan theophany through the scrim of Christian orthodoxy. So, according to Klossowski, when Actaeon literalizes the scene he stumbles upon, he seeks in it "an irrefutable demonstration of the *real presence*"— of Eucharistic transmutation. Or "the Twelve [Olympian] Gods, being identical in essence, but distinct in person"—just like the Trinity of Christian creeds. Or Diana is mirrored by her simulating demon in a "communication of idioms" (another Trinitarian reference) or a "hypostatic union" (a Christological one).[51] Foucault doesn't underscore these phrases any more than he underscores the Christian resonances in his own text.

Second, Foucault and *the sex of the goddess*. Diana is emphatically a goddess, not some marble Apollo with a petite, ornamental penis or that distant Father endowed with a merely official masculinity who is represented by His resolutely sexless Son. The myth of Actaeon and Diana emphasizes a difference in genitals. The hunter commits sacrilege as a male. What he must not see—cannot be allowed to see and speak—are the *labra Dianae*, the goddess's lower lips. It is the exposure of these that Klossowski features in the drawing that he completed in 1955 and would later attach to the text.[52] For him, the myth stages the contradictions of the epiphany of a divine female: Diana, virgin huntress, "dazzling and murderous," is still the object of fantasies of bestial rape.[53] For a goddess to consent to be represented in a body is to accept the assault of male eyes. Indeed, she depends upon them to clothe herself in the bodies pressed on her by their fantasy. Never possessed, she can appear to Actaeon only as subject to male possession. Klossowski emphasizes Diana's virginity only a few years after he had written a Christian analysis of Sade's hatred of virginity.[54] More important, the figuration of Diana here as an invisible divinity who can appear through male fantasy becomes the animating monomania of Klossowski's trilogy about Roberte.

The contradictory female-divine is everywhere in Klossowski's retelling of Diana, but the specificity of sexual difference drops out in Foucault's retelling. It is too simple to claim that Foucault unknowingly universalizes the male perspective or that he is simply unaware that there are women in the world with distinctive desires.[55] The elision of the goddess suggests instead an abstraction or universalization in Foucault's writing about Klossowski. It is not just Diana's genital anatomy that disappears. It is the rhetorical specificity of Klossowski's mediation, his mythological staging.

Third, Foucault's apparent disregard for *Klossowski's many voices*. Foucault attends of course to Klossowski's techniques of composition. "A perilous space" begins to open where Klossowski's "discourses, fables, trapping and trapped ruses" can teach us "how what is most serious in thought should find, beyond dialectic, its illuminated lightness."[56] That lightness can appear only through discourses, fables, and ruses. It needs a text, like *The Bath of Diana*, that arranges theatrical devices to redepict the scene; that moves its view from character to character, imagining thoughts and supplying speeches; that always keeps an expert eye on the reader, who is sometimes included in an "us" but most often solicited as an implied "you." Klossowski's text is not so much the prose of Actaeon, the speech that Actaeon would have delivered after the vision, as the restaging for the reader of Actaeon's entrapment. Even in the original edition of *The Bath*, before he supplied his own illustration, Klossowski included a sequence of photographs of a famous statue of Diana. In the photographs, she first appears as the fierce huntress. The final image shows the draped cloth that covers the goddess's sex above an exposed leg that is counterposed with the rump of a stag— the changed, tamed, shrunken Actaeon.[57] The reader's final gaze falls on the almost entangled bodies.

Is Foucault's appreciation of Klossowski also an entrapment for the eye? Or is it only a paraphrase of lessons read, an effort to report on a book while surveying the corpus? Does Foucault mean to set the trap better than Klossowski by presenting a more dazzling simulacrum before his text, a supplementary lure for torpid readers? Or does Foucault rather stand above the Klossowskian corpus, noting its themes and situating its philosophical importance with respect to other authors— especially Bataille and Blanchot?[58] I've noted three points at which Foucault seems to overlook important elements of Klossowski's theater. I suspect that he doesn't overlook them so much as mark his distance from them. Foucault writes a critical appreciation of Klossowski's work. He means to represent it but also to insert it into a story about Western thought. Foucault's own genre is constrained by notions of literary criticism and philosophic renarration. He translates Klossowski into another genre. The new genre—the achieved form of his essay—

is the most obvious answer Foucault gives in it to the challenge of Klossowski's writing. *I will admire you,* the choice of critical genre says, *but I will not imitate you without reserve. I will interpret your theater without surrendering to its devices.* This is indeed a compositional answer to Klossowski. It is not, of course, Foucault's last.

ON BLANCHOT: OUTSIDE LANGUAGE

Bataille, Klossowski, Blanchot: Foucault repeats the triplet whenever he describes the condition of our language after the (Nietzschean) death of God. But when he comes to write the appreciation of Blanchot, he accords him a special place. Blanchot is not just another witness to the fate of our language but somehow the recorder of "language in its brute being."[59]

Foucault's essay on Blanchot is the culmination of the hunt across all the panels of a triptych. The hunt has tracked certain images: desert, void, empty space. Or it has followed a track through them to a place of recognition. With Blanchot, the space being sought is no longer the lightning-lit theater for the appearance of divinity in relation to sexed bodies. It is the space of the page of modern Western fiction, which is "neither a mythology nor a rhetoric."[60] On it, Foucault describes not the death of God as the death of the speaking subject who seeks after God. The only thing that speaks into the void is the void of language itself.

On its surface, this third appreciation is like the other two in its scope and procedure: Foucault explicates an entire corpus of essays and novels by tracing central topics.[61] But his difficulties over language return more forcefully here because less vividly. If *History of Madness* wanted to bend down to the earth, following a poet's admonition, to hear an impossible murmuring, here murmuring itself is lost irretrievably in the undoing and redoing of language. Foucault quotes Blanchot at length—the longest quotation in his essay:

> Not a word, barely a murmur, barely a *frisson,* less than silence, less than the abyss of the void; the fullness of the void, something that cannot be silenced, occupying all of space, the uninterrupted, the incessant, a *frisson* and already a murmur, not a murmur but speech, and not any speech, but distinct, exact, within my reach.[62]

With Blanchot, Foucault moves beyond mad murmuring but also beyond the desires for its archival transcription (or so it seems).

Foucault begins the essay with an old paradox of self-reference in Greek logic, one that can be resolved by sorting semantic levels. He uses it to distinguish the problematic of reference or representation from that of utterance, of speaking. There is a nonrepresentative space of language in which it relates to itself not by reference but by separation. "Literature is not language approaching itself to the point of burning manifestation; it is language putting itself farthest from itself. . . . The 'subject' of literature (that which speaks in it and that of which it speaks) is not so much language in its positivity as the void in which it finds its space when it enunciates itself in the nudity of the 'I speak.'"[63] For Foucault, this space is the subject of Blanchot's writing, in which he writes and about which he writes.

The space of language, its being, appears only after the speaking subject disappears. Foucault notices the disappearance in a number of other contemporary projects: the formalization of language, the study of myths, psychoanalysis, and the (Heideggerian) search for the Logos that is the birthplace of Western reason. Yet language without a speaking subject, without that subject's supposed meanings or interior motions, appears for Foucault most strikingly in another canon of authors that culminates in Blanchot. The "experience of the outside [*le dehors*]"— the title of Foucault's essay, a reference to a charmed term in Blanchot— first appeared "for us" in Sade's monologue of naked desire. Foucault emphasizes the way Sadean speech opposes the interiorization of moral law demanded by Kant and Hegel. He links it with Hölderlin's manifestation of "the scintillating absence of the gods," understood as a new obligation to attend to the endless consequences of "God's failure." Sade and Hölderlin leave behind floating reminders of the impossibility of a stable I. The experience is reiterated in Nietzsche, Mallarmé, and Artaud. It appears again in Bataille, whose thinking, "instead of being discourse about contradiction or the unconscious, becomes that of the limit, of ripped subjectivity, of transgression." The outside registers again in Klossowski "with the experience of the double, the exteriority of simulacra, the theatrical and lunatic multiplication of Me."[64]

The thought of the outside then culminates in Blanchot, who had written during the 1950s on each of the authors already named. Blanchot is "for us this very thought itself—the real presence, absolutely distant, scintillating, invisible, the necessary fate, the inevitable law, the calm vigor, the infinite, measured vigor of this thought itself."[65] "Blanchot" means, of course, Blanchot's writing, since Blanchot himself is, Foucault notes, famously absent. The absent God has become the absent author, and Blanchot is not so much its prophet as its sacrament, its "real presence." Reading Blanchot well, we receive the communion of authorial language, consume the thought of outside.

So Foucault's image implies—except that he has already forestalled the implication. A page earlier he has warned against a fatal confusion. Blanchot's writing may look like the negative theology of Christian tradition. It may somehow resemble the famous mystical texts of Pseudo-Dionysius. But while negative theology pretends to pass outside the self, according to Foucault, it does so only to find the self again at the end, wrapped in the "dazzling interiority of a thought that is fully Being and Word." How different Blanchot is from (Christian) mysticism, which always ends by recuperating any temporarily lost self in the presence of the communicating Word! Blanchot's protagonists regularly refuse to perform actions that might seem like those of a god willing to die precisely to show the emptiness of the divine law's promises. The cultural death of God liberates language not in order to record the lightning strikes of a new sacred, or the theatrical play of divine simulacra, but to speak its empty non-self.[66]

Here Foucault seems to fend off not only a confusion with (Christian) mysticism but the lingering religious echoes in Bataille or Klossowski. He uses the essay on Blanchot to reinterpret transgression. It is not primarily what calls down the law or constitutes it by violation but what is called endlessly into the empty space that law is. Again, when writing on Blanchot, Foucault explicitly sets aside the language (from Klossowski, from Nietzsche) of mask and theater. There is nothing higher, nothing hidden, no goal or secret. There is only the outside, the emptiness around language, of language. More interesting to Foucault than Hölderlin's vanished gods or even Nietzsche's death of God is the death in Blanchot of the subject supposed to be speaking language. That subject, the endlessly iterated I of speech, is nothing more than a fold in language. Indeed, Foucault seems by the end of the essay to have disclosed a sort of joke in his original juxtaposition of the ancient philosophical paradox built around the alleged assertion, "I am lying," and the modern novel's puzzling over the claim, "I speak." "I speak" is always a lie when it suggests an interior I above language.[67]

Something else seems now to be excluded: the body. The very possibility of distinguishing the body as another space (say, of resistance, of encounter) is rejected as part of the logic of (false) interiority. Foucault almost follows Blanchot's conceit in which bodies are invaded by words, are replaced by words. Or he underlines Blanchot's reminder that the bodies in a novel are constituted by words. If Artaud once hoped that "the body and the cry" might undo language so that the subject could become "material energy, the suffering of flesh," Foucault reading Blanchot attenuates bodily images and muffles cries in favor of a thin voice that promises only its own speaking.[68] The already spectral face of Eurydice must be forgotten. The self-absorbed song of the Sirens is only the rumor of another song.

With Blanchot, Foucault reaches the end of a trajectory of thinking about the sacred as the outside of language. The negation of reference and interiority, the refusal of divinities or the bodies they desire, transfers any number of sacred powers back from the deceiving boundary to the text itself, but only to flatten them. Is this final desire for empty language Foucault's own or rather his admiring mimicry of Blanchot?

One way to pursue the question is to compare this reading of Blanchot with what Foucault had already written or would go on to write about bodies. Consider first his writing in *History of Madness*. Years before, Blanchot distinguished two sorts of novels. There is the Balzac-type novel that "introduces into the system of fiction enough recognizable elements so that the real existence of the reader can find, if necessary, a place in it." By contrast, the Lautréamont-type novel "ignores those lifelike factors that ordinary existence presupposes; without taking account of habits or customs, it wants to fashion the form that will manifest it." The second type, which is characteristic of the twentieth century as opposed to the nineteenth, "composes the new ensemble of its figures and events around a unity that it has chosen in relation to references that it does not need to justify."[69]

Where might *History of Madness* fit into this distinction from Blanchot? Given its panorama of detail, its professed reverence for archival voices, the book would certainly seem Balzacian. Of course, the whole range of detail is subordinated to unusually cyclic forms and indeed to a preoccupation with form. The exercise of writing *History of Madness* is to find a form in which madness can have an antihistory. So perhaps Foucault's book is closer to the second type of novel—and, indeed, it cites Lautréamont but not Balzac. Still Foucault's preface to that book suggests that its form will acknowledge Reason's historical tyranny over language even as it listens for sounds from unreasonable bodies. The language exposed in Blanchot is controlled or poisoned by modern Reason's sciences that exhaust Self. It is not the language of Bataille's sacrificial experience or Klossowski's mythic theater. It is also not the whole of the language of *History of Madness*. Foucault's extravagant praise of Blanchot is the excess of a fandom that has already refused simple identification by writing otherwise.

Consider then what Foucault will go on to write. He is once reported to have expressed the wish to write like Blanchot, but his essay on Blanchot doesn't predict the course of his own writing.[70] Foucault's texts from the 1970s resemble in diction, topic, and some devices the account he gives of Bataille and Klossowski, not of Blanchot. (I note only to set aside the question, how far the *Archeology of Knowledge* is writing "like Blanchot's.") In particular, Foucault's future writing plays, as Klossowski does, with ironic yet urgent retellings of inherited texts about bodies, their punishments and disciplines. Foucault will continue to be preoccupied with limit experiences but also with the endless fabulations around bodies, especially as they encounter divinities. He will also be preoccupied with what Klossowski calls demons. (In Foucault, they come to bear the name "Power.") So if Foucault's appreciation cedes to Blanchot (for the moment) the term "literature" or agrees to a certain narrative of exhaustion for the modern novel, it only surrenders a single word and a certain genre. It does not mean that Foucault will stop writing about bodies, using other arts.

The arts for representing bodies may be more theatrical than novelistic. In this appreciation, Foucault agrees with Blanchot in rejecting— or despairing of—Artaud's wish to display the hot energy of suffering flesh. Yet elsewhere, a few years earlier, he had paired Blanchot and Artaud around Zarathustra as oeuvre and experience, two coupled continuations of Nietzsche. Perhaps the theater, as Artaud understood it, can suggest forms for representing bodies when a particular sort of novel no longer can. Put together with the suggestions in the essays on Bataille and Klossowski, the mention of Artaud points toward a return of bodies through theater, in the multiplication of their simulacra.

Later Foucault will add Artaud to the trio of Bataille, Blanchot, and Klossowski.[71] If he did not write an equivalent appreciation of Artaud, he did contribute to *Critique* an appreciation in which Artaud's notion of theater figures centrally. Titled "Theatrum philosophicum" (the philosophical theater), it is a praise of Deleuze. It takes the meaning of "theater" partly from Klossowski, who figures prominently at beginning and end.[72] But the descriptions of theater derive more importantly from Artaud. When Foucault describes a theater that is "multiplied, polyscenic, simultaneous, portioned out into separate scenes that while unknown to each other sign to each other . . . [in which] masks dance, bodies cry out, hands and fingers gesture," "a theater of mime with multiple, fugitive, and instantaneous scenes in which unseeing gestures signal to each other," he could be paraphrasing Artaud's appreciation of Balinese theater.[73] The phantasmatic body of active, material surfaces that Foucault evokes when writing on Deleuze is a *theatrical* body. If the means for its representation are rejected when Foucault writes on Blanchot, they are adopted when he writes later in his own name.[74]

With the benefit of longer hindsight, looking back over all of Foucault's books, Blanchot had clearer eyes for his differences from Foucault. Blanchot praises the other's "grand baroque style," marked at once by "its splendor and its precision." He claims to find in Foucault a kindred spirit, a restless solitary who nonetheless "distrusts the pomps of interiority." But Foucault's best writing describes a power "that comes from below, from the depths of the social body, driven from forces that are local, mobile, and transitory, occasionally minute." I add: Foucault does write the social body, but also the body straining to be antisocial, to escape control, to transgress the boundary, which is one reason why there are in Foucault, as Blanchot notices, so many of the formulae of negative theology.[75] Foucault writes not about the sovereign I but about the transformation of subjected bodies. He needs, like Klossowski, a language suitable for the metamorphoses provoked when divinities traffic in bodies. He needs, like Artaud, a space to multiply and disarticulate bodies in history.

Bataille, Klossowski, Blanchot, and then Artaud: Writing about them, Foucault confronts what it is to pursue the sacred in language after Nietzsche. He negotiates a textual inheritance obsessed with how gods treat bodies. He also prepares—by a series of imitations and tacit dissents—an alternative future for his own scenarios.

CHAPTER 2

THE DISMEMBERED ASSASSIN AND THE
WELL-SCRUBBED DELINQUENTS

DISCIPLINE AND PUNISH opens with a gruesome tableau of
the public torture of Damiens, condemned in 1757 for attempting to
assassinate Louis XV. The tableau is usually remembered as if it were
a picture. It seems to call up other bloody images in Foucault's genealogy—like the dismembered emblem of *Acéphale* or the photograph of a
Chinese death by a thousand cuts that fascinated Bataille. Yet Foucault
doesn't represent the execution of Damiens through a picture. There are
illustrations to *Discipline and Punish*; in the French edition, they appear
on glossy pages at the front. They do not include the opening scene.
Foucault begins the book not with an image or the verbal paraphrase
of one but with a string of quotations. The first twelve paragraphs excerpt archived descriptions of the public torture—trial proceedings, a
newspaper account, firsthand testimony by a police official. The reader
is confronted from the beginning with the relation of public displays to
words. Both claim to represent bodies in extremity.

A squeamish reader, I prefer to avoid these excerpts. I refuse to
recount them. My reaction is one of Foucault's reasons for beginning
with the archived texts. I am meant to find them revolting, barbaric,
and (above all) old-fashioned. I am expected to feel relief when I pass
from such gruesome testimonies to something tidier, like a list of asep-
tic penal prescriptions. In *Discipline and Punish*, the description of the
tortured body is half of a pair. The other half consists of excerpts from

rules, published in 1838, for a Parisian house of young prisoners.[1] The rules determine every period of their day—not for gruesome punishment, of course, but for rehabilitation. Of course.

Foucault juxtaposes the texts to ask how we understand the change from gruesome public executions to lifelong rehabilitation and whether we must understand it as progress. The texts also give us two ways in which language responds to bodies under duress. So the juxtaposition here recalls another of Foucault's openings. More than a decade earlier, he began *Birth of the Clinic* by presenting two specimens of writing that also mark a before and after in bodily description. It is worth recalling Foucault's earlier pairing of texts, in part because it treats so many of the same elements, in part because it seems to tell a different story about them.

"It is a question in this book of space, language, and death; it is a question of the gaze."[2] A deft opening sentence—aphoristic in its balance and rhythm, aphoristic too in its double twist. Space, language, and death: two abstractions punctuated by a fleshly fatality. Then a second turn: gaze, which requires a gazer rather like the reader, who is implicated at once in voyeurism. The sentence could appear at the head of *Discipline and Punish*, but Foucault affixes it in fact to *Birth of the Clinic*. There it is followed by two medical descriptions separated by fewer than a hundred years. The first, from the middle of the eighteenth century, describes the (supposed) results of a regimen of baths ordered by Pommard for nervous desiccation. The patient's body, observed only from outside, begins to reject pieces of itself—in the urine, from the rectum, by vomiting. The second description, from the first quarter of the nineteenth century, depicts a lesion in an anatomized brain.

How do the two medical texts differ? Not by quantity of imagination, however much we have been taught to believe that the earlier text is driven by absurd fancies, while the later is a sober report of unimpeded observation. We were taught, in other words, that truly modern medicine "liberated" the space of seeing from the "fantastic figures" that once blocked our view on reality. That story of progress is itself an obscuring fantasy. There is indeed a change in view from one of the juxtaposed medical texts to the other, but it doesn't result from removing old screens of dogma. One change comes in how recent medicine conceives space—how it places illnesses in described space before suffusing them with clarity. The taste in medical language has also changed. Doctors take up a new style—meticulous, measured, minutely attentive, fastidious in the drip of adjectives. Despite what its myths of origin assert, modern medicine isn't a new commitment to seeing things clearly. It changes the domain of what is to be seen. Instead of stopping with human suffering, the medical gaze now passes beyond it—skillfully breaking open the skull, for example, to liberate, at last, the "sad, fragile pulp" as a proper "object of knowledge." The new medicine takes as "the first face of truth the grain of things, their color, their marks, their hardness, their adhesion."[3] Medicine claims now to register the truth of particular bodies by cutting them open to see them better.

Read this way, the movement from the first text to the second in *Birth of the Clinic* appears almost to reverse the beginning of *Discipline and Punish*, not least in placing the dissected body. In *Discipline and Punish*, the archived accounts of Damiens's judicial torture show a particular body dismembered. They are contrasted with later texts that step away from any individual to set rules for a group. In the regime for young offenders, bodies are barely described while being ceaselessly directed, put into calculated motion or brought to orderly rest. If the accounts of Damiens's death acknowledge the failures of speech before his mangling, the rules for young offenders prescribe a daily routine with prattling fluency. Isn't this the opposite of the juxtaposition in *Birth of the Clinic*, which passes from bodily regimen to anatomized brain?

Consider the two pairs of texts again, paying attention to how they render suffering. The accounts of the public dismemberment recall an intolerable spectacle staged on a particular body. Pommard's account of the hydrotherapy is certainly more laconic, but it admits some slight pain (discomfort, our doctors would say) in the unfortunate patient's coughing up or vomiting the detaching membranes. Suffering is not mentioned in the two later texts. The language that sets rules for young offenders resembles in its affectless clarity the fastidious description of the unfeeling brain. The young bodies are so many specimens on the dissecting table of the institution that confines them. A loss of the capacity to write suffering is a loss in representing human bodies. If it sounds odd to accuse an anatomy of ignoring the body, we might still say that it doesn't treat its corporeal object as one of *our* bodies.

Consider again how these four texts give voice to bodies or else deny it. In the opening of *Discipline and Punish*, the archival excerpts multiply corporeal words around Damiens. He is body, flesh, skin, hand, thighs, until he is only butchered pieces dragged apart by straining horses. But the regicide is also a voice. He is asked repeatedly whether he has anything to say. He refuses to answer, yet he begs God for mercy until he can only cry out his agony. The body voices its own torture. The body, still living, becomes a cry. In the model regulations for young offenders that Foucault quotes, there are no samples of their speech. Presumably they are allowed to talk in the intervals of "recreation" or else compelled to recite in classes or after evening lectures on morals. But their days begin and end in silence. Their bodies are corrected in silence. The offenders are scheduled to wash their hands four times throughout the day, their faces once. They wash; they do not speak. The contrast between voice and voicelessness may be less clear in the texts from *Birth of the Clinic*, but it does appear. The victim of hydrotherapy is allowed to give voice in vomiting and coughing, and she may be supposed still to speak with the tongue that begins to show the side effects of her alleged cure. The anatomized brain has lost its voice once and for all in becoming an object of knowledge.

However we arrange these four texts, their comparison makes clear that Foucault allows no simple relations of words to bodies. A single bodily event can be described in multiple genres. The body itself may participate in them or may flee from language into sound or scream. Language about bodies is not stable: the most scientific language has its history and its fashions. Nor is the relation of language to bodies innocent. Words may order torture or washing. Indeed, they may describe a torture of endless washing while calling it a cure. Words make attempts on bodies, especially when they pretend only to describe them.

RELIGIONS OLD AND NEW

After opening *Discipline and Punish* with the collage of archived words about bodies that are seen or locked away, that cry out or retire in silence, Foucault offers at once his large lesson: the emergence of modern systems of incarceration conceals the body under a network of new speech. The body disappears from view, but it also disappears as the designated target of penal concern. The modernized judicial system no longer touches the body except to get at something else—to work through the body on the soul. It teaches the body by discounting it in favor of the soul. It replaces the body that can scream, that can be ripped apart, with a "juridical subject" (*sujet juridique*) to which it directs its ministrations and its discourses.[4] The juridical subject that displaces the "real body" is made into a subject for a new form of power, but it is also the subject matter of new systems of expertise.

In what may be the most famous aphorism in *Discipline and Punish*, Foucault writes: "The soul, effect and instrument of a political anatomy; the soul, prison of the body."[5] A clever reversal of the old Socratic saying, though not a simple one. What after all is the body that is imprisoned by the soul? Or which body is it? And how do we describe it if not with the dictionary of one political anatomy or another? Power makes and remakes languages for describing bodies while drawing targets on them. Managing bodies requires writing about them in certain ways. How to write about them otherwise?

Early in the book, Foucault lists a series of four "general rules" that his study "obeys." He gives them just after quoting and mocking the genre of the rules list in the house of young offenders. So Foucault's own rules aren't offered as methodological principles, as a system for historiography.[6] They are more like practical counsels for how to read in archives—or else narrative conventions for retelling what you find there. A few pages later, still in the mood for admonitions, Foucault describes his work as a "micro-physics" of the body that "presupposes that the power exercised there is not conceived as a property but as a strategy, that its effects of domination are not attributed to an 'appropriation' but to dispositions, maneuvers, tactics, techniques, functions . . . that one should set as its model the perpetual battle."[7] The body is a network of tense relations, a field for perpetual battle. This micro-physics is a series of battlefield reports from a war that is not officially taking place.

Any new arrangement of power-knowledge projects a new object on which it may exercise itself, not least by talking. The object supplied for the new penal system is a kind of soul, a fresh referent for that old theological term. "Objective of this book: a correlative history of the modern soul and of a new power to judge; a genealogy of the present scientific-judicial complex in which the power to punish finds its support, receives its justifications and its rules, extends its effects, and masks its exorbitant singularity."[8] The modern soul is a necessary correlate for a modern form of judgment, the protagonist for its explanations and verdicts.

The modern *soul*: the opening juxtaposition of scenes in *Discipline and Punish* displays two kinds of religion. On one side, a liturgical Christianity justifies and attends the public torture of Damiens. On the other, a legal-clinical religion manages young inmates within the pristine reformatory. The old religion does of course put in an appearance for the lads. The rules speak of a chapel in which the almoner, as we used to say in English, leads a morning prayer followed by "a moral or religious reading." At night, public reading of a passage with "some instructive notions or some touching tract" leads to evening prayer.[9] If these elements are vaguely Christian, their merely moral content contrasts with the incarnational detail of the torture of Damiens. He calls out to God, begs Jesus for forgiveness, kisses a crucifix, and asks for prayers at the attending priest's next Mass.

The torture inflicted on Damiens is called in French *supplice*, a word that descends from the Latin *supplicium*. The Roman word included among its many meanings both the action of sacrificing and the thing sacrificed. Foucault shares the French word and the sense of its etymology with Bataille, who uses it as a religious frame for his decisive discovery of "inner experience."[10] In Foucault, *supplice* under the French monarchy is a bodily spectacle that assigns many roles to Christianity. Confessors accompany the condemned. The judicial torture is performed at Christian sites, often in front of a major church or shrine. It is punctuated by Christian speeches: admonitions, confessions, cries for divine mercy. The judicial torture is meant to connect human judgment with divine: it is an earthly anticipation of eternal punishment, a theater of hell. So Foucault frequently describes the monarchical *supplice* as a rite or liturgy, a ceremony or even a festival. At some public executions, he notes, the accused becomes not only a popular hero but a folk saint.[11] The gallows issue a compelling summons to sanctity.

To talk about the suffering body of a condemned criminal as the hero in the theater of hell, but also as the revelation of divine truth, is to summon the memory of a very particular execution, as Foucault and Bataille both know. On certain theologies Foucault would have heard while growing up Catholic, the *supplice* of Jesus's crucifixion is endlessly reiterated on every Catholic altar.[12] The Mass is a sacrifice. Bataille recalls such theology in many places, but perhaps most extensively in that section of *Inner Experience* titled "Le supplice." The section puns on the word's relation to "supplication" and "sacrifice" but also gestures repeatedly, for contrast, toward Christ's suffering and its repetition in ritual and willed imitation. In *Discipline and Punish*, though Foucault's section "Le supplice" is not so explicitly theological, it still evokes the Crucified One stretched out behind Damiens.

Compare this latter-day crucifixion once again with the second scene of Foucault's opening, the rules for the model penitentiary. The embodied spectacle of redemptive punishment has been replaced by rational calculation of endless rehabilitation, in which an early diagnosis of criminal tendencies can lead to one's being remanded to expert supervision for as long as it takes to treat them. Overcoming the barbaric excess of the old monarchy and its unreformed religion, the modern state creates a vast system in which a new priesthood of clinicians imposes penances for lifelong tendencies.[13]

PUNISHMENT AS PURE SIGN

The scene of the body under judicial torture is, of course, only the beginning of Foucault's story. From it, he goes on to tell three later stages: the reform of cruel punishments, the general extension of discipline to the whole of society, and the construction of an empire of prisons— or, rather, the construction of a society in which the prison is the hidden engine of the whole. Our society, where social warfare should not be mentioned in mixed company.

The story as Foucault tells it is detailed and absorbing. It is also controversial. In this book and the rest, scholars delight to find historical errors. My reading steps around many details of Foucault's historical narrative and all the historians' controversies. I am not concerned with whether he got each of the facts right. On many pages, his historical narrative means not to report facts so much as to represent the fantasies of certain forms of power—forms of power that alter facts or invent them. Strong power tells vivid stories. Writing the history of power requires an ear for fictions and a talent for re-creating them. Its historiography must be more like theatrical criticism than a historical almanac.

Foucault's narrative displays the mutations of power. Historical contrasts help dislodge the "facts" that have been fixed by present power. It is necessary to retell not only significant changes in arrangements of power but the origins of our present system, which we have been taught to regard as ungenerated because naturally right. Here then is the second stage of Foucault's penal narrative in simplest form: The severity of the *supplice* provoked various reform movements. Some reformers objected to the inhumanity of the spectacles; others, to their inefficiency. These calls for reform were actually preceded by broader social changes of uncertain origin. Crime became less violent but also moved its target from bodies to money. (The body disappears in another sense.) The shift from crimes of blood to crimes of fraud was matched by a growth in the police apparatus, which applied tighter "gridding" to the population for the sake of recording information about it. Reform—this becomes a regular refrain in Foucault—went along with "a closer gridding of the social body."[14]

The word I translate clumsily as "gridding" is *quadrillage*. Foucault uses the available French word to describe a modern relation of power to bodies that have been distributed in rationalized space. Later in the book the same word will name one of the basic functions of modern discipline. In roughly contemporary lectures, it becomes an elementary form of power.[15] *Quadrillage* is a successor to *partage* in *History of Madness*, the word that Foucault shared with the poet René Char. The terminological succession makes for a difference, because the two words carry different associations.[16] In *History of Madness*, Foucault links *partage* to ancient rituals for expelling impurity from a community: "the old mute rites that purify and reinvigorate the obscure consciousnesses of the community," "the immobile rigor of ceremonies."[17] If *quadrillage* is associated with a kind of quarantine, it is not some ancient ritual. It is modern control over spatially indexed information about bodies. It is imposed not by ritual horror but by geometric cognition: the lucid order of a clear-eyed and self-possessed desire to know. So *quadrillage* can't content itself with the single boundary of a *partage*, with the anxious line between inside and outside, acceptable and intolerable. *Quadrillage* requires a whole system of lines in order to capture everyone, each one, within a little square.

In *Discipline and Punish*, Foucault uses *quadrillage* alongside another salient word. *Dispositif* is ordinarily translated as "apparatus" or "mechanism," but then Foucault also writes of *appareil* and *méchanisme*. To translate the three indiscriminately is to ignore his diction. If I had to choose a single English translation for *dispositif*, I would probably adopt "disposition." I would mean it not in the psychological sense (a sunny disposition) but in the military one: the disposition of forces on a battlefield linked to what used to be called the "table of officers and equipment." Military meanings recur in historical uses of *dispositif*, and they are accented in *Discipline and Punish* by a more general recourse to military analogies or metaphors. *Dispositif* replaces the chaotic carnage of actual battle with its projective or retrospective narration at a military academy—say, in an advanced seminar on strategy. Instead of the mired field of screams and stench, analyses in monotone punctuated by drawings with unit numbers and time markers.

A few years after publishing *Discipline and Punish*, Foucault offers what is sometimes taken as a definition of *dispositif*. It is, he says, the network that can be traced through "a resolutely heterogeneous ensemble, containing discourses, institutions, architectural arrangements, regulatory decisions, laws, administrative measures, scientific statements, philosophical, moral, charitable propositions—in short: of what is said, as well as what is not said."[18] As so often in Foucault, this is not so much a definition as an elaborate refusal to define. The meaning of *dispositif* is transferred to the simile or metaphor of the network (itself equivocal); then the simile or metaphor is stretched over a disordered (Borgesian) list of unlike things. The term *dispositif* issues a conceptual or imaginative challenge: Find the kind of pattern that might link all of these things—all that is said and all that is not said. The challenge may be less explicit in *Discipline and Punish*, but the function of *dispositif* in describing strategic power is no simpler.

In Foucault's penal narrative, the reformers of *supplice* and their reeducated police apply *quadrillage* to bodies aggregated into a population. If the *supplice* of Damiens culminated in the quartering of his tenacious body, the gridding of reform is applied to the confident fiction of a whole population, of individual bodies summed by new forces of control and measurement. The rebuilt language suitable for describing the social body is some combination of numbers, models, and policies. It performs efficiency. So it wants, among other things, to replace the excessive expenditure of torture with more economical means, seeking not only the maximum of predictable return but the simplest formulation of its own policies. It wants to be elegant in the mathematical sense, to have policies that are both cost-effective and beautiful in their generality.

Penal reform requires rational elegance for its success because it operates directly on minds—on the minds of those who support it, even more on the minds of those subject to it. Long justified as a deterrent, punishment must now be calculated exactly as the set of minimalist signs able to forestall future crimes of various sorts. The *supplice* was a liturgical response that wanted to show both the horror of offense against the sovereign and its ultimate futility. Deterrence required excess. Under penal reform, the punishment is a minimalist sign, set to indicate as discreetly as possible both the crime and the state power just far enough to prevent recurrence. Punishment becomes a rationalized code in several senses: a codification but also an abbreviating cipher legible to citizens. The mind is "a writing surface for power, with semiology as instrument; the submission of bodies by the control of ideas; the analysis of representations, as principle for a politics of bodies much more effective than the ritual anatomy of *supplice*."[19]

Foucault dwells on this fantasy of the punishment as sign. He may mean to tease those who classify him as a structuralist. He surely wants to evoke the way in which the displacement of bodies is both registered and aided by a change in the conception of language. To be effective as a deterrent, the idea of the sign punishment must be linked naturally to the idea of the crime. The transparent language of penalties demonstrates the error of the crime while exposing its false incentives. Literal and invariant, it will act soberly on chastened imaginations with predictable results. It won't falter before screams or scatter before divinity. It will emulate the tranquil description of an anatomized brain.

Reformed punishment is not a liturgy of redemptive suffering, no theater of hell. It arranges its scenes, its tableaux, for public instruction. The sight of prisoners engaged on public works should not produce terror. It should reaffirm the analysis of crimes against the social body while showing how to repair them. "Public punishment is the ceremony of immediate recoding," of bringing the surd of crime back into the general calculus.[20] The punishments are sad, of course, because they result from an insult to the social body, a gash in the rationalized mock flesh that we all now share by curious communion. Some of the reformers imagine elaborate costumes and choreography for this group melancholy, but only as supplements to sober episodes of didactic theater. Children will be required to attend public punishments as part of their moral formation. Adults will come for review. Indeed, these scenes will be much more profitable morally than some religious pilgrimages. (The example Foucault quotes from a penal reformer is Mecca, but the reformer doubtless has in mind nearer sites and more familiar religions.)[21] The new public displays will surely find their poets, even their missionaries, so that their stories can pass down through families the way tales of a religious legacy once did. The whole city, the whole nation will become a living and properly moralized scripture, a vast *Pilgrim's Progress*, without a melodramatic and vindictive God.

It goes without saying that the fantasy of the city-as-allegory remained fantasy. Even the reforming proposals for a system of transparent punishments fell quickly—instantaneously—into the reality of prison as the common remedy for every serious crime short of capital punishment. Still these were to be new prisons, reformed prisons. If they abandoned public punishment as education cognitively linked to the crime, they carried forward the sentiments of rehabilitation and the habits of calculation. They also applied the notion of service to the social body in the form of compulsory work.

The architects of the modern prison, as much as the reformers of barbarous punishment, were resolved to avoid liturgies of terror. They wanted, like their reforming predecessors, to include religious elements only for their moral effects. While they avoided sacraments of sacrifice or the Christian liturgies built around them, they ended up borrowing other practices of the old religion. Their new penal system consists of "exercises, not of signs: timetables, uses of time, obligatory movements, regular activities, solitary meditation, common work, silence, application, respect, good habits." This is, Foucault notices, a description of Christian monastic life. Protestant prison reformers even find themselves borrowing the basic unit of monastic architecture, the cell, which becomes in the new prison schemes "the instrument by which one can reconstitute at once *homo economicus* and religious conscience."[22] Indeed, the exemplary prison foundations—in Amsterdam, Gloucester, Gand,

Philadelphia—fit religious exercises for "pedagogical and spiritual transformation" into the expansive system of modern imprisonment.

DISCIPLINE AS RELIGION

The exercises are pedagogical and spiritual. They are also plainly physical. They render bodies "docile" by synchronizing movements. Bodies are distributed exactly in space so that their actions can be concatenated into a single, long sequence. Some of Foucault's strongest images for this fantasy are military. Techniques of military training spread beyond the barracks as "a military dream of society." He adds another line of metaphors and analogies, another genealogy for the techniques of the new discipline. Discipline applies to all citizens the lessons once learned in the confined space of the monastery. So Foucault will say that modern society generalizes the techniques of the monastery, that a modern school is another monastery, that the modern timetable is the monastic *horarium* or schedule—in short, that vowed asceticism has become citizen exercise.[23]

Bodies rendered docile by physical exercise and careful spatial distribution must be trained. The phrase Foucault uses as a section heading is *bon dressement*.[24] The slightly archaic *dressement*, like "dressage" in equestrian English, can mean training in the double sense of taming and making presentable. *Dressement* can also mean drawing up a list or register. The results of training are shown by examination, by specified trials that yield recorded results. If trainers need standardized manuals, examiners need required tests and registers of successes and failures. These can be combined into a profile for any given individual (like the form for a racing horse). A scheme of examination brings individuality "into the documentary field." "The examination, surrounded by all its documentary techniques, makes of each individual a 'case'"—a dossier that captures the individual, not least as an instance for future studies. "This putting into writing of real existences" makes human lives subjects of a progressively refined disciplinary power.[25]

The training of docile bodies is a circuit of writing. It arises from regulations or instructions to end in results and recommendations. All this writing intends to capture individual bodies in order to direct them. The general regime of discipline "is aimed neither at expiation nor even exactly at repression."[26] "Expiation" is a theological and ritual term; it is one of the stated purposes of the superseded liturgy of horror. Discipline claims to need no liturgies of that sort. Of course, it doesn't abandon ritual so much as complete it. The great public spectacles are relinquished because ritual now penetrates every part of life. This was clear already in the juxtaposition that opens the book: The regime of the model reformatory ritualizes every moment of the day. It writes rubrics for every action of its inmates, down to the timed washing of hands.

Discipline places all "acts, performances, conducts" within a field that allows them to be sorted and measured. Individuals count in this space not as unpredictably stubborn bodies but as instances measured against a valorizing rule. They are grades or scores. The rule becomes a "constraint of a conformity to be achieved." Whatever cannot appear on the scale is rejected as decisively, defectively outside its purposes. As penal logic made embracing and perpetual, discipline "compares, differentiates, hierarchizes, homogenizes, excludes. In a word, it *normalizes*."[27] Differentiation and hierarchization are also the bases for much liturgical action. Homogenization and exclusion are aims in some rituals. Normalization—that seems to be neither sanctification nor ritual purification.

What does it mean to use religious techniques for secular reform? Is that a change in institutional motive, in the stories to be told about it, or in the kind of power that constitutes the institution? Since Foucault's narrative emphasizes the generalization of monastic techniques, a reader might also want to ask, What restraints are removed in the shift from monasteries to penal discipline? Or what changes in the quality of the surrounding space and the modality of compulsion within it? There is no bright line between the old religion and the secular state, however much the latter prides itself on being utterly distinct. In many ways, the secular is another mode of religious reform, the latest reformed religion.

A related error that Foucault means to avoid, here and elsewhere, is that of conceiving the birth of disciplinarity as the bright beginning of a new epoch, a *revolutionary* beginning. He affirms instead the interaction of old and new. "There appears, through the disciplines, the power of the Norm. The new law of modern society? Let us say rather that since the eighteenth century, it has come to join other powers in obliging them to new delimitations; that of the Law, that of the Word and the Text, that of the Tradition." The Norm functions alongside the older sources of

Christian morality, but it also obliges them to change. One of the most interesting causal circles implied by Foucault's analysis is the effect of the Norm on the religious moralities that continue to compete with it, often now from a position of social inferiority. "'Discipline' can be identified neither with an institution nor with an apparatus; it is a type of power, a modality for its exercise, comprising a whole set of instruments, techniques, procedures, levels of applications, targets; it is a 'physics' or an 'anatomy' of power, a technology."[28] Discipline can be—has been—taken up by a wide range of institutions, including churches. To compete with the state or to win its favor, churches practice discipline too.

The dream of discipline is fulfilled in Jeremy Bentham's model prison, the famous Panopticon. Its circular arrangement allows every cell to be kept under constant surveillance from a central command post. Here the grid has become fully architectural: each individual allocated to a single cell, all cells equally in view. Uniform isolation makes each one knowable as a unique and transparent position. There is no place for a recalcitrant body to hide, not even in the command post. The Panopticon "automates and disindividualizes power. It has its principle less in a person than in a certain concerted distribution of bodies, surfaces, lights, gazes. . . . The ceremonies, the rituals, the marks by which the sovereign's surplus power was manifested are useless. . . . In consequence, it matters little who exercises [disciplinary] power."[29]

The cell within the enclosure of the Panopticon might seem to lie at the furthest point from the public torture of Damiens. Yet the cell remains a little theater.[30] Its whole aim is to bring the isolated body under perfect surveillance. So doing, it performs another sort of dismemberment—cutting off the body from all others, but also reducing its gestures to so many isolated incidents for observation. The backlighting of each cell encourages a stroboscopic analysis of the minutest movement, an exhaustive cartography of gestures. The body is not only exposed to the gaze but taken apart by it in the *supplice* of penal theater.

DELINQUENTS AND OTHER DISCIPLINARY PRODUCTS

The final step in *Discipline and Punish* tells how the general scheme of disciplinarity works its way out in prison reform, in the actual copies of the Panopticon. Foucault describes these modern prisons with a phrase from Baltard: they are "complete and austere institutions."[31] Remembering the correlation between forms of power and the subjects they form, the reader may ask, Which subject does the power of the prison require? For whom is the prison prepared as the complete and austere stage? The last part of *Discipline and Punish* gives an answer. It comes in an easy version and then a more accurate one. The easy version says, The new subject is the Delinquent! That answer must then be explained as yet another doubling, as the assignment of another role or character to the body when it passes from the court to the prison—or, more precisely, from conviction to sentencing.

Any power overwrites bodies with the fictions that its mechanisms require. The power of disciplinarity overwrites bodily peculiarity as measurable and controllable instantiation. It recognizes as usefully individual only what it can normalize. To accomplish this, it posits just the individual subject that it needs. Much like the Eucharistic body of Christ in traditional Catholic theology, the stipulated presence of this subject is asserted against admittedly contrary appearances. But here the subject posited by punishment, the "punished individual," is not characterized by miraculous transubstantiation or divine immutability. On the contrary, it is characterized by its availability to the processes of disciplinary power.[32]

To secure a conviction, penal law posits a legally responsible agent, what Foucault calls "the juridical subject." To carry out the sentence, another sort of subject must be found in the very same body. "This other character [*personnage*], whom the penitentiary apparatus substitutes for the convicted offender, is the *delinquent*. The delinquent is distinguished from the offender by the fact that it is not so much his act as his life that is pertinent to characterizing him." To operate, the penitentiary apparatus "must totalize the existence of the delinquent, making of the prison a sort of artificial and coercive theater in which it will be reviewed from top to bottom."[33] The spectacle has been reconvened. No longer a theater of hell, it is merely a scientific display of abnormality. Like the sanitized amphitheater of a medical classroom, this new theater doesn't mean to provoke horror in its audience. It aims rather to increase usable knowledge of the deviations on display. It hopes, in other words, to perfect its own operation.

The penitentiary apparatus reads the criminal act up into the whole of a life—backward to a morbid past, forward to a recidivist future. "The correlative of the penal system is doubtless the offender, but the correlative of the penitentiary apparatus is someone else; this is the delinquent, a biographical unity, a nucleus of 'dangerousness,' representative of a type of anomaly." The genre suitable for describing this subject is the clinical history that concludes with a prognosis. The shift in subject and in the language appropriate to it moves the body too. "Just where the branded, cut up, burned, destroyed body of the tortured [*supplicié*] disappeared, just there appeared the body of the prisoner, doubled by the individuality of the 'delinquent,' by the little soul of the criminal."[34] Going through such an analysis, a reader may wonder why the emergence of the new subject—of another legible secret inside the body—should matter so much. Indeed, a tenderhearted reader might object: *I don't care what the victim is called; I just want to change the victimizing institution!* To which Foucault has a double reply, which might or might not console.

The first reply underscores a complication that has run through the analysis. Names like "delinquent" are powerful templates for forming individuals. Any serious political critique must engage this level of subject formation, partly so that it sees the extent of the power it opposes, partly so that it recognizes how much of the victim it means to rescue has been created by the victimizing system. To dismantle the system is to dismantle its subjects. How do you save subjects from a system without preserving them as subjects of that system? Rescue becomes too easily repetition.

A second reply, perhaps more consoling, points to the failure of so many schemes of reform. As Foucault repeats, objections to prisons are as old as the modern prison movement. Everyone knows that prisons don't work, yet all attempts to reform them fail. This might suggest that other forces are at play, such as economic incentives built into a subeconomy that profits from delinquency. It may suggest further that reformers misconceive what prisons are meant to do. "In place of the observation that prison fails to reduce crimes, one should perhaps substitute the hypothesis that prison has succeeded very well in producing delinquency."[35] Prisons aren't meant to reduce crime. They are meant to control it by redescribing it. They are in the business of producing new characters, instruments for the exercise of disciplinary power.

PRISON AND UTOPIA

Foucault's fable of disciplinarity shows the transfer of monastic techniques from Christianity to other contexts and other purposes. It concludes with the carceral society, a social body invisibly regulated by the prison in its modern form. The last chapter of *Discipline and Punish*, titled "The Carceral," begins with another sort of church practice: the making of liturgical calendars. Foucault singles out the death of a child inmate at the penal colony of Mettray as the date on which the carceral system was achieved. (On old Christian calendars, a martyr's feast is often kept on the date of the final suffering, since death brings birth into eternal life.) The boy's last words are preserved by the colony's chroniclers: "What a pity to have to leave the colony so soon!"[36] The sanctity of this "first penitentiary saint" is proved by his regret at having to depart from the penal system. He is an anti-martyr who testifies by wanting not to die. The blessedness of life on a carceral earth must exceed any blessedness in heaven. If only one could be a prisoner here forever!

Foucault's religious allusions don't end with the generalized ritual of discipline or the exaltation of its bound saints. In the last pages of this book, as counterpart to the diptych of Damiens and the young offenders, there are some fantastic tracings of another plan for human life. Foucault keeps quoting the Fourierists, those extravagant social critics.[37] Indeed, the Fourierist newspaper, *La phalange*, supplies the last quotation in *Discipline and Punish*, the exact structural complement to the archival accounts of the public execution of Damiens.

Phalange: it derives from an ancient Greek military word, *phalanx*, and it was later picked up by fascist groups. In the 1840s, enthusiastic utopians still took their title from Fourier's name for the ideal community, constructed by balancing exactly calculated human differences in economic, sexual, and ritual harmonies. Fourier's vision is religious not only in its projection of a complex ritual system and an attendant mythology but in its eschatological predictions. When Foucault brings forward Fourier at the end of *Discipline and Punish*, he gestures ironically toward an imagined speech that might yet represent a mythological alternative to present power.

Or precisely not. In this book, utopia is frequently associated with Bentham and the Panopticon.[38] Bentham's plan wants perfect control over bodies. Like so many other reformers, he proposes it for the common good. Fourier's proposals are much more elaborate than those in Bentham. That makes them more frightening. After all, *Discipline and Punish* is a study in failed utopias. The society of benign moral formation becomes so quickly the carceral society. Surely the Fourierists are only one more dream on the heap of history.

Perhaps so, but there is something in the excess of Fourier's imagined alternatives that draws Foucault—or implicates him along with others. Foucault is hardly the only thinker of the last century to keep Fourier in mind. Fourier's way of writing bodies was studied by writers as different as Zola, Leconte de Lisle, Wyneken, Walser, and Breton. Walter Benjamin counted Fourier a regular conversation partner for the grand project on Parisian arcades.[39] There is no need to reach so far back. In 1971, four years before Foucault published *Discipline and Punish*, Roland Barthes had produced *Sade, Fourier, Loyola*.

Despite their doctrinal differences, Barthes claims, these three authors share processes of writing. They join in the same "desire for classification," for cutting things apart and numbering them; in the same practice of using images; and even in the same impulse to costume the social order.[40] They are all three "Logothetes," language fabricators. Fabricating language requires four operations: self-isolation, articulation by detailed distinction, ritual ordering, and theatricalization or endless staging. These appear with different inflections in Sade, Loyola, and Fourier. I would add that they also appear in Foucault, as topics and as practices.

Barthes selects from Fourier's writing some distinctive topics: sensual pleasure, money, utopian architecture, and the predicted transformation of human bodies. Across all the topics, Barthes stresses Fourier's endless calculations and obsessive arrangement of details. Fourier becomes the emblem of the penchant for writing in systems. Here again, Barthes's description of Fourier's style fits some of Foucault's stylistic tics exactly. Foucault shares with Fourier (as Barthes describes him) a zeal for nomenclatures, hierarchies, progressions, and their implied architectures. Especially in *Discipline and Punish*, Foucault might seem to fall victim to the impulses of classification and enumeration that he identifies with disciplinarity. Foucault may be drawn to Fourier's writing despite his suspicion of utopias. Or he may be too adept at imitating styles for arranging bodies.

Certainly Foucault sees in the Fourierists that critique requires dense counter-imagination—for perception, not persuasion. The microscopic infiltration of discipline can be exposed only by an equally microscopic depiction of human life. The excess of Fourierist description would risk becoming a worse disciplinarity if it were ever enacted, but that very risk must be run to make clear the ruses of prevailing power. The vividness of the fantasized alternative shows by contrast how things stand with us, with our bodies. It is not just that we are denied the erotic festivals of Fourier's Harmony or its perfect weather. We stand under a system that punishes while claiming to reform, that pretends to be utopian while outsourcing the mass construction of hidden hells. We feel fully that horror by juxtaposing it with a happier fiction, with the colorful dream of festivals of human bodies at the play of pleasure.

In *Discipline and Punish*, the passages quoted from the Fourierist newspaper attack modern penalty as false reform. The first quotation retells a courtroom scene: the sentencing of a delinquent. Foucault notes that the Fourierists favored such scenes because the penal system revealed to them the deepest antagonisms of our so-called civilization. What the courts count as great crimes, the Fourierists see "not as monstrosities but as the fatal return and revolt of what has been repressed." So-called petty crimes are "not at all . . . the necessary margins of society"; they are "the central groaning of the battle that unrolls there."[41] Foucault concedes that Fourierist journalism isn't typical. He doesn't want it to be typical. He offers it as a forerunner to the anarchists' radical critique of the prison system.

At the very end of *Discipline and Punish*, Foucault quotes from *La phalange* the letter of an unnamed correspondent. It lays out an imaginary map of Paris with hospitals, asylums, and prisons at its center. This is not the map of a city; it is the battle plan of the "pitched war of all against all."[42] The map condenses Foucault's analysis of disciplinary society. It also explains his writing from the *History of Madness* through the end of *Discipline and Punish*. The Fourierist correspondent unmasks the machinery of disciplinary society by which war is generalized, routinized—normalized.

The "body" of the text of *Discipline and Punish* ends with a correction to some of our favorite categories for analyzing power. Foucault writes that "the notions of institution of repression, rejection, exclusion, marginalization, are not adequate to describe, at the very center of the carceral city, the formation of the insidious inducements, the barely avowable petty cruelties, the little ruses, the calculated procedures, the techniques, the 'sciences' that permit in the end the fabrication of the disciplinary individual."[43] The mechanisms of disciplinary power are more complicated than the binary spatial metaphors we use to describe them. They are also more cunning. Discipline operates best by inducement rather than rejection; by infiltrating the smallest bodily interstices rather than guarding the obvious borders; by elaborating its knowledge and its skills rather than calling in the hired muscle—though it keeps muscle on call for special occasions. Our standard vocabulary for analyzing power is too cartoonish.

Then Foucault picks up the Fourierist metaphor of hidden battle. It responds to the opening texts about the execution of Damiens. "In this central and centralized humanity, effect and instrument of complex relations of power, bodies and forces subjected by multiple dispositions of 'incarceration,' objects for discourses that are in themselves elements of this strategy, we must hear the rumbling of battle." Underneath the manipulation of desire, the microscopic infiltration, and the learned manipulation, battle rumbles still. It is the hidden battle of all against all. It is not seen but heard, like the murmurings of the mad. It is another turn of madness, pretending to be perfectly sane. The sound of battle subtends the whole of this book as the mad murmurings accompany the entire *History of Madness*.[44]

Foucault's writing is Fourier in reverse. I don't mean that it is dystopian while Fourier is utopian. The reversal is more in temporal relation than in scheme of values. If Fourier must describe the combinatorial possibilities for Harmony, his society to come, Foucault must decode them for a society that has been, that *is*—that arose in utopian dreaming and that continues with utopian justification. He agrees with Fourier that languages of power are extravagant mythologies. The luxuriance of categories in Fourier, the grandeur of historical schemes, the obsession with decorative detail—there is something of that in all systems of power.[45] Utopian fiction is the preferred genre of power, though it affirms its fictions as facts of nature. So the student of mutations of power, the writer of histories of power, must be a lover of mythography, an apprentice Logothete (to recall Barthes on Fourier).

Does Foucault's writing in *Discipline and Punish* have no relation to the future? In the years of writing it, as in some of the years to come, he would be actively involved in various movements of prison reform. Is that the future intended by the text? The only future he mentions in it is a future of writing. *Discipline and Punish* ends not in its "body" but in a curiously placed footnote. (The effect is lost in the English, where the footnote is incorporated into the main text as its last few lines.) In the note, Foucault writes, "I here interrupt a book that must serve as a historical backdrop to various studies of the power of normalization and the formation of knowledge in modern society."

Consider first the use of a footnote to make such a gesture. In academic writing, despite the rules, footnotes often contain the most interesting material—the essential qualifications and the revealing confessions. So here we might take Foucault as citing and mocking a convention of expert knowledge. As if he were to say, at the foot of the last page, *By the way, everything you have been reading is background*.

What we have been reading is a story about the displacement of bodies. They are moved from the spectacle of the church square to the education of the prison, from the language of pathetic testimony to the toneless enumeration of rules or the precision of the official report. We have been reading a book about how language conceals bodies but also how it creates a series of substitutes for them. This terse footnote seems to perform its own substitution, even as it marks the furthest distance from the horror of the opening description. A book that begins in lengthy extracts from the archive of torture ends with scholarly reframing that is also scholarly narcissism.

Still the most striking words in the note are "I here interrupt." Interruption is precisely what is not allowed by the gridded time of discipline. Any interruption is diagnosed in its causes and assigned to appropriate penal therapy. *I interrupt*: The performative utterance either acknowledges or introduces a waste of time. Either we have already been engaged in needless speech or we are about to embark on a digression.

I here interrupt. What space, which cell is marked out by "here"? Where, indeed, is the space of this interruption—or of the speech that it interrupts? Is it the space of an imagined future, or a utopian topography, or the margins of Fourier's books?

I here interrupt. Foucault gestures toward a gap in the regime of disciplinarity. The gap is carried by another writing of bodily existence. The writing may seem more remote from bodies, as if it were only writing about the writing of bodies. It is in fact an interruption of the scientific concealment of an endless war of all against all.

CHAPTER 3

THE BUFFOON-KING AND THE POSSESSED NUNS

MOST OF FOUCAULT'S TEXTS ARE RECITALS, but they take place on different stages. I have been reading texts that Foucault prepared for publication and then committed to print. Now, and often in what follows, I turn to reconstructions of public lectures that he gave at the Collège de France between the inauguration of his chair in December 1970 and his death in June 1984.

These lectures were obligatory performances. As a condition of his appointment to the Collège, Foucault had to deliver twenty-four hours of public instruction each year drawn from his original research. So he did—on Wednesdays, from January through March. Foucault's appointment to the Collège brought him not so much security or publicity, which he already had, as a happy combination of academic standing with a minimum of obligation. He was tied neither to curricula nor to committees. Still he was obliged to speak in public at set intervals, and on a stage propped up by academic authority. He became the center of a serialized melodrama of magisterial instruction.[1]

FOUCAULT ON (THEIR) STAGE

With the exception of the inaugural lecture, Foucault's obligatory speeches at the Collège were not published during his lifetime. The institution's annual report printed only summaries. Yet from the beginning Foucault's lectures circulated in bootleg audio versions and student notes or transcriptions. Since Foucault's death, more complete transcripts have been redacted in French and then translated into other languages. Strictly speaking, these are editions of what Foucault said, not publications of his lecture scripts. The editions transcribe and collate various recordings. There are gaps in some places, though the scripts are sometimes consulted to fill them. But the editors determine punctuation and paragraphing. They supply annotation. They eliminate the speaker's repetitions and correct his grammar. While I am glad as a fan to have the lectures in print, I read them with some shame, because I was meant only to hear them.

In these lectures, I am charmed by Foucault's voice—by the authorial voice, not the actual sound of Foucault's rapid tenor on muffled recordings. (How frequently we are disappointed on first hearing an author we have long read, to whom we assigned a more appealing voice inside.) The authorial voice of these lectures plays with its audience more obviously and perhaps more congenially than in the books. If Foucault complained about the crowds lying in wait for him every Wednesday, about the little thicket of recorders in front of his lectern, he nonetheless spoke *to* them. He taught against the institutional frame within which he stood. The author who had used the evolution of the classroom as a prominent example of modern discipline might be expected to approach any lectern with irony. An overflowing lecture hall at the Collège de France is evidently not the prison-classroom. It is as free as any academic space can be. The members of the audience are auditors, not students. They are not required to attend. They don't follow a curriculum or seek a degree. They are not being graded. Envy their freedom! Then recognize, with Foucault, how completely the space is invested with academic authority. Its "freedom" is a pharaoh's chamber at the apex of an immense pyramid of discipline.

Foucault begins one series of lectures with a reflection on his situation before the audience. "You know that the institution in which you are, in which I am, is not exactly an institution for teaching." Foucault is only required to give "public reviews" of his research. "I consider myself as absolutely held . . . to tell you more or less what I do, where I am, in which direction . . . this work goes." He insists that he has no control and no desire for control over what his anonymous listeners do with what he says. Yet, he confesses, he spends more and more of his time worrying about his lectures. "How can I, in an hour, an hour and a half, make this or that trick work, in a way that it does not bore people too much?" How can he conduct this "spectacle," this "circus"—but let me quote: "The fact that I have to do this sort of circus every Wednesday evening is a true—how to say it—to say *supplice* would be too much; annoyance is a little too weak. Well, it's a little between the two"—that is, between a *supplice* and an annoyance.[2] Foucault has already published *Discipline and Punish* when he says this. He has described the performance of monarchical *supplice* in gruesome detail. So his listeners are expected to hear that these public reports of writing in progress, which are not supposed to be acts of teaching, have almost become for Foucault public rituals in which a sovereign power is displayed and reaffirmed through his visible body. It would be "too much" to say that he is dismembered for the sake of showing something to his auditors, but he considers saying it.

ABNORMALS AND THEIR EXPERTS

Foucault gave thirteen series of lectures after his inauguration as a member of the Collège de France. The lectures on abnormals are the fifth. The series was delivered in the spring of 1975, after two series on penal institutions and one on psychiatric power. *Discipline and Punish* appeared midway through the lectures on abnormals. From prisons to the clinic, by way of the courtroom, certain questions press on Foucault. They were sketched as an abstract topic by that promissory footnote at the end of *Discipline and Punish*: "various studies of the power of normalization and the formation of knowledge in modern society." They might be described more vividly as questions about capturing bodies by writing—or writing power into bodily personifications.

Foucault opens the lectures on abnormals without prelude, according to his taste, by reading extracts from two psychiatric reports in criminal cases. The reports are recent or current; he dates them to 1955 and 1974. They are juxtaposed not to show a change from before to after but to illustrate continuity. The opinions apply a self-satisfied erudition to categorize defendants in criminal proceedings before punishing them. In the 1955 opinion, the accused—whom Foucault calls A for fear of violating regulations on disclosure—stands trial for complicity in the murder of his mistress's child.[3] (The mistress herself committed the crime.) The expert provides a psychosocial profile of A, who has (inevitably) been deformed by various unhealthy social conditions and then emboldened by artsy contempt for the bourgeoisie. A came to adulthood in milieus marked by Alcibiadinism, Erostratism, Bovarism, Don Juanism. These -isms personify supposed psychological traits or types by reference to literary characters.[4] They also characterize A as the bearer or instance of a sort of personhood that encompasses many individual bodies. His (shared) traits led A to believe himself a superman, above nature and society. Of course, none of this diminished his legal responsibility. On the contrary, the expert story is meant to guarantee that he will be held responsible—as much for a host of distasteful social problems that he now personifies as for his own crimes.

Foucault passes quickly to the second set of opinions, drawn from a case of sexual blackmail in 1974 ("last year"). Here one of the accused, X, is described by another expert as "homosexual since the age of twelve or thirteen."[5] "Homosexual" carries out another sort of personification, assigning X to a fixed species of (fictive) pathology. Foucault will return to this term's personification in *History of Sexuality* 1. Here he passes over it as he continues to read from the opinion. If X is a precocious and pathological homosexual, it cannot surprise us to learn that he is "totally immoral, cynical, indeed even gossipy. Three thousand years ago," the expert pronounces, "he would certainly have inhabited Sodom, and the fires from heaven would have punished him very justly for his vice." Implicit here is a much older personification, the millennium-spanning rhetoric by which bodies that express same-sex desire are labeled descendants of the biblical Sodomites. X's aged lover, Y, is evidently worse than a simple Sodomite: he makes the learned expert want to vomit. Z, who is involved with X and Y in a love triangle, works only as a DJ and hustler because he is exceptionally lazy. "He is," the expert concludes, "particularly repugnant."

As Foucault reads the two opinions, his audience laughs. Their laughter is recorded on the audiotapes. A reader of the published text knows about it because Foucault takes it up. He cites the laughter as evidence when characterizing the power of one species of expert speech.

In societies like ours, Foucault explains, certain discourses combine three properties. They have, first, the power to influence a verdict of freedom or confinement—at the limit, a verdict of life or death. Yet, second, they are not really judicial discourses so much as discourses that bring scientific authority into the courtroom through expert testimony. Third, these discourses make audiences laugh. Foucault says to his audience, "You are the proof and the witnesses of this."[6] Foucault mimics judicial language, reminding his audience not only that they are guilty of laughter but that they are seated in something like a judicial space, in which Foucault plays the roles at once of the prosecutor and the defendant. His expert discourse has made them laugh; his expertise is always on trial. So are they. Wherever they sit in societies like ours, inside or outside the theater of the renowned Collège, they will find themselves in a quasi-courtroom, subject to the pompous personifications of lethal expertise.

A few minutes later, Foucault tries again to describe this third feature of expert speech, its capacity for comedy. He calls its discourses "grotesque" just because they have, "by statute, effects of power of which their intrinsic qualities would deprive them." He adds that they might also be called "Ubu-esque," assuming that his audience will catch the reference. Foucault insists that the tag is something more than a counter-joke or an insult. He is after something important: "Ubu-esque terror, grotesque sovereignty, or, in other more austere terms, the maximization of the effects of power from the disqualification of the one who produces them." Grotesque sovereignty, vile sovereignty—but the hearer is not to think only of monarchs. "The administrative machine, with its imperative effects of power, [passes] through the mediocre, negligible, imbecilic, scruffy, ridiculous, worn-out, poor, powerless functionary." The functionary can be negligible because this power doesn't have to personify itself convincingly in order to be effective. In the functionary, the dictator, or the courtroom psychiatrist, a certain kind of modern power can afford "to give itself the image of having issued from someone who was theatrically disguised, depicted as a clown, as a fool."[7] The power is comic when it pronounces so pompously its extravagant personifications, and comic again in its clownish deputies. It also has the last laugh: it can kill you. The comedy of personifications ends in what some of us account a tragedy.

THE STAGECRAFT OF KING UBU

Foucault presumes that his audience has already met King Ubu, the protagonist of an infamous play by Alfred Jarry first performed eighty years earlier. The character is based on one of Jarry's secondary school teachers (a teacher of physics), and the source of the play is a tradition of student verses and plays begun before Jarry arrived at the school. (The name "Ubu" muddles the teacher's name: he was called "Père Hébert" or "Ébé," among other things.)[8] Jarry's play begins as an adolescent satire of academic power—indeed, of the peculiar disciplinary status of science in secondary schools. In Jarry's reworking, Ubu becomes a fantastic figure for all adult authority, pompous, feckless, and brutal.

Though Jarry's *King Ubu* is sometimes likened to the more familiar tale of the emperor's new clothes, Ubu's rise from military obscurity to the throne is much bloodier. His crimes resemble what we now call (with startling candor) "cartoon violence." In the first act alone, there is the depiction or threat of bashing in brains, tearing out eyes, sharpening teeth on a living leg, and cleaving a body with a sword. The play about Ubu also differs from the fable of the emperor in its farcical obscenity, amped-up schoolyard taunting. The dirty words aren't about sex: they name hungers, digestions, excretions. From the play's infamous first word (*Merdre*, Shitit), the audience hears a litany of turds, farts, other stinks, and the organs that produce them. The play's effect on its first audiences may have had less to do with the violent plot than with the forbidden words streaming from the bodies on a public stage.

Comic-book violence, schoolyard slang—there were still other affronts. The thrashing, cursing bodies were not properly represented according to theatrical conventions. At the first staged performances, a single backdrop juxtaposed incoherently times, places, and things.[9] Scene changes were indicated by crude signs. A full orchestra had been replaced by a piano and lone cymbal. Wicker figures stood in for armies of soldiers and squads of cavalry horses. Most important, Ubu's grotesque body was evoked by a great wicker stomach and a huge mask. Jarry himself was perhaps more interested in the revolutionary staging than in any particular version of the script.[10] *King Ubu* is a play about a grotesque, monarchical body that wants to change the rules for representing bodies. The king's pomps are contradicted by the shabby means for depicting them. The endless offense of the royal speech, modeled after Jarry's own intonation, is delivered with self-conscious artifice—as if the construct-body had never quite learned to speak, even when disgorging obscenities.

These means of representation can be described as caricature. I suppose that the term fits, though it remains opaque. Nor do I find it helpful to debate whether *King Ubu* is best described as symbolist, modern, modernist, or proto-surrealist. Jarry is after something more than the identity politics of aesthetic movements. He wants to undo conventions of embodied power by recalling for adults, in the very adult space of an avant-garde theater, the fantastic bodies projected during childhood and adolescence. The performed recollection reminds us that our bodying forth of power always remains fantastic. The formal strangeness of Jarry's play reveals the comedy that lurks whenever power is personified. Attaching this fantastic force to a living human body required, in older regimes of power, that the body be covered over, exaggerated, and concealed. In modern power, the aesthetics of personification can be reversed: a body chosen for its banality becomes the bearer of a superbly invisible and objective science. In both cases—the king in his regalia, the expert in the polyester suit—power has to make the individual body its artifact. The discrepancy between power and body can become comic in old or new regimes, but the comedy is especially visible in modern forms. The discrepancy appears in older forms as grotesque, in modern forms as clownish.

What makes Foucault's auditors laugh, I presume, is not just the implausible multiplication of technical terms spoken with ponderous certainty. It is the contradiction between high science and the banal prejudices that so evidently animate it. The first expert parades his diagnostic personifications to justify his bourgeois detestation of existentialism and avant-garde art. The second expert—brought forward as the voice of objective analysis—is repulsed by a lazy hustler. He wants to vomit when he thinks of an older homosexual. Like any pratfall of a pompous ass, this provokes laughter. But the laughter forgets that this pompous ass has power over the bodies that repel him. The discrepancies in power's representations don't forestall a lethal effect.

So with Ubu. He is a caricature of the repulsively individual body; he is also a murderous plotter who becomes a blood-soaked king. Ubu's play is more than a satire of a tyrannical teacher precisely because it is performed by adults for adults in a way that undoes theatrical convention to reveal much larger conventions—the conventions of *real* power, as we would say. Putting childish means for representing power on an adult stage directs attention to the wide world's childish means of figuring power in bodies, over bodies. Childish and potent: this magical thinking casts spells. It mangles bodies offstage. Or, more precisely, it treats all bodies as if they were only wicker bellies and masks, only pieces of stage scenery.

How much of this does Foucault presume in naming "Ubu-power" for his audience? Most of it, I think. Jarry belongs to the frame of reference in which he writes—and not least because of connections with Artaud. Foucault doesn't often speak of Jarry, but there are signs that he carried the author's works in mind, especially when thinking about bodies. A decade before the lectures on abnormals, Foucault begins an essay on literary pornography with the line, "The scene is set in Poland, that is, everywhere."[11] Jarry had famously concluded his opening remarks at the play's first performances: "As for the action, which is about to begin, it is set in Poland, that is, nowhere." In the essay Foucault takes Jarry as his companion for a meditation on "modern perversity" marked by the contrast between two eighteenth-century novels of terror, Crébillon's *Égarement* and Reveroni's *Pauliska*. Foucault's contrast between them concerns Desire and Knowledge (both capitalized); he lays it out schematically and in some detail. I mention only the first element in the comparison, which concerns speech. Crébillon's hero must be taught a "science of the world," which is nothing other than the "use of speech"—the skills of impertinence, fatuity, and bon ton, of the unending formalities that say nothing and accomplish much. By contrast, Reveroni's heroine, Pauliska, is educated by "mute myths," by "wordless complicities": never initiated into the circles of power, she is kept "in the hard and monotonous status of the object."[12]

Applying the contrast to Jarry's most famous character, we might conclude that King Ubu is more mute than Pauliska, because he comes later in the history of modern perversity. Perhaps he is, so far as his crude oaths and angry commands shrink language to shouts. Still if Ubu scandalously violates the rules of courtly language, he confirms the courtly conviction that language matters not for what it says so much as for what it does. Ubu's bellowing erupts from his artificial body as commands to be executed on other bodies. His speech breaks all the rules except the rule of royal speech itself—the rule that rewards the speech of some bodies with such consequences.

Ubu was not all stage body, of course. He was distinguished by his mask and his belly, but also by his manner of speaking. That is what made it so irresistible to perform Ubu in other settings without the costume. It was enough to revert to his speech, to the mixture of obscenities and courtly paraphrases, the circumlocution punctuated by curses. Indeed, it was altogether too easy to talk like Ubu. Jarry seemed unable or unwilling to stop himself, and the habit spread.[13] Just here Foucault's aesthetic may be more varied than Jarry's. For Foucault, one of the most interesting things about power is that it has no fixed idiom, no single set of linguistic mannerisms. Its speech is characterized instead by the capacity for rapid change through copying, annotating, absorbing. Power is polyglot. It must be. If it likes sometimes to recall the old formulae, the settled liturgies, it will at other times—in the next minute—ape the slang of the latest science. Onstage at the Collège, Foucault runs through a whole series of languages about power. He has already declared his recital a didactic satire of efforts to capture power in languages. It is also, with and against Jarry, something like a series of period pieces from power's sordid linguistic history.

INHERITED IMAGES

"In Poland, that is, nowhere." "In Poland, that is, everywhere." The curious nowhere of the speech in the expert psychiatric opinions has become our everywhere.

Psychiatric opinion is nonjudicial speech that has power in the courtroom and so beyond it, through verdicts and sentences. Foucault's investigation proceeds from the hypothesis that its normalizing power is "not simply the effect of the encounter, of the composition, of the interconnection of medical knowledge with judicial power." It is some other type of power, "neither medical nor judicial," that colonizes medicine and law even as it finds its place "on the theatrical scene of the tribunal."[14] The sort of expert psychiatric opinions that Foucault began by reading invade medical and judicial institutions—or stitch them together as their seam, joining them—or unite them at their border, as an insertion between them. Foucault changes his metaphors from sentence to sentence as he tries to evoke the space of the normalizing discourse in which the abnormal is created as the only proper object.

The labor of locating this new power, which makes us laugh even as it decides our fate, leads Foucault to caution against three errors in imagining power. First error: "to consider that power is essentially a negative mechanism of repression; that power has essentially the function of protecting, conserving, or reproducing the relations of production." Second error: "to consider that power is something that locates itself, in relation to the play of forces, at the level of a superstructure." Third error: "to consider that it is essentially linked to effects of ignorance."[15]

The question of where to look for power is obviously tied to questions about how to recognize power or to describe it once seen. The three errors mislead the search, then garble any analysis of a discovery. To judge from Foucault's cautions here and his practice of writing everywhere, systems of power are not well described either by a settled list of literal propositions or by simple plots. They are glimpsed rather through mobile juxtaposition, the rapid change of scene or script, so registered in language that is at once vivid and ephemeral.

Or perhaps languages about power should take up a mocking or adversarial relation to it, as Jarry did with *King Ubu*.

Or perhaps power appears most strikingly through our frustrated efforts to describe it, since it has always already formed the bodies that talk about it.

The string of alternatives is Foucault's own. He presents them and others across the lectures on abnormals not as steps of a single proof, not even as perspectives on a single object, but as ongoing efforts to write the flows of power.

Foucault's refusal of a single language should be recalled whenever a reader feels the impulse to explain him by looking to his sources. Of course, Foucault inherits theological, philosophical, and scientific languages for describing power. He never pretends to be writing about power for the first time (or the last). If Foucault criticizes previous languages (as he criticizes Hegel in enumerating these three errors), he also adopts their metaphors. It can be tempting to turn to his predecessors in hope of fixing his usage. The temptation should be resisted. The sources closest to Foucault speak complex, idiosyncratic languages.

Foucault makes their usage more complicated still by refusing ever to adopt just one of them—indeed, by refusing the wish for a single and satisfyingly technical vocabulary for power. I can show this by recalling quickly his negotiations with the widely circulating languages of three obvious predecessors.

A first vernacular for power would be Hegel's description of the master-slave relation in *Phenomenology of Spirit*, especially as it was translated and interpreted by Kojève, whose Parisian lectures on Hegel during the 1930s were attended, it sometimes seems, by every significant French thinker of two generations.[16] Since the master-slave dialectic actually serves him as a key to the whole *Phenomenology*, Kojève augments his French translation with paraphrases and supplements. In the section on master and slave, to speak superficially, Kojève's Hegel narrates the origin of properly human self-consciousness in the relation of domination established after a combat almost to the death. The word "power" appears throughout the description, but what Kojève's Hegel calls "the feeling of absolute power" is the experience of the slave in defeat and forced service.[17] Kojève glosses this (first) sense of power as the "anguish" and "terror inspired by the Master." It resembles in many ways sovereign power at the beginning of *Discipline and Punish*. That is one reason why Foucault associates Hegel with the error of conceiving power anachronistically as domination.

Nietzsche would supply a second vernacular for power around which Foucault must write. Setting aside *The Will to Power*, that pastiche assembled after Nietzsche's death, it can be helpful to recall passages from the great trilogy—*Gay Science, Zarathustra, Beyond Good and Evil*. They often identify the deepest form of power with life itself. Consider the single line from *Beyond Good and Evil*: "Life itself is will to power."[18] From this overrich remark, draw only the sense that power is intrinsically productive, that its incessant productivity is life. This gives a second meaning of power in the learned vernaculars: power is making, especially the making that is living. For Foucault too, power is evidently productive, but often not in the sense that Nietzsche intended—and without Nietzsche's Romantic allegories of Life herself.

A third inherited language, perhaps the most obvious, is found in Freud.[19] Foucault's account here of the nineteenth-century origin of instinct means to undo one of the central Freudian terms for motive power. Still Foucault inherits Freud's language as a learned vernacular, not least because of the prevalence of psychoanalytic terminology in his Paris. However we sort the historical sequences, a Freudian term like "psychic energy" can suggest a third meaning of power: a quantum that circulates by redistribution within a closed system. Foucault sometimes flirts with this notion, but then he immediately rejects it.

Hegel, Nietzsche, Freud: the authorial names are sufficient warning against thinking that Foucault wished for simple languages about power. Especially when these authorships are reduced to vernacular slogans (as I have just done), it should be clear that Foucault doesn't *choose* among them. He adopts no inherited language as his own. He refuses to impose a single vocabulary in their stead. Rather, he revises a number of dissonant languages. One after another, he presents different stories about power compressed into alternate clusters of metaphors. Not a new technical vocabulary, then, but a dramaturgy of power's images.

FROM METAPHORS TO PERSONIFICATIONS

Foucault stages a succession of metaphors on many pages of his writing. The deliberate variation of metaphors is one of his most familiar stylistic devices. Precisely because it is so familiar, so much a habit of Foucault's writing voice, it can be easy to skip over. A reader should pause every now and then over some of the sequences. There are many of them in the lectures on abnormals. I take just two, from about a third of the way into the series, somewhat after the presentation of Ubu-power.

The first passage describes the invention of instinct as a crucial concept for the discourse within which abnormals will appear. Instinct ushers the abnormals onstage to replace older categories such as the monster. Just before this passage, Foucault has claimed that the new category of instinct arises not by brave discovery, with a ringing Eureka!, but out of changing "conditions of possibility" for the term's rule-bound use. The concept of instinct is not discovered so much as elaborated in between earlier discourses of power.

> Importance of this meshing [as of gears' teeth, *engrenage*] on the basis of which the notion of instinct can appear and be formed: because instinct will become, of course, the great vector [*vecteur*] of the problem of the anomaly, or even the operator [*opérateur*] through which crimi-

nal monstrosity and simple pathological madness will find their principle of coordination. . . . [The concept of instinct makes it possible to
organize] the whole problematic of the abnormal, of the abnormal
at the level of the most elementary and everyday conduct. This passage to the minuscule, the great drift [*dérive*] by which the monster,
the great cannibalistic monster from the beginning of the nineteenth
century, is finally minted [cashed out, exchanged, *monnayé*] under the
form of all the little perverted monsters who have not stopped multiplying [teeming, sprouting, *pulluler*] since the end of the nineteenth
century, this passage from the great monster to the little pervert could
not happen except through this notion of instinct.[20]

Foucault returns to the recitation of metaphors a few minutes later. Listen again for the sequence of images.

This transformation has as linchpin [joint, *cheville*], as gear mechanism [*mécanisme d'engrenage*], this problematic, this technology
[*technologie*] of the instincts. . . . If my demonstration is correct (because it wants to be a demonstration), you see that all of this, all
of these epistemological effects—or rather technological [effects]—
from what did they appear? From a certain play [interplay, shared
functioning, *jeu*], from a certain distribution and a certain meshing
of mechanisms of power [*mécanismes de pouvoir*], some characteristic of the judicial institution, others of the medical institution—or
rather of medical power and knowledge. It is in the play of these
two powers, it is in their difference and their meshings, in the needs
that they had for each other, and the supports that they found in
each other, it is there that the principle [beginning, *principe*] of the
transformation was made. That one has passed from a psychiatry of
delirium to a psychiatry of instinct . . . the reason is there, I believe,
in this interlocking [*enclenchement*] of power.[21]

Consider now what you have heard, perhaps for the twentieth time.

In these two passages, the most obvious metaphors are *mechanical*:
meshing of gears, operator, stamping out coins, linchpin, gear mechanism, technology, interplay of parts, distribution, interlocking compo-
nents. The hearer is placed inside one of Piranesi's imagined prisons.
Massive constructions, unlit, catch a minute human body, barely visible
in the gloom. Reinforcing these metaphors, Foucault uses others, which

might be called *geometrico-logical*: point, vector, operator (again), principle, problem or problematic, (spatial) organization (as around an axis), elementary, and (with emphasis!) demonstration. It is as if Foucault were seeing modern power as an interaction of forces exerted through an engineer's space, for precise fractions of time, in exceptionless conformity to equations.[22]

Does Foucault criticize the picture of power vested in the inviolable body of the monarch or the hierarchical brutality of the slave owner only to vest it in a Victorian fantasy of steam engines? He unrolls these images in aid of his own warning about misconceiving power. They help him undo the metaphors of deliberate agency contained in the three errors. They suggest the scale or complexity of power relations, cautioning against utopian reveries of easy revolution. But Foucault doesn't stop with two sets of corrective metaphors. In the self-revising flow of his speech, neither the mechanical nor the geometrico-logical metaphors stand in last place. There is no last place because there can be no complete lexicon for power.

Look at the metaphors again. *Démonstration*, for example, also has a medical sense: it is what happens in the kind of medical classroom called an anatomical theater. Similarly, the most common sense of *cheville* is ankle, a biological joint. *Opérateur* is an old word for surgeon. *Vecteur*, which could mean the calculated resultant of mechanical forces, has here its pathological sense, the vector that carries a disease. *Pulluler* is typically used of insects or animals. A range of other words can take a biological spin, such as "use" and "functioning." Most unusual are the implicit biological personifications in Foucault's talk about the reciprocal need and mutual support of systems of power. So the mechanical or geometrico-logical metaphors are brought into opposition—into a play of forces—with medical and biological metaphors. Remember the backdrop for the first staging of Jarry's *King Ubu*: all the settings scrambled, all seen at once. Foucault's metaphors for power are like that. They are modernist pastiche or surrealist reverie or the random juxtapositions of the archives—which is to say, of lived history.

If Foucault often imitates the metaphorical habits of the language he is trying to describe, the next moment he quotes metaphors from deliberately incompatible accounts. The juxtaposition allows certain terms to be used under erasure, half canceled. We learn from the juxtapositions here that any biological metaphors for power have to be understood without an implication of agency or fixed teleology. If the sequence of metaphors in the two passages seems to imply a personification that culminates when Foucault tells how power needs support or offers it, the very movement through the mechanical and geometrico-logical language has rendered those locutions all too evidently metaphorical. If personification has its risks (and more about those in a moment), it also has its favored plots. They can register in language some of power's changes.

Let me say this again, from the side of the hearer. When the deliberate mixture of Foucault's metaphors is unsatisfying, the reason might be that a hearer has been deceived by the academic theater or haunted by the memory of experts in courtrooms. She might still be awaiting an expert opinion that will summarize speeches about power before rendering a final judgment on them. She might expect the theories of power to be lined up as so many diagnostic -isms, like Alcibiadinism, Erostratism, Bovarism (in its several degrees). Indeed, Foucault's academic fame—he is onstage at the Collège de France—reinforces an expectation that he will settle the true and final verdict on power with an expert opinion of his own. This is an illusion or, more exactly, a genre mistake.[23]

Models for Foucault's speech about power are to be found not in the standard genres of academic philosophy that he mocks, much less in expert opinion rendered as if for a court. They come from his favorite novels. In them he finds narrative containers strong enough to hold together the mutating languages of power. I think of Blanchot, of course, but also of a book like Julien Gracq's *Le rivage des Syrtes*. A few years before he delivered the lectures on abnormals, Foucault is reported to have said that this book was "one of the most beautiful novels that I have ever read." In an interview given the same spring as the lectures, Foucault mentions the novel again as one of the few that has stood out from his limited reading.[24] I will take those mentions as sufficient excuse for recalling Gracq's novel as another parable about languages of power.

THE LIVES OF POWER

On its surface, Gracq's novel is a first-person narrative, told in retrospect, about an incident that renews an old war or disrupts an illusion of peace. Aldo, the hapless protagonist, is a young aristocrat who abruptly tires of life as an aesthete-libertine in the capital city. A decaying commercial republic like Venice, Orsenna clings to the forms of its lost empire. On an impulse, Aldo asks for posting to a remote province. He is sent as an "Eye" or civilian observer to a dilapidated naval outpost. Neither astute nor bold, he is engulfed from the first by events that he does not understand. When he recklessly leads a ship into the territorial waters of the ancient enemy, his folly appears to spark a disastrous renewal of hostilities. Of course, the enemy had already been preparing an invasion, and his recklessness may have been anticipated by a clique within his own government.

Just below its surface, the action of Gracq's novel occurs less in ambiguous diplomatic intrigues than in descriptions of power as it animates events, people, and landscapes. From its first page, the novel rehearses analogies or allegories for changes in power. Orsenna's governing body, the Signory, is likened to a bankrupt nobleman living in seclusion, safe from his creditors yet fallen into "decrepitude and enervation." The distant province of Syrtes, to which Aldo is assigned, has already atrophied: "life has withdrawn from these distant extremities, as if the too parsimonious blood of a mummified political body no longer reached them."[25] Power is like life in a body and just as mortal. Or not. The novel soon enough complicates bodily metaphors. Orsenna doesn't decline in protected solitude. Its internal processes are influenced—undone, decided—by other forces. Orsenna's ancient rival, Farghestan, encircles and infiltrates its territories. Whatever power is, it is *not* a single process in an isolated body.

Perhaps that is why Gracq also notices from the novel's beginning the discrepancies between power's names and the things it pretends to govern. Consider Orsenna's relations to Farghestan. An inconclusive naval bombardment three centuries earlier gave way first to a lull in fighting and then to decades of silent disengagement in which it finally seemed too provocative even to negotiate a peace treaty. Yet in the official language of Orsenna, the states are always "at war" (if not quite in a "war on terror"). Not a single sheet has been removed from the ancient dossier that enumerates the seventy-two distinct justifications for the attack upon Farghestan. Aldo is dispatched with all formality to keep watch over "the Admiralty," the official name for a sagging shell of a fortress that smells of "ancient power and mold." It sits on "the front," a landscape of forgotten marshes and silted harbors, where a handful of vessels is kept afloat to patrol sponge fishing. The same discrepancy appears at every level of official language, from proclamations to gossip. Aldo is told in Orsenna that the officer in charge of the Admiralty is "boring." From their first encounter, he realizes that Captain Marino is a disconcertingly canny and forceful "unknown."[26]

In Gracq, as in Jarry, the distance between the official formulas and the material realities can become comic. Aldo originally describes his posting as "a ceremony grown half clownish over the years." Welcoming Aldo ceremonially to "the Syrtes front," Marino lifts his glass "just to the height of a smile of visible irony."[27] Yet Gracq's irony is not Jarry's buffoonery. The novel registers changing power in the way that the play does not. As power recedes, it clings most tenaciously to its language. If the official formulae no longer work for Aldo or on him, they circulate more rapidly still in the capital. Returning to the city, he finds not a condemning silence but histrionic debates about future victories: "the sign retained authority, survived the thing it signified."[28]

Aldo is brought at last before the head of the Signory for what the reader expects will be his chastisement. It becomes instead a last study of the tropes of power. At an advanced age (of course), a certain Danielo has been brought by subtle manipulations from his rural study to what claims to be the center of authority. As a historian, he has studied power. A latecomer to its exercise, he speaks of it with a convert's melodramatic fervor. Aldo himself remarks on the calibrated "mise-en-scène" of their conversation.[29] In the novel's longest monologue, Danielo befriends Aldo, chides him, threatens him, and gives him new instructions. But the heart of the speech—its true "State secret"—is Danielo's confession of love. "I have loved power. . . . I shall not struggle against my pleasure. . . . It has distracted me for years." After a lifetime of scholarly restraint, Danielo relishes the experience of "the disconcerting ease with which things are done. There was also for me this practically inexhaustible amusement: to realize that the machine works, that a thousand gearwheels [rouages] play and function when one presses the button. . . . Then there comes another pleasure, the pleasure of arriving at a single goal by several circuits. One doesn't get tired—one doesn't tire for a long time of seeing that these gear assemblies [engrenages] mesh. . . . I've had pleasure from this machinery [mécanique]."[30] The similarities with

Foucault's language are obvious. I note them not to offer Gracq as Foucault's true source but to show how richly a novel like Gracq's can register competing languages of power and their pleasures. It does so by a range of personifications. In them, the metaphors coalesce and change, desire and release. Performing a series of languages in the narrative of his lectures, Foucault not only multiplies metaphors; he shows too their mutation through personification.

Aldo tells the reader in the novel's first chapter that the banality of Orsenna's old "victory" over Farghestan was no impediment to the poets who continued to sing it. On the contrary, they took an "excessive liberty . . . to add here without measure to the known facts, to pile giant episodes onto this third-rate war one after another, as if they had found there, for their genius, an inexhaustible source of renewal."[31] One could say the same of the discourses of many modern powers as Foucault rehearses them. The banality of domestic life—of a love triangle, say—incites the poetic genius of the experts. It must also incite anyone who means to represent their new power. Foucault, bard of all our Orsennas!

What then is the difference between Gracq's novel, which Foucault so admires, and Foucault's own epics of aging power? It is not helpful to say that Gracq writes fictions while Foucault writes facts, or even that Gracq writes novels while Foucault writes histories. A serious reader of Nietzsche, Foucault is quite ready to affirm that he writes fiction and only fiction. He will even claim sometimes to write novels, then proceed to redefine the novel and to undo its sense of authorship.[32]

When he is not speaking the high tongues of Nietzsche or Blanchot, Foucault does sometimes admit a little rivalry with novels. Over dinner on the terrace of his apartment, Foucault denies to Claude Mauriac ever thinking of writing novelistic fiction. Instead he has made "fictional use [*usage fictif*] of materials that I assemble, bring together, mount, making by design fictive constructions with authentic elements."[33] This is a remark about a constraint of sources and forms. It associates Foucault with modernist makers of collages of found objects, as if his books were like the little boxes of Joseph Cornell. The association could lead to another series of questions about the aesthetics of the *objet trouvé*—or, more precisely, the *enoncé trouvé*. A reader could wonder, for example, about the difference between Foucault's quotation from archives and

Gracq's Venetian references. Or about how Foucault's archival citations are and are not like the elements of daily life that Blanchot finds in the kind of novel named after Balzac. But it may be more helpful to ask about the effect of writing fictions from found speech.

In an interview conducted late in 1976, Foucault underlines the importance for him of the "problem of fiction" and insists that it's quite distinct from questions about truth. "It seems to me that there is a possibility of making fiction work in truth, of inducing effects of truth with a discourse of fiction, and of proceeding such that the discourse of truth elicits, manufactures something that didn't exist before, thus that it 'fictions.'" Here Foucault emphasizes not the formal constraints on his fictions but their effects of novelty. History is fiction: that's trite. History *fictions*: that may be both more interesting and more consequential politically. Foucault continues: "One 'fictions' some history on the basis of a political reality that makes it true; one 'fictions' a politics that doesn't yet exist from a historical truth."[34] Politics makes historical fictioning true—so illuminates our politics. A truth from history fictions a new politics—so shows something important about the politics of writing. Or speaking it onstage.

PERSONIFICATION AND HISTORIOGRAPHY

In the lectures on abnormals, Foucault shows that power can be described only in contradictory metaphors. The metaphors carry compressed stories about how power moves in time, but they are also themselves mutable, mobile. They contain histories, and they are caught up in histories. Foucault, like Gracq, will juxtapose in a single recital various languages about power to emphasize their succession. If succession can be suggested in metaphors (especially biological ones), it is enacted more clearly through personifications. In Gracq, the most striking representation of power is not so much Danielo's monologue as Danielo himself. He stands both for the city's power and for all those who love it. He is the fictive body of power as desiring and desirable. In Foucault, almost as vividly, power not only changes or redirects itself but seems to want or need things, to seek them. Don't those personifications lead us to believe in a single power personified behind all the clusters of metaphors, controlling them and grounding their succession?

The personification of power would seem to be a more dangerous temptation for Foucault than for Jarry or Gracq. He is not restaging a marionette play from the Poland that is nowhere and everywhere. He is not reciting a memoir of an imagined Orsenna. He writes out the power that courses through the bodies before him. So why does he run the risks of personifying power rather than always debunking it or actively urging action against it?

Foucault is not unaware of the dangers. He takes them so seriously that he refuses easy antidotes to them. It is not enough to change doctrines of power if the metaphors, narrative plots, and personifications that pretend to describe it remain unchanged. But most of his hearers don't believe that power resides in metaphors, plots, and personifications. They suffer errors in imagining or representing power. They don't know where to look for power in the world, in themselves. They laugh unthinkingly at the power that can condemn them. Teaching them about power requires showing them where to look for it. They have come to witness the academic power of Michel Foucault. So he begins there. They want a performance. He performs for them. He shows them how power works by speaking all the words of power while reminding them from lecture to lecture that he is an impersonator. His impersonations may reveal to the hearers—to us—not only the means for enabling power to speak through personification but even more the expectations we bring to that speech from our favorite stories.

Foucault has argued in these lectures that our imagination of power lags behind power's mutations. We still use images of absolute monarchies or slave societies to depict the much later forms of power that actually shape us.[35] This belatedness is an effect of power, which requires plausible concealment. Structures of power-knowledge conceal themselves in many ways, including by citing or miming past forms of power. They erase their origin by pretending not to have had an origin. They pass through history unchanged, or they stand outside history. They personify themselves, in other words, as divine.

Foucault writes against representations of power as permanent and inevitable by stressing the origins of particular representations of power or by framing them with earlier and later representations. He forces the historical contrasts in order to unsettle the presentations of power, as he jumbles metaphors to remind that they are only metaphors. When

Foucault indulges in striking contrasts and dramatic reversals, he does so to contest power's penchant for false accords and concealed transitions. He risks hyperbolic history by way of personification because power prefers to hide its entrances and exits. So, in typical passages, Foucault is less interested in precise firstness than in dramatic appearances.[36] Modern power in particular prefers slow and silent invasion. So Foucault selects his examples of its origins for dramatic effect, not chronological precision. He historicizes power by casting it as a protagonist in gaudy narratives because he means to highlight the stagecraft, the scripting, the mythology—I mean, the theology.

Many Western theologies retail stories of a divinity at once immutable and historical. They shape the expectations of Foucault's hearers. So he mocks the craving for stories of divine birth. Describing the rise of the notion of instinct, for example, he presents a nativity scene. This episode of "psychiatric holiness" restages the Christmas story in considerable detail:

> At the center, the instinct of death appears nude; it has just been born. To its side, the patient who is its bearer, its generator; on the other side, the forbidden woman who is the object; and then, behind them, the judicial ox and the psychiatric ass. This is the nativity, the nativity of the divine child, the instinct of death that is now in the process of becoming the first and fundamental object of the psychiatric religion.[37]

A delicious parody of the official historiography of scientific discoveries, it also shows how far Foucault associates the desire for certain kinds of stories with Christianity.

The risks of hyperbolic personification in history writing are real. Foucault runs them, decries them, and runs them again even in this single series of lectures. He does so especially when it comes to Christianity. Its entrances and exits are some of the largest events in our cultural histories. More important, Christianity is a story of grand beginnings and endings that has settled our culture's taste for how to tell all stories about powers and bodies. A bit before the scene of the God who is born in a manger, the Gospel according to Luke restages an angelic visit to Mary. Gabriel announces that she will conceive and bear a son by divine will. She says, "How can this happen, since I do not know a man?"

The angel replies, "The Holy Spirit will come over you, and the power [*dynamis*, Vulgate *virtus*] of the Most High will overshadow you" (Luke 1:34–35). Foucault knows the widespread taste for stories of birth by a divine power working from the shadows. Or he knows how fully we have based our notion of powerful personifications on Christian plots.

CHRISTIAN PERSONIFICATIONS

Before the late 1970s, Foucault succumbs regularly to the temptations of personification when narrating Christianity. The habit begins long before his lectures on abnormals. Consider a small example: in *History of Madness*, he had relied for church law on Paolo Zacchia, *Quaestiones medico-legales*, composed in the first half of the seventeenth century. Foucault says of Zacchia that he "drew up the exact balance sheet of all Christian jurisprudence concerning madness" and then, more astonishingly, that he was "the inheritor of the whole tradition of Christian law."[38] This is a startling simplification for someone so attentive to shifts and ruptures in fields of knowledge—because, of course, Zacchia no more sums up the traditions of Western church law than Tuke and Pinel sum up earlier discourses about madness. On the contrary, Zacchia subscribes to a peculiarly modern project that evacuates the penitential subject into its discrete acts.

In the same way, Foucault's lectures on abnormals present an admittedly schematic history of Christian penance: from the Irish penitentials, to Scholastic sacramental theories, to the reforms of the Council of Trent and the spread of spiritual direction.[39] His narrative of decisive changes blurs a series of survivals, returns, and reversals. Foucault seems to relish Romantic notions about the curious timelessness of church institutions. He suggests that Counter-Reformation confessional practices have persisted into our present. "The whole sacramental economy of penance, as one will know it not only toward the end of the Middle Ages but down to our own days, is more or less fixed." Or he says to his audience about the confessional: "an institution, or rather a little object, a little piece of furniture that you know well."[40] As if, in a fit of Romantic medievalism, he believed that the Catholic Church could still practice late medieval or Counter-Reformation forms of power. As if he had forgotten his own remarks in *Discipline and Punish* about how the new modality of discipline infiltrates all of the earlier forms of power—how Norm reacts upon Law, Word and Text, Tradition. As if he were unaware of how claims of persistence underwrite church power in the present. An unbroken transmission of power in the church guarantees the power of the church.

There will be occasion to think later about why this might happen for Foucault precisely with regard to Christianity. It is worth remembering, here as elsewhere, that Foucault's historical tableaux are always didactic. In the lectures on abnormals, for example, the history of the Christian confessional appears to illustrate three lessons. One is about sex and speech. Another is about the contribution of Christian pastoral practice to modern disciplinarity, especially forensic psychiatry. The third lesson is about bodies as a site or an occasion of resistance to discipline. I will rehearse the first and second lessons quickly since they will return at greater length in Foucault's later writing. I will then underline the importance of the third lesson, the one about bodies.

Foucault turns to his *first lesson* about Christianity two-thirds of the way into the lectures on abnormals. The transition can appear abrupt or artless, but it is not haphazard.[41] The jerky transition results from Foucault's regular use of a nested or circular construction when he turns to Christian topics. They appear not as sidebars or digressions but as embedded reflections. In the lectures on abnormals, the jerky transition is motivated by the topic of sex. Having described how the concept of instinct came to cover the whole field of psychiatry, not least in expert opinion, Foucault picks up another thread of inquiry: the field of abnormality was crossed from the beginning by "the problem of sexuality."[42] Through notions of heredity and degeneration, sexual reproduction became the causal matrix for abnormality. More important, familiar or scandalous sexual abnormalities offered early material for psychiatric expertise. Soon enough, they were being treated as the root of other abnormalities. What accounts for this sudden interest in sexuality, which had played a much smaller role in the earlier sciences of mental alienation?

Foucault wants to persuade his audience that the answer is not the sudden disappearance of a prohibition on speech. Sexuality gains prominence with the handing over to the new science of abnormality of well-established procedures for controlling speech. These procedures come from the pastoral practice of Christian churches, where distinctively modern forms of control had been cultivated for several centuries and older forms for millennia. Sexuality appears in the new science of abnormality during the nineteenth century because the site of its articulation has changed. We talk about it no longer in the confessional but in the clinic. Whatever the site, sexuality as such has always been articulated. "In a general way, I would say this: sexuality, in the West, is not what one silences; it is not what one is obliged to keep silent but what one is obliged to confess."[43] To confess—once ritually and sacramentally, now medically and legally.

For his *second lesson*, Foucault inserts a schematic history of Christian confession in the genealogy of nineteenth-century abnormality. The Christian practice has a long history across which confession means many different things. In the modern period, it develops in tandem with the new forms of discipline in armies, workshops, and schools. The early modern intensification of sacramental confession leads to the development of another practice, what we call in English "spiritual direction" but what Foucault knows in French as *direction de conscience*, direction of conscience. From the second half of the sixteenth century on, this new technique requires increasingly more detailed speech about sexuality and increasingly greater vigilance over the body. Since a new form of power-knowledge must posit a correlative object (recall *Discipline and Punish*), it is not the same old body that is the object of spiritual direction. It is a body double called the flesh (*la chair*). The desiring body—the concupiscent body, to use the technical term—is coded or gridded as a flesh that can be endlessly monitored and copiously described.[44] Flesh is a way of personifying a new power through or behind the body. Like its successor, sexuality, it is defined from the first in relation to speech: "Flesh is what one names; flesh is that of which one speaks; flesh is what one says. Sexuality is essentially ... not what one does but what one confesses."[45] There are rules for this speech. On the one hand, it must be exhaustive, a gridding applied to the whole of one's life, since fleshly concupiscence can insinuate itself anywhere. On the other hand, the speech must be exclusive: one says everything, but only to one's director.

Foucault concedes that the techniques of spiritual direction were applied only to a small segment of the population, chiefly in seminaries, monasteries, and convents. Still he urges their general importance. They are connected with the origin of modern forms of Catholic mysticism. They also reveal a new degree of pastoral power, of thorough Christianization, that produces the early modern phenomenon of demonic possession. Foucault spends the greater part of a lecture analyzing the emergence and the consequences of that phenomenon. The account is a limit case in the staging of speech and its bodies.

BODILY CONVULSIONS

For this *third lesson*, about Christianity and bodies, Foucault takes as his dossier Michel de Certeau's *The Possession of Loudun*.[46] The book contains a commented selection of documents from a notorious case of demonic possession during the early 1630s at an Ursuline convent north of Poitiers (Foucault's birthplace). The case provoked a large literature, beginning with polemical pieces written as it unfolded. It is often familiar now through the fictionalized account by Aldous Huxley, John Whiting's play, Ken Russell's film, or the opera by Penderecki. Certeau's book is different from all of these—in its attention to the surviving historical records, in its emphasis on their uncertainties. Certeau emphasizes the competition of narratives applied to the bodies of the possessed and the increasing complexity of the scripts they were forced to perform. Foucault does not disagree with Certeau, but he wants to impose his own reading on the assembled archive. He will construe the case as a lesson about how bodies resist the incursions of new powers of personification. The result is a clarifying example of Foucauldian historiography.

Foucault contrasts possession with witchcraft. While witchcraft is rural and outside the church, possession is urban and within church institutions. While witchcraft sells the witch's body to copulate with the devil in exchange for powers, possession is a constant struggle that divides the body itself. The contrasts continue, but Foucault is most interested in renarrating what he repeatedly calls, following Certeau, the "theater of possession." Theater it certainly was. At Loudun, large crowds gathered for the exorcisms, and measures were taken to ensure a good show. It was an approved pornography: the nuns were mostly young women, constrained and taunted. But theirs was no routine scene of bondage. The bodies onstage performed the contest of the world's great powers.

In possession, the central figure is the "sacred character" of the spiritual director become exorcist.[47] He is triangulated with the devil and the (female) possessed. Reading the records from Loudun, we might expand Foucault's three figures into five or six. The director-exorcist stands in for the person of the church, which draws its power in turn from a thoroughly personified God. The devil, another person, often employs a sorcerer as intermediary: in this case, on the official account, it was the parish priest. So the stage is filled with characters, each refracted in various relations. Most important for Foucault, the nun's body is doubled as passive receptacle and source of resistance, at once subject to demonic power and struggling against it. Her body must be repersonified by the director-exorcist through the category of flesh. The flesh is the miniature stage for spiritually significant pleasures or culpable desires. Only by its superimposition does the body become legible as a theater of mortal combat, "citadel-body, battle-body."[48] Flesh is a distinctive form of Christian power, but even more the great example in the West of the body double. It shows how to control the body by personifying it through a script.

Unexpectedly, the nun's body begins to convulse. Its convulsions are "the plastic and visible form of the combat within the body of the possessed."[49] The combat is not only between the flesh and the devil: the body also rejects its assigned role as flesh. The main combat is indeed not between God and the devil or the exorcist and the invading (lesser) demons. It is between the body underneath the flesh and the power of the spiritual director. The flesh is projected by the pastorate of the sixteenth and seventeenth centuries as the focal point of an extended surveillance. Bodies must be coached in its scripts, since they are expected to talk about themselves in the ordinary administration of confession and the extraordinary performance of exorcism. When the new ecclesiastical technology for controlling souls pushes too far, it encounters first the disordered speech of possession and then the cry of convulsion. Indecency, blasphemy, and babbling are possession's regular indices. Whenever the demons are presumed to control them, the Ursulines are permitted to say all sorts of forbidden things. Afterward they deny responsibility by professing not to remember any of it. The technology of pastoral speech also meets less comic resistance: the body that groans or screams. "Convulsive flesh is the effect of resistance to this [pastoral] Christianization at the level of individual bodies."[50] The official demand for endless speech is contradicted by a dramatic interruption, a somatic refusal of the script.

What sorts of convulsions are these? Do the nuns produce them in order to resist? Or do their bodies, pushed too far, react as it were by themselves against the encroachments of priestly violence? Neither description is adequate. There is no bodily agency in this resistance—as there is no simple description of the bodies under possession. It would be both accurate and inaccurate to say that the convulsions are a kind of counter-speaking, a counter-theater, yet without a (human) claim of authorship. On the one hand, Foucault has emphasized the theatrical character of the proceedings at Loudun and the ambivalence of the nuns' role in them. On the other hand, "convulsive flesh" (flesh, not body) "is the effect of resistance." It is an effect of material resistance, not a choice. It startles pastoral power by revealing power of another sort—startles it but doesn't thereby elude it. Nor does it create a unity behind the convulsions: there is no author for these fleshly reactions.

Ignoring these subtleties, the ecclesiastical theater at Loudun won't permit convulsion to throw off personifications. It judges it a counter-performance. So the church imposes increasingly detailed scripts on the interactions of director and possessed. The assembled exorcists map the demonic presences within the body as an aid to interpretation. They gather guidelines for reading facial expressions or gestures. They even permit what would otherwise be intolerable displays of physical offense against their own power. At one public session, a nun mocks one official with caresses before kicking another. These bodily expressions of resistance are tolerated because they are recuperated—by interpretation but also by asserting final control over the resistant bodies. The demons "inside" the nuns are first made to obey the exorcists' commands to assume all sorts of positions (like trained animals).[51] They are then cast out of the bodies, leaving the nuns exhausted and docile. More dramatically, most violently, the disobedience of these bodies is recuperated for churchly meanings when the body of their alleged sorcerer, the parish priest, is tortured and burned at the stake. The old theater of the *supplice* is recalled to reinforce the new theater of spiritual direction.

Loudun is a theater in which convulsing bodies are brought to heel by policing personifications. The nuns' resistance is personified in the devil, his demons, his sorcerer. Once personified, it is interpreted and then restrained until it can be replaced by the opposite power, mediated through divine personifications. As Certeau notes, Jarry himself was interested in some aspects of the performances at Loudun, perhaps especially the symmetry of divine and demonic personifications together with their bodily concomitants. I'm more interested in the curious resemblances of the theatrical aesthetic of *King Ubu* to the public displays at Loudun. Certeau speaks at one point of the tragicomedy in the convent.[52] Tragic, certainly, in its consequences for those involved—the exposed sisters, the condemned priest, even the famous inquisitors. (The most remarkable writer among them, the Jesuit Surin, offered the demons his body in exchange for that of the possessed Jeanne des Anges. More than a decade later, after ferocious suffering, Surin attempted a dramatic suicide.) Tragic, then, but comic too—in the verbal and bodily antics of the demons, in the exorcists' (pretended?) credulity, in the deployment of a bureaucratic science of demonic proofs.

The comedy provides one link between Foucault's remarks on the possessions and his preoccupations throughout the lectures on abnormals. Another is found in the invention or improvisation of power languages that the case required. The outbreak at Loudun ends in one sense with the *supplice* of the local priest. It ends actually, says Foucault, with the adaptive modification of ecclesiastical power. If every extension of power elicits resistance, every resistance incites the rhetorical genius of power.

According to Foucault, the Roman Catholic Church learns its lessons from Loudun. Realizing that it has pushed too far, spiritual direction contrives ways to practice its interior gridding without provoking convulsion, without producing such theatrical resistance. One contrivance moderates the intrusiveness of pastoral speech, especially into the body's desires. So the general demand for confession is modulated by "a rule of style, or rhetorical imperatives" that limit the detail of sexual confession.[53] If an overly aggressive demand for reporting desire provokes unwanted bodily resistance, then the demand will be qualified, though never abandoned. Another contrivance, more important for Foucault's larger story, is to exclude the convulsive body from the purview of spiritual direction. The paroxysms of flesh must belong not to Christian confession or spiritual direction but to another system of power. So convulsion passes from spiritual direction to medicine, and eventually to a new specialization in nervous disorders. Here is "the great and famous passing of power to medicine," a decisive episode in the centuries-long negotiations between doctors and priests.[54] When religion cedes convulsion to medicine, it endows medicine with new power, including the power to elicit speech about sex.

In the spring of 1975, Foucault speaks for three more Wednesdays about the further development of sexuality within medicine. In the last minutes of the series, he returns to the contemporary French courtroom and King Ubu. A court is supposed to pose a triple question to the psychiatric expert about an individual brought before it. Is the individual dangerous, indictable, curable? Neither judicial nor medical, these questions have meaning only in the middle space of the science of abnormality. The abnormal degenerate is dangerous, cannot profitably be indicted, and can never be cured. The "Ubu-esque descriptions" that still constitute expert opinions—the descriptions with which Foucault began these lectures—recall and perpetuate the nineteenth-century science of abnormality each time they are spoken. The opinions constitute "a literature at once tragic and zany." A literature at once convulsively tragic and convulsively comic—or, as Certeau would say, a literature that veers unpredictably from fear to laughter.[55]

In Jarry, Gracq, and Certeau, Foucault finds eminent students of such literature. He reads them as examples of how to reperform and so expose the machinations of power. He has noticed in each, but especially Certeau, the moments at which bodies refuse to perform their personifications. Of course, it would be too simple—too deceptively comforting—to put full faith in a *real* body, knowable before all personifications, that could serve as the fulcrum for overturning power. Power keeps writing its curious poetry, keeps changing its scripts at any sign of surprising resistance. Power tends not toward true science but toward more cunning poetics.

CHAPTER 4

CHATTING GENITALS

A COMMON MISTAKE IN READING—funny or fatal—is to take an ironic passage for a literal one. The mistake can arise from faulty writing but more often from faulty reading. A reader misses cues by reading too quickly—or ignores them in wanting the text to deliver something it never meant to give. Readers who demand certainties will ignore a text's ironic disclaimers. Readers who require that a text deliver a specific brand of knowledge—a science, a theory—will hold the text down until it changes into what they seek.

When Foucault's *History of Sexuality* 1 appeared in English in 1978, it arrived out of sequence among his works and in an inattentive translation. It also reached readers eager to regard Foucault as someone who could accomplish mighty feats for them.[1] So, in English, Foucault's little book was first required to empower gay history, as if Foucault had written a history of sex; then to guide revolutionary action in the present, as if Foucault had proposed a political plan; and finally, to supply axioms for queer theory, as if he had delivered the fundamental knowledge of sexuality, when he had in fact done everything to show its insubstantiality, its spectral mystifications. Foucault's writing was somehow combined with the urgent certitude of identity politics and its testimonies. Liberation and identity always make an odd couple.

Conditions of reception like these cannot be overcome by more pedantic translation or by helpful sidebars on Foucault's career. The conditions result less from ignorance than from desire—from the pious investments that constitute a certain sort of reader. Such investments led many to the newly translated book but did not prepare them for its ironies.[2] The readers most likely to be interested in *History of Sexuality* 1 were those least likely to receive it as ironic. Yet the book begins not by denouncing the churches and their anathemas on sex, not by decrying hypocritical rulers and their prudery police, not by urging revolt against the complicity of courts and expert psychiatric witnesses, not by dismissing Freud or socially compulsory psychoanalysis. The little book begins by mocking Foucault's political allies: the proponents of sexual liberation and, indeed, of gay pride. Its ironies fix on the most pious readers by debunking the scriptural story that grounds their felt righteousness.[3]

The tone in these passages is not subtle. Foucault lets himself go whenever he paraphrases fervent faith in sexual revolution. He mimics the portentous tones, the hortatory cadences, the resort to theological hyperbole—to the extravagance of scriptural speech. Sex has become, he remarks at one point, "the secret, the omnipotent cause, the hidden meaning, the fear without respite."[4] These are all attributes of some versions of the Christian God and His (!) revealed Word. Foucault's irony culminates during the concluding peroration, when it attacks the whole regime that endows sexuality with such awful powers. "Irony of this disposition: it makes us believe that it concerns our liberation."[5] Irony is the book's final lesson, but also its constant manner.

The effects of irony in *History of Sexuality* 1 are aided by two other devices that resist pious readers who come in search of a caucus platform or sure steps toward self-improvement. The book is resolutely abstract. (Foucault would later describe its argument as *en pointillé*, in dotted outline.)[6] It seems to presume acquaintance with its cases and sources or else to suppose that their details don't really matter, because it offers them only as examples rather than as evidence. The book provides nothing like a detailed reading of individual episodes. Its most extensive report, the case of Jouy, is delivered with an allusive casualness likely to give offense. The book's section on method lists "propositions" that are specifically antirevolutionary, and its "rules" are labeled as (anti-Cartesian) "prescriptions for prudence."[7]

To make matters worse, *History of Sexuality* 1 stands in confusing relation to the series of historical studies that it supposedly inaugurates.

Part of the confusion is the English subtitle, *An Introduction*. The phrase is an artifact of translation. The French subtitle says, more substantively, *The Will to Knowledge*. *An Introduction* can seem to promise a methodological foundation or at least some solid axioms and principles. Read that way, the book will disappoint. *The Will to Knowledge* suggests, more aptly, that this little book considers the very impulse to know sexuality, a will to knowledge that moves both its readers and its writer.

REMAINING VICTORIANS

The title of Foucault's first chapter puns on the title of another book. As he will shortly explain, *Other Victorians* is a study by Stephen Marcus of figures not ordinarily included in common myths about Victoria's reign: "the prostitute, her client and pimp, the psychiatrist and his hysteric." Foucault plays on Marcus's title, expanding it and repunctuating it as "We Others, Victorians."[8] This means several things. We others, who count ourselves as still trapped by Victorian repression. We others, who imagine that we are rising up from the margins of society to protest repression, like prostitutes and hysterics in revolt. We new Victorians, compelled still to tell our stories—just as they were—for moral edification and public health.

Foucault carries forward the play on words as he begins to recite the pious story of Victorian repression and present liberation. He offers only a few clues that he will reverse it. The first comes three sentences in: "Still at the start of the seventeenth century, it is said [*dit-on*], a certain frankness was current." We are reading not historical fact but a recitation. It imagines that in the imagined era of free speech, an early modern Eden, there was no need for secrecy: "words were said without excessive reticence, and things without too much disguising." For us, by contrast, because of Victoria, sexuality is (said to be) "mute" and "hypocritical." "The decency of words bleaches [our] discourses."[9]

Foucault rehearses a story about a disconnection between words and things, a story about muteness and hypocrisy. Then he steps back to consider what makes the story about silence so satisfying to recite. The text gives no typographical cue for his transition: there is only an invisible shift of voice. Foucault explains that the story satisfies because it conforms to our favorite schemes of analysis while representing us as not only perceptive but courageous. We have seen through the great repression and now dare to speak it! The "we" here is particular: it includes those versed in leftist economic analyses, dialectical criticism, and the prophecy of revolution. Foucault has sprung a trap on his likeliest readers. He has further suggested that speeches around sexuality ought not to be offered as earnest political critique or urgent revolutionary manifesto. Talk about sexuality ought to be more like the speeches of— but which models does Foucault's ironic writing actually commend?

The first word of the book's body is one of the most famous opening words in contemporary French letters: *Longtemps*, for a long time. In case we should miss the significance, Foucault repeats the word at the opening of the last chapter. *Longtemps*: the first word of Marcel Proust's torrent of a novel-chronicle, his pouring into words of a life's memories, including (notoriously) memories of human desires, their silences, and their fulfillments. In the opening section of the volume titled *Sodom and Gomorrah*, Proust registers the relatively recent appearance of the category "homosexual" in France by juxtaposing it with much older vocabularies, biblical, racial, and biological. But the evocation of Proust also reminds a reader of the salience of struggles to speak sex in European literature. Scientifically tutored politics is not the only available rhetoric for talking sex.

The figure of Proust, writing and rewriting nameless desire, is paired in Foucault with another figure of unrestrained writing: the anonymous author of the Victorian erotic memoir *My Secret Life*. The endless pages of that work, eleven octavo volumes in the first edition, show not only the impulse to write across years but an insatiable fascination with naming sex. As Foucault explains elsewhere, the memoir is "an immense verbal cloth," "a tapestry" of words about a sex life.[10] Foucault knows Gershom Legman's argument that the anonymous author was in fact Harold Ashbee, collector of erotica and compiler (under a Latin pseudonym) of a taxonomic bibliography of pornography. Still Foucault views *My Secret Life* less as a bibliophile's *hommage* than as an experiment in applying language to lived sex. He compares it to Protestant practices of keeping a spiritual journal. For the anonymous memoirist, language has a function that is "instrumental, physiological, exciting, strictly corporeal."[11] Prepared beforehand, inhaled during the act, words remain in memory afterward as a perfume. The compulsive memoirist uses language the way "we" use amyl nitrate—presumably, as a vapor that acts on the body to intensify pleasure. A reference to gay sex in the 1970s, but also, in its emphasis on remembering, a chemical repetition of Proust.

The word flow of *My Secret Life* is a better emblem of our Victorianism than the supposed silence of the widowed queen. We late Victorians have not been forced into silence; we are compelled to speak. The contrast between the memoir's compulsive author and the tight-lipped queen serves Foucault well; so does the implied association between that author and Proust—or the contrast, elsewhere, between that author and Freud. The "immense verbal cloth" of *My Secret Life* is not clinical speech. It is produced under another impulse than therapeutic reporting, an impulse like the one that pushes Proust to write and rewrite. When Foucault urges his readers to notice how much of our supposed repression consists of talking, he also urges us to hear his speech as something other than political declaration or positivist historiography.

Later in *History of Sexuality* 1, Foucault will recall the story of Diderot's *Les bijoux indiscrets, The Indiscreet Jewels* (that is, *Genitals*). In the story, as Foucault abbreviates it, a "good genie," Cucufa, delivers to a "curious sultan," Mangogul, a neglected silver ring that compels women's genitals to speak.[12] The story has more layers than Foucault's brief summary can describe. Published anonymously, it satirizes the French court, but it also attacks European tastes and customs with scathing generality. It dresses itself up in the exotic garb of Afro-Orientalist fantasy, then mocks the tedium and falsehood of travel literature. The book pretends to be translated from the journal of an "African author" and affects philologico-historical scruples. Setting most of its delightful detail aside, Foucault takes just the conceit of talking genitals—with one significant change. In Diderot's novel, the genie's magic ring works only on women. If various pseudo-anatomical speculations are presented to account for this sexual specificity, the novel's answer is much simpler: men do not need to be compelled by a ring to boast of their sexual exploits.[13] They do so regularly and sometimes even candidly. It is Foucault who tacitly generalizes the magical conceit to include both sexes. He writes as if all bodies were female and subject to the whimsically sadistic curiosity of a monarchical and decidedly male Power.

Foucault says that the point of the studies he is about to undertake is nothing other than "to transcribe into history [*en histoire*] the fable of the *Indiscreet Jewels*."[14] What does it mean, to transcribe "into history" a fable in which magic compels bodies to speak through and about their sexes? Apply that question to the title of Foucault's book, that famously misleading and disappointing title. *History of Sexuality*, we say in English, and then (if we have been well taught) quickly point out that sexuality is not sex. This is indeed not a history of *sex*, as so many frustrated readers have discovered after handing over money in pursuit of learned titillation. They might be just as frustrated by the implicit promises of "history" in ordinary English. Without further specification, the French *histoire* means both history and story. Diderot's tale of the talking genitals, for example, calls itself on many pages an *histoire*. If Foucault writes an *histoire* of sexuality, it is history that is inseparable from storytelling. Proust, the anonymous author of *My Secret Life*, and the masked Diderot are more important guides for Foucault's writing than either clinicians of sexual syndromes or statistical historians of sexual acts. Foucault is not interested in counting and classifying orgasms over an interval of European time. He scrutinizes instead the sciences that have been built around a category. He dreams the play of alternate languages over sexed bodies in ecstasy—as they anticipate, enact, and remember.

The play of language fascinates, but so does the collusion of language with the projects of administrative knowledge. The subtitle of this book was the main title of Foucault's first lecture series at the Collège de France.[15] It is obviously a Nietzschean phrase—or, rather, a condensation of a whole series of Nietzschean phrases, of Nietzsche's investigations into the wills, the cravings, the physiologies that stand behind placid claims of objective knowing. Foucault uses some of Nietzsche's other formulations (such as "will to truth"), but for the subtitle he chooses "will to know."[16]

The obvious reference would seem to be to *scientia sexualis*, the sexual science that constitutes sexuality as its object and our desiring selves as its subjects. On this reading, the subtitle suggests that the central task of this little book will be to acquaint us with the operation of the will to sexual knowledge in its several forms, behind the scrim of Victorian "repression," but also within our earnest claims to sexual liberation. This reading stops short. Is there a difference between the will to sexual knowledge and the will to knowledge *about* sexual knowledge? What motivates the writing of *History of Sexuality* 1 if not a will to knowledge somehow preoccupied with sexuality? Is *History of Sexuality* 1 an analysis of that will or an exhibition of it?

I don't pretend to catch Foucault out in a simple contradiction. I think that he chose the subtitle precisely for its double meaning. He analyzes sexual knowledge by eliciting it in his readers and performing it himself.[17] Foucault uses our will to sexual knowledge to lure us into reading him. He wants to show us something about our will. So Foucault deliberately indulges his own will to knowledge about sex to exhibit for our sakes its necessary transformations. He gives in to writing sex even when he writes it ironically. The book's schematic structure is both an image and an undoing of the will to know through writing. Why, then, keep on reading? Everything depends on how the text can redirect the desires for knowing that it activates. Foucault's language must hold us in place while our wills are turned. With Proust, *My Secret Life*, and *The Indiscreet Jewels* as his (anti-)pornographic models, Foucault teases the reader's desires with language that refuses to sate them.

THE PLAN FOR STUDYING SEXUALITY

Having dislocated expectations about language, in his ironic trap and in his allusion to a literary exemplar in Proust, Foucault turns after beginning to something like a declaration of positive purpose. A book's self-descriptions are not always reliable. It can fail to live up to them; they can fail to describe what actually happens in the book; they can be deceitful; and so on. Still it would be foolish to ignore them. One important self-description of *History of Sexuality* 1 comes at the end of the first part, after the turn from the ironic introduction. This is a stubborn passage, because its three sentences do not seem to say the same thing. I take them in order.

"It is at this point that I would like to situate the series of historical analyses of which this book is at once the introduction and something like the first overview: a reconnoitering of some historically significant points and sketches of certain theoretical problems."[18] This is what a reader expects in an introduction to a series of historical studies. Foucault seems to be saying, I am going to survey the principal historical topics or developments with an eye to underlying theoretical problems. So the first volume will combine a preliminary, large-scale narrative with methodological preparation. Even here a reader with a keen ear might suspect some tension between introduction and overview or reconnoitering and sketching. The words imply different spatial relations to the sequence, terrain, or appearance of the object of study. In Foucault, space matters.

"It is concerned in sum with questioning the case of a society that for more than a century noisily castigates itself for its hypocrisy, speaks with prolixity about its own silence, devotes itself to detailing what it does not say, denounces the powers it exercises, and promises to liberate itself from the laws that have made it function." Foucault suggests now that the book is about the "case" of our society, a case that presents conflicting motives and contradictory actions. This book will then be the self-interrogation or self-criticism necessary before the reader can proceed coherently to the historical studies. As if Foucault were saying, I am going to tell you what hides your own situation from you, what masks the operation of your versions of selfhood, before turning back to explore its genealogy. As preparation for studying history, we must untangle ourselves—yet we need the history in order to untangle.

Then the third sentence: "I want to explore not only [that society's] discourses but the will that carries them and the strategic intention that supports them." Here it seems that what is really at stake is the disclosure of a hidden causality. As if Foucault were saying, I am going to show you what actually holds up your ceaseless chatter; it is a will and a strategic intention.

Of these three sentences, the last two are better descriptions of what the little book has so far done. They capture some of its multiple ironies, its allusions, its insistence upon an "us" that very much includes the "you" of the reader. The pages up to this point haven't read like a historical outline. They prepare readers rather for unveiling secrets—not of sex but of why sex feels like our only secret. Here history is a new account of what brought us this far, an account that will replace the one we have been repeating.

Of course, the book's self-description becomes even more complicated as soon as we remember that this is an introduction, survey, reconnoitering, sketching of a series of historical studies that were never written. They were abandoned or indefinitely postponed in favor of other studies. No territory answers to this compositional map.

One plan for the series is presented in synopsis on the back cover of the first edition. There were to be five additional volumes, moving forward from the origin of the modern problematic (the conception of the body as opposed to the flesh), through the main nineteenth-century figures discussed in *Abnormals* (child, hysterical woman, pervert), to the problems of population and races. Within the text of *History of Sexuality* 1, footnote references point to some of these promised volumes, though also to other works that may or may not belong to the series. Foucault also provides a summary of the projected series as the culmination of his discussion of the domain of study.[19] They will first treat, he says, the (modern) formation of the disposition of sexuality on the basis of the Christian conception of the flesh. Then they will follow the development of the disposition through the four "great strategies" deployed in the nineteenth century: sexualization of the child, hystericization of woman, specification of perverts, the regulation of populations. *History of Sexuality* 1 does cover all of these topics, though differently and in various orders. For example, the specification of perverts is treated often and in detail, while questions of population and race are pushed to part 5 and the discussion of biopower. Foucault also rehearses the narrative arc of the whole series within this little book, though in the mode of promise. The chronological span is justified in the discussion of periodization, when Foucault again rejects the standard narrative of repression and liberation with his own story of the ceaseless inventiveness of sexual discourses since the beginning of modernity.

The series of six volumes that Foucault sketches here is not of course what he wrote. Later I will read Foucault's accounts of his change of plans. Now I notice that the structure of *History of Sexuality* 1 already complicates the proposed historical studies by subordinating them to a project of cultural critique and resistant self-fashioning very much in the present. This book does not outline a sequence of historical studies so much as it reformulates historiography as a locus of resistance.

The structure of *History of Sexuality* 1 is explicitly circular.[20] The book is divided into five parts: (1) a critique of our retelling of recent history, (2) a more proper retelling of the same story, (3) a recognition in this retelling of the ideal of *scientia sexualis*, (4) a methodological sketch for future investigation, broken into four subparts, and (5) a return to our own perilous situation under biopower, with a final hint of what might be an alternative story. If you try to tell this sequence more briefly, it might look like this: a false historical narrative, a truer narrative, this truer narrative placed in much longer historical perspective, a sketch of some forms of inquiry useful for redoing the narrative, and then a return to the beginning. The return is marked quite obviously by the repetition of the Proustian *Longtemps*. At each appearance, the *longtemps* is linked to an *aujourd'hui*: for a long time, even now.[21] The book's first words: "For a long time we have suffered, and we still undergo": historiography of and in the present.

The repetition of *Longtemps* at the start of chapter 5 brings the reader back to the present with wider eyes—with a clearer view of what actually shapes us. The corrective act of memory triggered in the present and brought back to it is a Proustian structure of memory return. The circle is also Nietzschean. A very similar circle links the end of *Zarathustra* to its beginning in an image of eternity. Repeating the action, Zarathustra plays his role differently, because he has fashioned himself into someone different along the spiraling transit of the interim. Reader, beware: circular structures mean to change you. You will return to your beginning as somebody else.

The interpenetration of present and past is more than a structural feature of *History of Sexuality* 1. It is built into its central category, sexuality. To repeat: This category doesn't mean the sum of sexual acts, feelings, or pleasures (assuming we could know what counts as sexual). Sexuality is the specific correlate of a recent form of power-knowledge, a science that characterizes the modern period. To explain our ceaseless speaking is to explain how we became subject to that science or, rather, how we came to be formed as subjects for it.

From *Discipline and Punish*, if not already from *History of Madness*, a reader has learned that Foucault is interested in sexuality as one of the prime categories of normalization. A history of sexuality is in some ways the most obvious kind of a narrative about it. So the logic that Foucault applies to the constitution of the objects of this science is one he has applied many times before. He rehearses his basic lesson about the relation of sciences to their objects. *Discipline and Punish* was "a correlative history of the modern soul and of a new power to judge."[22] So too, at the culmination of the first half of *History of Sexuality* 1, sexuality is revealed as the "correlative of that slowly developed discursive practice that *is scientia sexualis*. The fundamental characters of this sexuality . . . correspond to the functional requirements of the discourse that must produce its truth."[23]

Sexuality is just the kind of object that sexual science needs. Subjects defined by reified sexual desire come into being because the new science must exercise its power on them. The language of sexuality is not a representation of preexisting entities, of persons or their intrinsic properties. It is dictated by the shifting tactics, the adjusted operations, and the continuously calibrated effects that constitute science. Here as elsewhere scientific language is not primarily representational; it is artisanal. When Foucault says, "The history of sexuality . . . should be done first from the point of view of a history of discourses," he does not mean by "discourse" an unblemished mirror that reflects what already exists in the world. He means instead that the rules for constructing a scientific language drive its speakers to posit corresponding objects. Sexuality is not reflected in language; it is produced by linguistic operations.

Sexuality may of course come to contain more than science dictates and to function otherwise than science prescribes. A scientific discourse deployed to control a particular group may be reversed. For example, the specification of the perversion of homosexuality may become, by reversal, the language of homosexual liberation. More broadly, the relations of discourse to power are ambivalent. If discourse carries and produces power, it also strays beyond it, undercuts it, exposes its vulnerabilities. So too with silence: an effect of interdiction, it may create spaces for resistance.[24] Still the characteristics of the category of sexuality are determined first neither by reality nor by revolution. They are set forth by the power-knowledge that projects sexuality as such.

SEXUALITY AND THE AFTERLIFE OF CHRISTIANITY

It is possible to read *History of Sexuality* 1 as a simple fulfillment of the final footnote in *Discipline and Punish*. That would suggest, among other things, an expectation about the role of Christianity in its history. In this regard, at least, *History of Sexuality* 1 does not disappoint. From its first pages, it refers regularly to Christianity. As we would expect from the lectures on abnormals, Foucault emphasizes the relations between Christian pastoral practice and the modern project of sexuality. The reform of the Catholic confessional after the Council of Trent is the first example he gives of an explosion of sexual speech in the modern period (even if confessors were also cautioned against lurid description). Foucault suggests that this might be the first time in which the modern West's imperative to speak sex is imposed as a general obligation. The old monastic practices are generalized for all—at least, all who would be saved. Again, and predictably, Foucault launches his study of the multiplication of perversions with the three codes that persisted up to the end of the eighteenth century: canon law, Christian pastoral practice, and civil law (which often drew its sexual categories from the other two).[25]

Other Christian references are less predictable and perhaps more disconcerting for readers with secular prejudices. The language of sexual liberation is said to flatter itself with "an allure of deliberate transgression" (Bataille again), but also to reactivate traditional devices of prophecy, not least by promising life in a new sort of body within a garden of delights. Liberatory speech about sex carries forward many of the functions and varieties of Christian preaching. It has its subtle theologians and its popular, even lyrical exhorters. Again, we accuse ourselves of having *sinned* against sex in making it for so long a sin.[26] Here, as in the earlier essays, Foucault is interested in religious images or concepts that might survive into antireligious speech about sex, but much more in the continuity of religion's rhetorical energies. The idea that speech about sex tells its truth in order to overturn unjust oppression and open a new future is not just a prophetic idea: it reactivates the rhetorical motives of prophecy.

Foucault also insists on the contrasts between sexuality and earlier Christian moralities. The continuities are conditioned or transformed by the constitution of a new regime of power and knowledge. *History of Sexuality* 1 betrays sometimes a sort of nostalgia in alluding to Christianity. If Foucault teases advocates of the repressive hypothesis for believing in a before-time of sexual freedom, he sometimes seems to posit the Christian Middle Ages as that other time, the period of another regime.[27] He indulges a morose delectation of old churchly moralities, especially when he wants to emphasize that sexuality closes a system around sex much more tightly than Christianity ever could. Christian speech serves in *History of Sexuality* 1 as an abiding contrast, though not in the way that it will in the later volumes of the reconfigured series. Here it is the legendary *before* to which the modern regime of sexuality is the more ruthless *after*.

THE SODOMITE AND THE HOMOSEXUAL

Nostalgic contrast is nowhere more visible than in Foucault's juxtaposition of the modern homosexual and the late medieval or early modern sodomite. This is perhaps the most tediously familiar passage in Foucault for English readers. It is also one of the most badly interpreted. It begins:

> Sodomy—that of the old [*ancien*] civil or canonical laws—was a type of forbidden acts; their author was nothing other than the juridical subject. The homosexual of the nineteenth century became a personage [*personnage*]: a past, a history and a childhood, a character [*caractère*], a form of life; also a morphology, with an indiscreet anatomy and perhaps a mysterious physiology. Nothing of what he is in total escapes his sexuality.[28]

This is the passage that is supposed to authorize (American) queer theory's indispensable distinction between homoerotic *acts* and *identities*. Of course, the authorizing passage doesn't address that distinction. The word "identity" doesn't occur. It appears elsewhere in *History of Sexuality* 1 only rarely, and then with its arithmetical meaning (identity as equality, sameness) or in ironic quotation of adversaries (identity as misapprehension).[29] If not acts and identities, what does Foucault have in view? The reader need only remember some earlier texts. The central contrast is between the sodomite as "juridical subject" of forbidden acts and the homosexual as a medicalized "personage" or character. The contrast is between the personifying imputation of legal culpability and the scientific construction of a whole new self beyond mere culpability.

This distinction has appeared at least twice before. In *Discipline and Punish*, Foucault wrote that under penal theory punishment is applied not to the juridical subject of the individual as offender but to the individual in detention conceived as a new character, the delinquent.

The delinquent is a biographical "nucleus of 'dangerousness.'" The prisoner's body is endowed through its double, the delinquent, with the little soul of the criminal. The new soul is the point of application of penal science.[30] Again, in the lectures on abnormals, Foucault argued that one function of nineteenth-century psychiatric expertise was to double the "author of the offense" with a "new personage of the delinquent, previously unknown to the eighteenth century." The psychiatry of delinquency goes beyond the expertise required by earlier legislation, which sought only a determination of whether the "author of the act" was still a responsible "juridical subject." In just the same way, the character of the homosexual doubles the sodomite as "author of the act"— creates an "ethico-moral double," as Foucault says in the lectures, an "individual" who is the "bearer" of a "character" with required traits rather than the "juridical subject" of a legally defined offense.[31] In *History of Sexuality* 1, the doubling is accomplished by positing a perversion hiding behind certain sexual acts. Like its nineteenth-century cousins instinct and degeneration, perversion commits its unfortunate bearers to lifelong medical surveillance as members of a pathological species.

These and other parallels clarify the central contrast in the frequently misread passage about sodomites and homosexuals. They also help resolve a long-running exegetical dispute: What is the contrast's historical range? Controversy over the passage has scoured the last twenty-five centuries of Western history in support of ingenious arguments about how the modern homosexual might or might not differ from all earlier figures. (I have tendered some myself.) The parallel passages suggest that Foucault is offering a very restricted comparison and a typically ironic claim of newness. Foucault here juxtaposes a nineteenth-century medical character with an eighteenth-century legal subject. The word *ancien* does not refer to ancient or premodern texts but only to the immediately previous period of jurisprudence. That much is clear not just from the language of the passage but from the general chronological frame of *History of Sexuality* 1, with its emphasis on the deployment of new strategies in the nineteenth century in contrast not with antiquity but with the eighteenth. Tightening the historical contrast, we can avoid some of the sillier complaints against it.[32] Foucault is not saying that there were no females before the nineteenth century who preferred sex with other females rather than males; that there were no earlier homoerotic habits or institutions or artworks or discourses; and so on. Nor is he saying only that the nineteenth-century homosexual differs from the eighteenth-century sodomite because the homosexual belongs to nineteenth-century science. Without further explanation, that would be a tautology.

One way to explain this tightened contrast is to insist again that the kind of doubling performed here is created for the sake of exercising a new power. The real difference is between church power over the sodomite as a biblically imagined sin character and the psychiatric power over the homosexual as a pervert who emerges in the space between law and medicine. The homosexual is not only assigned to a different sort of narrative but placed under a different sort of power.

A second explanation, argued by David Halperin, holds that the modern homosexual combines earlier features. Surveying a range of ancient, medieval, modern, and contemporary texts, Halperin analyzes same-sex categories into eight properties or elements: constituting an orientation, involving gender deviance, involving same-sex genital contact, being a sexual preference, representing a character type, involving homoerotic desire, classifying women and men together, and remaining constant across sex or gender transition.[33] Halperin argues that homosexuality is distinguished from all earlier categories not only by its combination of answers to questions about these elements but as the only category that answers Yes to most of them and Maybe to the others.

A final explanation of understanding Foucault's contrast between homosexual and sodomite is to say that it continues the original rhetorical strategy of *History of Sexuality* 1 by reversing the assumptions of gay liberation. Homosexuality is not what you are; it is only a clinically imposed diagnosis. This diagnosis is not the hidden truth of your desire; it is an artifact of juridico-clinical systems of power. Our conviction of declaring innermost truth when we come out as gay is the product of an epistemic system, not the evidence of redemption. The historicization of the sexual category applies to our speech too. The liberationist project, for all its invocation of Marxist dialectic, pretends to stand above history—or after it. It wants to speak the language of a postrevolutionary future.[34]

Recall the little book's subtitle: *The Will to Knowledge*. *History of Sexuality* 1 provides a mocking antidote to our epistemic prejudices about the sort of narrative a history of sex must be, but also about what sort of doctrine a revolutionary ideology of sexuality must supply. Surely it will pass from ignorance to knowledge, beginning as a grim tale of repression only to culminate in the sexual revolution of our enlightened present. I mean, we proclaimed gay liberation as of June 28, 1969! Indeed we did. Through that proclamation we confine ourselves more completely within the will to sexual knowledge, to *scientia sexualis*, that also animated the forensic psychiatry of the nineteenth-century perversions. It is our will to knowledge that must be exposed before we can even begin the history of sexuality.

Exposing the history will require a turn once again toward the European past understood as predominantly Christian. In later volumes, Foucault will vanquish his nostalgia quickly enough in order to stress the continuities between early Christian and modern sexual science. Even then, when it becomes a figure for a decisive shift in power, Christianity will persist as an indispensable contrast.

THE ANALYTICS OF POWER

Foucault is not writing a memory novel, or scribbling out a record of his sex life, or confecting an Orientalist fable. His text offers knowledge about our knowledge; it surveys the knowledge that it elicits and enacts. So his book cannot convey a theory. Foucault disowns both the word and the project. "The stake of the inquiries that will follow is to advance less toward a 'theory' [*théorie*] than toward an 'analytic' [*analytique*] of power: I mean to say toward the definition of the specific domain that the relations of power form and the determination of the instruments that allow it to be analyzed."[35] A few years later, further along in recounting sexuality's *histoires*, he will be more emphatic— and more teasing. He will remind his auditors at the Collège de France that he is not going to give them "a general Theory of Power (with all the caps) or explications by Domination in general." In other contexts, Foucault mocks "our" need for such theory.[36]

Refusing to supply a theory of power, Foucault invites readers to an "analytic." There are many possible meanings for that term in philosophical and scientific traditions. Let me recall four of the most obvious as cardinal points against which to plot Foucault's usage.

Cardinal Point 1

Foucault may have in mind two famous works of the Aristotelian canon, the *First* and *Second Analytics*. Some clues in the passage suggest this link. The Aristotelian works are concerned with definition and demonstration. They mean to delimit the domain of knowledge properly speaking, and they form part of Aristotle's collection of preliminary logical works known as the *Organon*, or instrument. A reader does find throughout Foucault's book mentions of logic or references to logic as a body of study. There are also mathematical terms that a modern reader might associate with contemporary formalizations of logic.[37]

If this is what Foucault has in mind, then a reader must face the notorious problem of the Aristotelian *Analytics*: although they are supposed to describe the form of scientific knowledge, Aristotle doesn't go on to write his own scientific works according to their prescriptions. They come to seem either impracticable or falsely abstract. More important, the "propositions" that Foucault offers about the history of power are hardly like rules for syllogisms. Indeed, when he calls them "rules for prudence," he invokes not the *Aristotelian Analytics* but the *Nicomachean Ethics* and its treatment of intellectual virtues. Foucault's method is not a formal analytics of demonstrable knowledge. It is more like a set of admonitions intended to help the reader acquire the virtue of seeing into ethical situations.

Cardinal Point 2

Foucault may be thinking of Kant, and specifically of that section of the *Critique of Pure Reason* titled the "Transcendental Analytic." In that section, Kant rewrites Aristotle's *Organon* as a description of the rules by which human experience is constituted. Here analysis seeks to discover the constitutive regularities that enable us to recognize categories and to pass judgments. At the very least, critique aims to prevent dogmatic mistakes about the grounds of experience that can lead by overreaching to metaphysics or its twin, moral skepticism. Foucault is evidently concerned with how we represent power to ourselves, with the regularities of our experience of power. He wants to undo the errors of representation that lead us to put power out there or up there, in some remote causal ground (the King, the Law, the State). Just as clearly Foucault analyzes this experience of power as the imaginative sediment of previous forms of power. The interesting thing for him is the contrast between the present forms of power and the anachronistic forms in which we speak of them. His analytics is thoroughly historical. So when Foucault uses the great Kantian phrases, as he sometimes does in this book, they have always to be understood as referring not to the unchangeable grounds of human consciousness but to the languages and imaginations of subjects formed under particular regimes.[38]

Cardinal Point 3

Perhaps Foucault thinks of psychoanalysis as appropriated by Gaston Bachelard, who was, among other things, a teacher of Foucault's academic mentor, Georges Canguilhem.[39] Bachelard transposed the setting of psychoanalysis to his studies in the foundations of science. He wrote, for example, *Psychoanalysis of Fire*. It concerns the "psychological problem posed by our convictions about fire"—or, rather, the disconnection between our affective convictions about fire and its historical disappearance as a scientific category or a laboratory entity. We imagine fire otherwise than contemporary science studies it. "We shall show precisely that the intuitions of fire—more perhaps than of anything else—are charged with a heavy load" that leads to the unconscious repetition of "the oldest and most chimerical philosophical theories."[40]

Bachelard's remarks resonate with Foucault's interest in the constitution of clinical or scientific objects of knowledge. They agree with Foucault's treatment of the imagination of power. Still, while Bachelard holds in *Psychoanalysis of Fire* to a separation between poetic imagination and objective science, while he contrasts imaginative error with scientific truth, Foucault offers the analytic of power as a way of correcting *power*'s self-distortions. He doesn't adopt Bachelard's contrast of inherited intuition with science but takes up instead the expectation that an analysis of conceptions of power will encounter resistance. Power makes itself tolerable by masking itself. The masks are quite varied. They include both threatening theologies and sweet promises of liberty.[41] If an analysis of power is going to do more than repeat power's own propaganda, it must be able to unmask it so as to make it less tolerable.

Cardinal Point 4

Foucault may be using "analytic" in relation to something like what Roland Barthes means by textual analysis. For example, in the opening pages of *S/Z*, Barthes justifies his method of breaking the text apart, line by line, according to its different "codes." Foucault is also fond of the word "code." It appears frequently in *History of Sexuality* 1, especially with regard to power and even when related words, like "law," are explicitly set aside. In *History of Sexuality* 1, though not in the later volumes, "code" refers to encoding rather than to codification (as of a system of laws).[42] Here power and resistance to it depend on coding: "it is doubtless the strategic coding of these points of resistance that renders a revolution possible, a little like the way that the State rests on the institutional integration of relations of power."[43] Because both power and resistance are everywhere, networks of power depend on the encoding of multiple points within larger strategies. One should then say the reverse: relations of power come to be power by strategic encoding—as quite ordinary words come to be a narrative when they are arranged according to decipherable narrative codes. On this reading, after Barthes, the analytics of power would be a study of how power writes itself, how it produces a coherent and compelling text, a text capable of scripting subjects. An analytics of power would disclose or depict power's narrative production on, in, and through bodies.

POWER'S ART

Foucault speaks the contrast between theory and analytic, but he implies in it and throughout the little book a contrast between theory and literature or *scientia* and *ars*. This Latin couplet renders two Greek pairings: *theoria* and *praxis*, *theoria* and *technê*. The contrast of *theoria* and *praxis* recalls centuries of debate over the status of various studies—philosophy, medicine, theology. The second pairing, *theoria* and *technê*, adds to the debates what we still call the arts, from craft through poetry. When he refuses to produce a theory of the power that runs through sexuality, Foucault suggests that his own writing wants to be practical and even artistic. If his is not the language of *ars erotica* in the ordinary sense, it is perhaps a first essay in the (hybrid or paradoxical) "ars erotica, ars theoretica, ars politica" that might provide an alternative to the scientific prose of sexuality.[44]

In *History of Sexuality* 1, as in earlier texts, Foucault evokes power lyrically. These passages have the rhythm of ritual speech. In the manner of negative theology or apophasis, they often list what power is not, what it cannot be said to be.[45] Sometimes, Foucault attempts more positive descriptions, though these too are often lists of terms without coordination. (Negative theologies will often multiply the names of God as a way of negating them.) For example, at the beginning of the section titled "Method," Foucault urges—in a single, Proustian sentence—that power be understood as a multiplicity of relations, their transforming play or interplay, their mutual support, their gaps or oppositions, and the strategies that organize them (with the implied bodily metaphor) into states, laws, or social hegemonies.[46] This is not a *definition* of power in any ordinary sense. It is not even a description of power. It is a set of instructions about where to look for what we so reductively call "power." The instructions begin by breaking apart the false unity of the single word.

Apply the instructions now to sexuality, the correlative object projected by a particular kind of power. Why is sexuality so important to us? Not because it is always and intrinsically important in human cultures. Most human cultures have gotten along quite well without the category or its cognate. Sexuality is important because it is "a particularly dense crossing point for the relations of power. . . . In the relations of power, sexuality . . . [is] endowed with the greatest instrumentality: usable for the greatest number of maneuvers, and able to serve as a support, a crossroads for the most varied strategies."[47] Like instinct in the lectures on abnormals, sexuality serves as a coordinating concept. Its flexibility, its blurry comprehensiveness, its unbounded multiplication—these are not defects but virtues. It is so useful to an emerging form of power precisely because it seems so mystifyingly applicable to everyone, in so many respects. The category of sexuality generalizes the deliberate confusion of the much older category, sodomy. If no one could be quite sure which acts were sodomitic, neither can anyone now know how far sexuality extends. The invention of sexuality, like the invention of sodomy, is an achievement in the consolidation of power over human bodies by deliberately irresponsible naming.

What kind of power does sexuality serve? The form of the question shows that the reader has been tricked again by monarchical narratives of power. These narratives demand a Protagonist, a Demiurge or Artificer, who forges the tools it needs for its plans. Better to think of an arrangement or alignment of already existing points—and better still, perhaps, to revert to the always qualified biomechanical analogies that Foucault favored in *Abnormals*. There he juxtaposed metaphors to describe the curious power that arose, as it were, between the court and the clinic, in the gaps of institutional arrangements. In *History of Sexuality 1*, sexuality arises in part from the space cleared by Christianity, but also in a space between two other patterns of organization. Sexuality is useful as the pivot between what become the two axes of biopower. A reader could say that biopower requires the concept of sexuality to hold its two axes together, but just as truly that biopower becomes possible when a concept is found that allows their efficient alignment.

Older forms of power could take life or spare it, often quite dramatically. Then brute exercises of power became scandalous to Enlightened sensibility and so to modern penal logic (at least according to power's own histories). The power of life or death had to be replaced with the power of total management over life—a power of fostering life that can entail, in certain regrettable cases, refusing it to the point of death. This power takes two forms. The first is an optimization of the human body as a machine, an "anatomo-politics of the human body." The second is a cultivation of the species-body, reproductive and durable, "a biopolitics of the population." In the eighteenth century, these two are still separate. In the nineteenth, they join to form biopower at the intersections of the biological and the political. If "biohistory" names "the pressures by which the movements of life and the processes of history interfere with one another," then "biopolitics" can designate what it is that brings "life and its mechanisms into the domain of explicit calculations and makes power knowledge an agent of transformation for human life."[48] Foucault emphasizes that the power-knowledge relations in biopower are historically unprecedented.

Within the new disposition (or dispensation) of sexuality, sex has three functions. First, as new code, it groups together a whole series of organs and functions under a fictive unity, which then explains them. Next, as epistemic genealogy, it allows the new science of sexuality to

borrow the cognitive prestige of its predecessor, the biology of reproduction. Finally, as perfect mask, positing sex allows the category of
sexuality to appear not as an artifact of power but as something external to power that must be subjugated. In these and other uses, sex is
transformed into the ideal point for the application of the power that
flows through sexuality, just as delinquency was the ideal point for the
application of penal power. A category like sexuality is thus indispensable for the progress of biopower. If the category didn't exist, biopower
would have to invent it. It did.

In the middle of these final remarks on the usefulness of sexuality to power, Foucault imagines an objection that he divides into two
questions. The first asks whether the analysis of sexuality as the production of a disposition of power doesn't elide the body's reality. As
if the objector were saying, But there really are bodies! To which Foucault replies that he is not trying to contrast the biological with the
historical so much as study their increasing interactions. "The aim
of the present investigation is rather to show how the dispositions of
power articulate themselves directly on the body—on bodies, functions, physiological processes, sensations, pleasures." More pointedly,
he says that he is not writing a history of mentalities; he proposes
a "'history of bodies' and of the manner in which one has besieged
what is most material, most living in them."[49] Unconvinced, the objector insists in a second question, Isn't this materiality precisely
sex? Isn't there really a sex onto which the power that flows through
sexuality must impose itself? To which Foucault replies, It's this very
idea of sex, of sex as the permanent anchor of sexuality, that must be
traced historically.

I don't know whether his reply convinces the objector, who seems
to personify the insistence of certain desires for consoling theory mas-
querading as robust allegiance to reality. The objector—perhaps the
reader—wants to cling to the reality of a sexuality inscribed on the body
in order to make late modern power tolerable. So Foucault's reiterated
reply denies the form of the question. We cannot oppose a history of
concepts to a timeless body as if we had access to a body beyond concepts, outside histories. Our experience of embodiment has been all
too effectively organized by concepts imposed on it from infancy. We
should surrender the pious hope that the perfect words of the right

theory would deliver our bodies to us, intact, unblemished. Theory, the last promise of direct experience, relic of the language of Eden.

BECOMING UN-VICTORIAN,
OR THE ESCAPE FROM SEXUAL SCIENCE

The little book's last section begins with a quotation from D. H. Lawrence that culminates in an Edenic exhortation: "Now our business is to realize sex. Today, the full conscious realization of sex is even more important than the act itself."[50]

This is the reverse of Foucault's view. Foucault quotes Lawrence ironically, if not mockingly. The book's end echoes the tone of its beginning. Foucault understands Lawrence to put knowledge of sex in place of sex, so unwittingly to proclaim the ultimate triumph of *scientia sexualis* in the name of realization. Sex as an object of knowledge has replaced sex as an act of bodies. From this quotation, Foucault proceeds to wonder aloud how our pious regime of sexuality will look from some unspecified future—how it will be remembered, not in Proustian reactivation but in astonished retrospect.

Foucault distinguishes two groups among us that already pass retrospective judgments on Freud. The first group consists of those who charge Freud with "pansexualism," which here means seeing sex underneath everything.[51] We tend to dismiss the members of this group as unthinking prudes; in fact, they are guilty only of a chronological mistake. What they think started with Freud was actually much older: it was our society's millennial elaboration of the disposition of sexuality. The second group (which includes most of Foucault's readers) comprises those who think that Freud restored to sex the rightful importance that had long been denied it. Theirs is a much worse mistake, because they misunderstand not the dating but the whole process. Freud in fact only relaunched, with a more-than-ecclesiastical efficiency, the "epochal injunction" to put sex into speech. Freud is not a new beginning. He continues an epoch.

What we take as the repressive Christian denial of sex is in fact the beginning of the construction of *scientia sexualis*, which tricks us into speaking sex as a way to discover its truth, our truth. The whole game should astonish us. Then comes the famous riddle: "And we should consider that one day, perhaps, in another economy of bodies and pleasures, one will no longer understand very well how the ruses of sexuality, and of the power that supports its disposition, succeeded in submitting us to the austere monarchy of sex, to the point of vowing us to the indefinite task of forcing its secret and of extorting from this ghost the truest confessions."[52]

The "austere monarchy of sex": In *Discipline and Punish*, modern prisons were described by Foucault (following Baltard) as "complete and austere institutions."[53] Here too "austere" refers not to a scheme of sexual renunciation, though it is that, but to the streamlined efficiency of disciplinary control. Yet it is an "austere *monarchy*." One reference goes back to the book's beginning, to the revaluation of the reign of Queen Victoria, who was supposed to be the emblem of our repression. Foucault had suggested, of course, that a better emblem would be the anonymous author of the endless scribbling of *My Secret Life*. He is our true monarch. We may thus suspect that "monarchy" is used here satirically. Indeed, it refers as well to the other monarchy Foucault has mentioned: the kingdom of Prince Mangogul, lucky owner of the ring that makes genitals gossip. Of course, the malicious prince may well put the reader in mind of still another monarch, Jarry's King Ubu. We live in the "austere" and grotesquely comic monarchy first proclaimed in the Ubu-esque power of forensic psychiatrists, who could spout sexual nonsense while taking lives.

As subjects under their rule, our endless task is to force the truest avowals of sexuality. There will come a time when the now reigning sexuality, the fetishized category of our innermost truth, will seem a ghost, as insubstantial as a shadow, but still capable of haunting—of mesmerizing and terrifying. That time will follow on "another economy of bodies and pleasures." This might mean different purposes for having sex, say, as nonprocreative, as pure play. Or it might mean different ways of having sex, of producing pleasure. Indeed, some readers invoke just here Foucault's remarks elsewhere about the gay discovery of erotic pleasures in new organs or sensations.[54]

I wish that these readings convinced me. I fear that they fail to appreciate how much is required to escape the economy of *scientia sexualis*. Both the Christian confessional and the nineteenth-century courtroom are acquainted with an enormous range of sexual tastes and activities. Remember the list of the species of "little perverts" that Foucault appends to the famous contrast between the homosexual and the sodomite: it contains ten entries, most of which need now to be deciphered with a specialized dictionary.[55] Foucault properly likens these perversions to "heresies"; they correspond in fact to the proliferation of types of sexual sin in the Christian confessional, including the seventeenth- and eighteenth-century subdivisions of the sin of sodomy. Even assuming that we could discover sexual acts that the Jesuit cataloguers had overlooked, adding to their lists is not going to get us out from the present economy of bodies and pleasure, the regime of *scientia sexualis*.

Escape from the regime will require removing bodies and pleasures from the purview of *scientia sexualis* so that they are no longer objects of scientific knowledge.[56] We need to undo the doubling of sexual acts with scientifically invented sexual characters. Can this be accomplished by reversing the pathological valuation—by proclaiming that the pathology was really normal all along? The very language suggests Foucault's answer: the normal and the pathological are central categories for forensic psychiatry and so for biopower. Reversing them leaves the epistemic project intact. Hence Foucault's critique of gay liberation conceived as the proud assertion of gay identity. The problem with "gay pride" is not the pride but the identity implicit in "gay." Overturning *scientia sexualis* requires giving up the desire for theories about sex—including the theories that underwrite identity politics.

So what does "another economy" imply politically, as prediction, prophecy, or exhortation? Turn at once to the adjacent phrase: "one day, perhaps." Foucault has used it before to disconcert assumptions about cherished categories.[57] If its effect is clear, it is still easy to mistake its sense. The phrase doesn't imply a utopian vision. It isn't an urgent exhortation to revolutionary uprising. It doesn't refer to other calendars in places beyond the reach of the West and its biopower. (Foucault's view of the rapid spread of biopower is pessimistic.) It doesn't imply, finally, what some Christian theologians call a realized eschatology. I cannot see that Foucault offers us a gospel of the kingdom at hand if only we tilt our heads.

"One day" in "another economy": these two phrases mark a limit to *representing* any alternative arrangement of sex within the languages now prevailing. Someday, perhaps, we will have another language for bodies and pleasures. We will praise or solicit them without also desiring their scientific truth. The only way to reach that other economy is first of all by unsaying, by apophasis. The apophasis begins already with the phrase "bodies and pleasures." In the lectures on abnormals, the bodies of the possessed rebelled by convulsion against new intrusions of pastoral power. Here, at the end of the dotted outline of a story about our sexuality, the body appears again to offer an alternative—or at least a resistant otherness. It now beckons as fluid occasion. Perhaps it promises to convulse in pleasure.

Two years after the publication of *History of Sexuality* 1, Foucault would say to an interviewer that for him "the word 'pleasure,' which in the end means nothing," remains "rather empty of content and clear of possible uses." "Pleasure" is a term of apophasis. With it, Foucault hopes to turn attention to "an event, an event that happens—that happens, I would say, outside the subject, or at the limit of the subject, or between two subjects, in this something that is neither of the body nor of the soul, neither outside nor inside."[58] The description sounds uncannily like what Foucault had written a decade earlier about Bataille, Klossowski, and Blanchot on the limits of language, the rupture of the subject, and the retreat of the sacred. So a reader might suspect that "economy" at the little book's end has after all an unusual meaning—one related to Bataille's notions of expenditure or to Klossowski's fantasy of bodies as living money. Most of all, the reader will see that Foucault is not describing a new regime so much as marking the limit of our capacity for description. We don't (yet) have the words.

Is this conclusion hopeful or hopeless? If it is an accurate rendering of our present subjection, then it is as hopeful as can be. As Foucault says in the last line: "Irony of this disposition: it makes us believe that our 'liberation' is at stake." The irony of the disposition is intended by the disposition. We have to recognize the irony not so that we can undo it immediately, since we lack as yet the means, but so that we can dwell in it as our very own irony. If our genitals must talk, let them at least not pretend to promulgate royal decrees or to issue revolutionary manifestos.

CHAPTER 5

THE SOBBING MATRON AND THE
LOQUACIOUS MONK

SOON AFTER IT APPEARED, *History of Sexuality* 1 was out-of-date. It no longer represented the project Foucault desired. He had promised in it to trace the genealogy of speeches and practices around the specifically modern category of sexuality back into the seventeenth or sixteenth century. He knew, of course, that there was a longer genealogy, a prehistory. In the lectures on abnormals, he had already sketched a narrative of Christian confession while interpreting the nineteenth-century reformulation of sexuality as the continuation of modern pastoral practice. In the book itself, Foucault gestured at several points toward Christian pastoral care for sex before modernity. He described a series of extensions by which the monastic discipline of chastity was applied to the clergy as a whole, then to all members of religious orders (male and female), then to zealous laypeople, then to laypeople simply. Foucault proposed that we could discern the birth of sexuality in the kinds of surveillance practiced within Catholic seminaries, religious colleges, and convents since the Counter-Reformation. The sexualities of nineteenth-century psychiatry were pastoral theology bequeathed to other kinds of pastors, to the agents of biopower. Repeating this, Foucault still conceived the project in *History of Sexuality* 1 within modernity's bounds.

Very soon after publishing the little book, Foucault begins to re-conceive that boundary.[1] The revision looks like another one of his attractions to beginnings that cannot be beginnings, to a Nietzschean ambivalence of origins. Foucault wants to start his *histoire* in the sixteenth century, but then the sixteenth century turns out to be too late— not a proper beginning at all. So where should he start? The question isn't easy. The ironic beginning of *History of Sexuality* 1 makes clear that stories about mutations of power are stories in which power takes a keen interest. Where to start is more than a puzzle of narrative technique. It is the critical question, how best to dislodge the narratives that power has always already circulated. If a story of power begins in the wrong place, if it fails to unsettle the prevailing narratives, it will find itself contending only with minor characters and peripheral plots. It will mistake the battlefield. Beginning a history of sexuality, Foucault must find a persuasive way to reveal that sexuality was manufactured as the object of a certain disposition of power. Having published the first volume, Foucault concludes that the best moment for disclosure is not early modernity. It lies earlier, in the invention of Christian speeches about sinful bodies and their souls. So he moves backward— writes backward.

Backward, but not in a single direction. During the years when he was supposed to be composing the later volumes of *History of Sexuality*, Foucault wrote across Christian texts on assorted topics that he drew from widely spaced times and places. He kept rearranging some of them, his favorites, as episodes in alternative stories. Others he skimmed and set aside. Foucault destroyed some of his pages on modern Christian topics; he left others as detached fragments in his files.[2] I doubt that his writing from these years could ever have been assembled into a single series of studies, much less into a single narrative. Some of Foucault's writing on Christianity evidently informs the volumes that eventually appeared as *History of Sexuality* 2 and 3. More of it would have found its way into the as-yet-unpublished (perhaps unpublishable) *History of Sexuality* 4: *Confessions of the Flesh*. But it is still a mistake to imagine that the missing volume could have fused Foucault's writing on Christianity by some alchemy. Only its absence encourages readers to expect such a fusion—its absence and our desire to have sex finally explained for us. The craving for knowledge about sex that Foucault depicts and resists in *History of Sexuality* 1 animates fantasies about its sequels, what his friends came to think of as "the infinite book."[3]

Other readers make sense of Foucault's pieces on Christianity by reading them into a plot about his intellectual development. The fragmentary writings are subordinated to a chronology of successive theories or the stages of refining just one. Yet Foucault denies the unity of theory when he gives reasons for writing in these years. In a series of lectures that is often described as a crucial turn in his thinking about Christianity, Foucault once again rejects theory production in favor of another description for his work: "My problem, or [rather] the only possibility of theoretical work that I feel, is to leave, according to the most intelligible layout possible, the trace of the movements by which I am no longer in the place where I was a moment ago." He means to show the "points of passage" at which each displacement affects the whole curve of thought and its reading. He aims to leave "a tracing not of the theoretical edifice but of the displacement by which my theoretical positions do not cease to change." If there are negative theologies, Foucault concludes, "let's say that I am a negative theoretician."[4]

Negative theologies are sometimes attributed to a conviction that God should be approached through denial rather than affirmation. It helps more here to describe them as a daily practice of rewriting. Negative theologies are an ongoing ritual of unsaying. They answer every positive claim about the divine with its corresponding denial. They must continue to do so for as long as there is theological assertion. Whatever a final version of *History of Sexuality* 4 might have accomplished, it could not have finished Foucault's devotions as a negative theoretician of Christian subject formation. There is always work for a negative theoretician in past, present, and future assertions of Christian power. There is work, too, in a theoretician's unsaying her own formulations. Negative theory is always ready to be displaced.

Daniel Defert likens the last manuscript of *History of Sexuality* 4 to Proust's famous drafts: "One finds [in the manuscript] a system *à la Proust*, without the paper strips glued to the sides, but with a system of superposition that means that only someone who truly has the habit of editing manuscripts could perform the work of truly saying what the final reading is."[5] I would reply: The true reading established by a true philologist is still not the final reading. It is a conjecture about the manuscript as Foucault last left it. It can seek only an accidental end of his writing. Reading what Foucault wrote on Christianity in the last five years of his life requires *not* reading the texts as belonging to the last five years. We read them better as anticipations of displacements to come.[6]

The *History of Sexuality* is a project in suspended time. The series was suspended, of course, by a death. We do not know how Foucault would have completed it. It is suspended more significantly by Foucault's chronological shifts as he pursues his motivating questions to recast sexuality or move beyond it. He will begin with early modernity—no, with early Christianity—no, with Greco-Roman antiquity. Each displacement moves under the suspended question about sexuality while redirecting it. The nested structure of the lectures on security, territory, and population model in miniature the quandaries of the *History of Sexuality* not only as we have it but as we must have it. Like the books in the series, the lectures move backward in a long excursus that is at once a detour and a redirection, a parenthesis and a peripety.

I won't try to reconstruct *History of Sexuality* 4 as if it could have been the last word. I read Foucault's writings on Christianity from 1978 on as part of an interminable sequence rather than steps in a single dance. So I concentrate on two clusters of lectures in which Foucault tells different stories about Christian texts. The first cluster takes pastoral power as its theme; the second analyzes truth telling in baptismal preparation, penance, and spiritual direction. Especially when stated so generally, the themes are less important than the variations Foucault plays on them.

The cluster of lectures around pastoral power contains a well-known text that Foucault read in French at Tokyo University during the spring of 1978. In it, he reframed the project of the *History of Sexuality* by pushing it back to the beginning of Christianity. The speech in Tokyo both recapitulated and rewrote lectures that Foucault had presented earlier that season at the Collège de France. Trying to understand the distinctively modern forms of political power over bodies, Foucault was led into an extended digression on the history of Christian pastoral care and its early modern crises. After recapitulating these explorations for the speech in Tokyo, Foucault summarized them more briefly still in the first of the Tanner Lectures at Stanford in October 1979. On each of these occasions, Foucault emphasizes the historical importance of pastoral power for modern subjectivity. He uses different collections of texts to make the point.

The lectures of the second thematic cluster have something like the reverse textual relation. In them, Foucault keeps writing different grand narratives around a smaller dossier of passages. In the spring of 1980, his lecture series at the Collège de France was titled "On the Government of the Living." That fall in the United States, he reprised some of the same material, especially in lectures at Berkeley and Dartmouth. He reprised it again, a few months later, in talks at the Catholic University of Louvain (April–May 1981). Some of the Christian passages appear once more in a lecture at the University of Vermont (October 1982).[7] On these various occasions, Foucault's penchant for multiplying explanatory schemata becomes clear. So does his relation to archives as interlocutors, as persistent motives for reflection. Far from trying to settle on the correct interpretation of truth telling in Christian soul making, Foucault shows how repeated reading multiplies associations.

A reader's caution for both clusters: Though they are all "lectures," the texts read at Tokyo, Stanford, Hanover, Berkeley, Louvain, and Burlington are not of the same genre as those presented weekly in Paris. Speaking to audiences that would assemble at best a few times, speaking sometimes in a language not his own, Foucault outside Paris is more sweeping and provocative. He performs deliberately startling historical inversions. He confesses—or invents—more of his own story. He pronounces gnomic conclusions. He proposes outlandish conceits to turn the event of a star lecture into some teaching for an audience of too many fans. In short, these traveling lectures show Foucault at what some readers judge his most irritating, especially when it comes to history.

I don't read Foucault for a basic history of Christian pastoral practices or anything else. I know that he delights in contradicting the standard histories. I see that he makes the mistakes of a brilliant nonspecialist or antispecialist. Still I read him, because Foucault mistaken often asks more interesting questions about Christian power than most specialists do. As usually practiced, philologically instructed history can be a great help in reconstructing the words that were originally in a text. It is not of equal help in understanding what the words do once they are put there. Nietzsche says it more sharply: "I for one would rather read Diogenes Laertius than Zeller, because in the former at least the spirit of the old philosophers lives, while neither that nor any other spirit lives in the latter."[8] I would rather read the ardent appreciations of a lover of wisdom than the currently certified conclusions of a textual statistician.

A CHRISTIAN UPBRINGING FOR SEXUALITY

In April 1978, in a paper prepared for what he thought would be a roundtable at the University of Tokyo, Foucault offers some of the "hypotheses" that are rearranging his project for the history of sexuality after the publication of its first volume.[9] One of these hypotheses is that Western society, since Augustine at least, has overproduced discourse about sex. This is the famous reversal from *History of Sexuality* 1. Many people would say that Christianity silenced talk of sex; the now familiar counter-hypothesis is that the advancing religion demanded new speeches about sex, obliging more people to talk about it more often.

A second hypothesis is that this discourse "very quickly and very early took a form that can be called scientific." This hypothesis moves the origin of *scientia sexualis* back to the origin of Christianity. Foucault contrasts a Western science of sex with an Eastern art of the erotic, a contrast that begs for qualifications and counter-examples. Less important to him than the forced contrast between cultural caricatures is the opposition between a science and an art. Foucault uses it to pose a reflexive question: "Why do we will, we others, and why have we willed, we European others, for millennia, to know the truth of our sex rather than to achieve intensity of pleasure?"[10] (Note that in declaring the topic, Foucault both assumes a group label and confesses a motion of his will. He thus performs explicitly what he suggests in the subtitle of *History of Sexuality* 1.) Foucault wants to examine the European claim that one has a sexuality, the truth of which can be known apart from arts for producing pleasures in bodies. The Freudian notion that one can be hysterically mistaken about one's desires is only the latest version of an old Western preoccupation with techniques for uncovering the hidden truth of sex.

A third current hypothesis holds that what was originally distinctive about Christian sexual science was not the content of its prohibitions but the form of their imposition. Foucault relies on the authority of Paul Veyne to argue that the features usually singled out as Christian in sexual morality are in fact taken from late pagan teaching. What distinguishes Christian ethical teaching? "It is then along the way of the mechanisms of power, much more than along that of moral ideas or ethical prohibitions—it is along the way of the mechanisms of power that one must do the history of sexuality in the Western world after Christianity."[11]

So Foucault turns to a Christian emblem of power. It is not a tableau or heraldic blazon but a sedimented metaphor: the shepherd, who lurks still in the very words "pastorate" or "pastoral." Talking in Tokyo, Foucault claims that the pastoral power preached by Christianity is distinguished from earlier forms of Greco-Roman power in four ways. It is *nonterritorial*. It conceives ethics as rules applying without boundaries rather than to the inhabitants of a particular place or even the members of a certain tribe. Again, Christian pastoral power promises to be a *power of care*. It professes not to be interested in conquest or punishment so much as the promotion of flourishing. The pastorate is supposed to be animated, third, by a spirit of *self-sacrificing* responsibility. The pastor lays down her life for the sheep, as opposed to the wolf, which grows fat on them. Fourth, pastoral power is *individualistic* so far as it affixes to the individual, to ensure her salvation. Foucault will emphasize this last point a year later in a phrase for the lecture titles at Stanford: *omnes et singulatim*, all and (yet) individually.

Nonterritorial, nonpunitive, self-sacrificing, individual. If this is the distinctive shape of pastoral power, a number of consequences follow for the Christian. To begin with, she is obliged to seek salvation always and everywhere under the pastor's authority. The pastor can demand absolute obedience from the believer in pursuit of salvation. What is more telling, the pastor can impose on the believer the demands of absolute candor. Indeed, the pastor trains the believer in techniques for finding and describing an inner truth. The essential contribution of Christianity to the history of ethical power is to be found in these techniques of interiorization, of cultivating the conscience by alerting oneself to the sources of sinfulness—to what Christians already begin to call "the flesh."

I concede that the schematic historiography of the lecture in Tokyo is irritating. Still, I resist the complaint that the lecture records Foucault's hasty (re)turn to Christianity—that it is the unfortunate prelude to years of amateurish poaching in texts and topics with which he had no legitimate business. Surely the trajectory of reading to this point makes clear that Foucault doesn't turn to Christianity for the first time in Tokyo. Christianity is always there in his thinking. Foucault is also quite candid about his status as an academic amateur in these studies. The question is whether that constitutes a weakness or a strength. Foucault has analyzed at length the operation of claims for academic expertise, especially when they restrict public speech about certain topics. To argue a priori that he cannot talk about such things because he is not an accredited expert would prove his analysis of power rather than undo it. The question should not be about his credentials but about the kind of rereading that might follow on his hypotheses.

CRISES OF THE CHRISTIAN PASTORATE

After Tokyo, Foucault's Christian writing is increasingly preoccupied by the techniques of speaking the self in relation to the flesh. It is still worth pausing over the characterization of pastoral power if only to trace how it arises from *History of Sexuality* 1. The schematic pronouncements in Tokyo can be filled in by looking back to lectures that Foucault delivered earlier that spring at the Collège de France. He had finished his obligatory public instruction barely two weeks before speaking in Japan. Portions of the paper presented there condense what he had laid out more fully at home.[12] The earlier lectures supply more detail to the analysis of Christian pastoral power across a broader range of examples. They also tell a different story about how Foucault came to be speaking of the pastorate at all. In Tokyo, the turn to Christianity is presented as the next step in a search for some beginning of the distinctively Western science of sexuality. At the Collège, Foucault turns to Christian pastoral power as a prelude to a distinctively modern form of power, which he calls "governmentality."

The announced title for the 1978 series at the Collège is "Security, Territory, Population," but Foucault announces its real topic as biopower. The series thus picks up from the final section of *History of Sexuality* 1. It is in fact the first lecture series pronounced since the little book's publication; Foucault had taken sabbatical leave the previous year. If the announced topic is now biopower, Foucault starts with warnings about any lecturing on power. (The warnings would seem ridiculously repetitive if they were not so regularly ignored.) He has never pursued a "general theory of what power is," since power is precisely not "a substance, a fluid, something that runs from here or from there." Power is rather "an ensemble of mechanisms and procedures that have as [their] role or function and theme just assuring power, even if they don't succeed in doing so." The ensemble is not "self-generating" or "self-subsisting"; neither is it set apart from other relations—of production, family, sex. Power relations are in all these other relations, as both cause and effect. Power is as specific as those relations are. Still, in a given moment or period, in a given field of forces, configurations of power are connected by resemblance or reflection. They can be linked across their specificities "in a way that is at once logical, coherent, and valid."[13]

With these reminders from negative theory, Foucault proceeds to analyze biopower under the three headings of his title: security, territory, population. He rehearses, as historical lessons familiar from *Discipline and Punish*, the transition from a legal code or juridical system to disciplinary mechanisms that project a new character as the ground of any crime and the target of ongoing surveillance. Security steps beyond discipline, viewing the crime within a series of events that can be assigned a cost and calculated against an acceptable average. Legal code, discipline, and security are aligned respectively, if roughly, with chronological periods: the medieval and early modern, the late modern (from the eighteenth century), and the contemporary. But Foucault immediately adds his usual cautions about not construing the historical sequence literally. The various mechanisms precede and outlast the periods of their dominance. Mechanisms of discipline have a long history before the eighteenth century, and the contemporary world is seeing an explosion of new legal codes. There is no succession of sharply delimited ages, as in some cosmogony, only the appearance of "complex edifices" in which one or another feature stands out.[14]

The lectures tell how security emerges in relation to scarcity of food, economic regulation, and population size. Foucault notices the rise of a new art of government, with its specific discourses and techniques, that seeks to control population through political economy by means of security apparatuses. He then proposes a revised title for the whole lecture series or reveals the title that he wanted to use all along: a history of "governmentality."[15] That neologism means at once this new art of governing populations, the long historical arc that grants governmental power such prominence in the West, and the process of governmentalizing by which the medieval state of justice became the modern state of government. "Governmentality" names an art for governing, a historical drive toward more government, and a specific historical transformation in modernity.

After announcing his more exact title, Foucault turns unexpectedly to the Christian pastorate, which occupies him for five lectures at the heart of the series. Whatever the plan might have been, the achieved structure of these lectures looks like a set of concentric circles, with modern governmentality on the outside. The innermost circle treats the pastorate. It contains the oldest material, the most remote, but somehow also the most revealing of the modern differentiation of biopower. Foucault will say later on, "I have done nothing else for several months than try to explicate for you those [modern] texts about grains and scarcity—the question was always about them through a certain number of detours." On this account, the central lectures on Christian pastoral power were only a detour, a sidebar or backstory. Foucault then suggests, at the very end of the series, that he has been conducting "a little experiment of method" through which the study of a local situation or circumstance unfolds into a much larger study of power.[16] This reverses the picture: the lectures on the pastorate are now the larger frame within which to situate the particular struggles over grain and scarcity.

Foucault hesitates still over the turn to the Christian pastorate. He redescribes his procedure in previous works, particularly *History of Madness* and *Discipline and Punish*. In both cases, he now says, there is a triple shift beyond the presuppositions of ordinary historiography. The first moves from institutions (the asylum, the prison) to the technology of power that subtends them. The second shift is from the explicit or measurable function of the institutions to a general economy of power flowing through and around them. The third looks beyond the objects assumed by institutions to the field of truth in which those objects are constituted. In short, Foucault writes about power as an "extrainstitutional generality, a nonfunctional generality, a nonobjective generality" that permits a glimpse of mutations in the fields of connected, mutually reflecting forces. By a similar shift of gaze, he will now try to discover a level of techniques (governmentality) that are to the State "what techniques of segregation were to psychiatry, what techniques of discipline were to the penal system, and what biopolitics was to medical institutions."[17]

Once shifted, the gaze discovers that governmentality applies not to a region, a constitutional entity, or a political structure but to people, to living bodies. This idea of a special art for governing living beings is not principally Greek or Latin. It comes rather from the pre-Christian and then Christian "East," where it takes the twin forms of pastoral power and spiritual direction. Foucault enumerates four characteristics of pastoral power just as he will at Tokyo, then emphasizes at the Collège the pastorate's uniqueness, describing at greater length differences between Israelite and Christian notions. In Christianity, pastoral power is institutionalized and "autonomized" as it never was in ancient Israel.[18] Before the modern period in the West, pastoral power also remains distinct in both conception and enforcement from politics, pedagogy, and rhetoric—even as it takes over some of philosophy's pedagogical functions. Having marked out this field of power, Foucault analyzes both the complexities of its institutionalization and the kinds of resistance to it.

This is an *analysis* or at least the "very vague, very rudimentary, very elementary sketch" of one.[19] The word is stressed again, as it was in *History of Sexuality* 1. Foucault is not writing a history of the pastorate. He is only trying to trace the shape of its power from a small selection of texts. I add: He is reading them both allegorically and tropologically, to borrow terms from Christian scriptural exegesis. He finds in particular reports the evidence of much larger patterns, which he sees as designs on and for human lives. In his chosen texts, Foucault reads that pastoral power is connected to salvation, to the law, and to truth, but in a way that overturns or oversteps each of them. Aimed at salvation, pastoral power is paradoxically distributive and reciprocal. The pastor is obliged to save all, but also to sacrifice anyone who would endanger the rest. Foucault circles around this paradox, in which he sees four unprecedented principles or mechanisms of power. The pastor is accountable for the acts of each member of the flock. This responsibility issues in an exhaustive, instantaneous transfer of the sins of the sheep onto

the shepherd, who will have to answer for them under divine judgment. In the present life, too, there is a sacrificial reversal by which
the shepherd must lay down his (or her!) life for the sheep. Foucault
also detects here what he calls the correspondence of weaknesses in the
shepherd and the sheep, which are bound together by experiences of
temptation and trial. The pastorate is a relation of total power over the
whole of life, then, but also a reversal that overwrites the shepherd's
life with the life of the flock. The reversal distinguishes the "styles" of
the Christian pastorate even from its closest antecedents, such as the
Hebrew notion of solidarity.[20]

Christian notions of obedience require subjection to an individual,
not to a principle or precept, and even to the point of absurdity. Obedience is not conditional upon a particular end: it continues indefinitely
until its subject is erased in humility. Here is another reversal, since the
one who commands can do so only because she or he has already been
commanded. Christian obedience is demanded in the name of a prior
obedience, in the pastor and in Christ himself.

The reversals of Christian pastoral power culminate in a lived connection to the truth. It is expressed in teaching about daily conduct,
but also, more significantly, as direction of conscience. In contrast with
ancient philosophy, Christian direction is neither voluntary nor circum-
stantial. The believing Christian is obliged to live under direction that
oversees all episodes and periods of life, not just particular troubles or
transitions. In this regard too, the new form of power replaces its predecessors. It changes notions of salvation, law, and truth, but above all
the notion of subjection.[21]

Foucault reasserts the now clarified claim that the pastorate is the
triple prelude to modern governmentality. He also offers reflections not
spoken in Tokyo about forms of resistance internal to the pastorate. He
wavers in naming them, calling them counter-attacks, resistances, in-
subordinations, revolts, then (finally) counter-conduct (*contre-conduite*),
deliberately setting aside the word "dissidence." Before enumerating
instances of counter-conduct, Foucault adds characteristic reminders
about how one should conceive this resistance. It is not consequent to
pastoral power, as if pastoral conducting came first and then produced
counter-conducts. Pastoral power views itself rather as acting upon
a contrary force so that there is "an immediate and founding correla-

tion between conduct and counter-conduct."[22] The revolts of conduct have their specificity, not least in their forms of representation and their dramaturgy.

Foucault names five themes in Christian forms of counter-conduct: unbounded asceticism, the formation of counter-community, mysticism as an alternative system for grounding truth, the direct interpretation of scripture, and enactments of eschatology. The themes are not external to Christianity. They arise within it. They also arise against it: Foucault draws the startling conclusion that Christianity understood as church, as an organization of pastoral power, is *not* ascetical, communal, mystical, scriptural, or eschatological. Since these elements are familiar as specifically Christian ideals, Foucault seems to be saying that Christianity has in fact not been Christian. The claim is familiar. It has been made across church history by radical reformers, who are typically condemned as arch-heretics.

Is Foucault merely siding with the heretics, adopting their reading of Gospel imperatives to convict structures of ecclesiastical power? It cannot be so simple as that. On one level, Foucault sees the Christian pastorate as the prelude to modern European governmentality. Christianity appears within his history of power *because* of its pastoral organization. Was that the sort of organization that Jesus intended for Christianity? The question matters to the student of power only so far as certain tensions within the founding documents about Jesus opened space for specific forms of counter-conduct. Of course, Foucault wants to stress alternatives to the pastorate, within the pastorate, for larger reasons of his own. The mutations of the Christian pastorate from its Jewish origin to its issue in European governmentality cannot appear as necessary or inevitable. Foucault is not preaching historical determinism of any variety. Power must be conceived not as an assured possession or decisive victory but as a tense and always mutable field of relations.[23] He sides with the heretics in their protests, not in their dreams of providential reform.

Paraphrasing Foucault's analysis of pastoral power in this first cluster of lectures, I have said nothing about his historical sources because Foucault himself says very little about them. In the Tokyo lecture, there are specific references only to Paul Veyne's studies on Roman sexuality and to Plato's *Statesman*. Tracing notions of pastoral power, Foucault refers in a few paragraphs to unspecified biblical sources on the kingship of David and the figure of the Good Shepherd.[24] Otherwise, he speaks generally of "a Christian society" in contrast to Egyptian, Assyrian, Hebrew, or Greco-Roman ones. In the more detailed Parisian lectures on the pastorate, Foucault cites a wider range of sources, many of which he found through articles in standard reference works for the history of theology.[25] He often leaps from text to text, from century to century, treating the few authors he does specify as examples rather than as evidence. So, for example, a single page in the printed version of the lectures takes Foucault from some New Testament verses through Cyprian, Gregory the Great, Benedict, John Wycliff, unnamed Catholic authors of the Counter-Reformation, and Marius Lupus, only to end in the middle of the twentieth century and the years before and after Vatican II.[26] The speed and range of citation are typical of this series of lectures at the Collège, especially in the typology of historical movements. Foucault does pay a bit more attention to two early Christian texts: the *Rule* for monks traditionally ascribed to Benedict, and Gregory the Great's *Pastoral Rule*.[27] Even these are cited more often than quoted, and quoted more often than expounded. For Foucault's more sustained engagement with Christian texts, a reader needs to go two years later, to the lectures clustered around that other theme, Christian practices of subject formation.

VERSIONS OF CHRISTIAN CONFESSION

Foucault takes up Christian practices for truth telling in at least five sets of intertwined lectures. Let me recall their sequence while emphasizing their range of topics. From January through March 1980, Foucault delivered his annual lectures at the Collège under the very general title "On the Government of the Living." In them, the Christian topics were baptismal preparation, penance, and the direction of souls. In October and November of that same year, at three American universities, Foucault read lectures in English that drew the main lessons from his investigation of Christian "acts of reflexive truth."[28] He illustrated the lessons using some of the material from the Collège; he introduced other textual discoveries. In April and May 1981, Foucault returned to some of the early Christian material—and even to portions of the lecture scripts used at the Collège a year before—when analyzing confession before the School of Criminology of the Université catholique de Louvain. Finally, in October 1982, he summarized his conclusions about Christian practices toward the end of faculty seminars on technologies of the self at the University of Vermont.

When these lectures are outlined side by side, the shared sources stand out, but so do differences in their arrangement and framing. Several of the lectures at Louvain mirror those at Paris, while the lectures at Dartmouth and Berkeley intercut texts and topics. More significantly, the Christian material is framed by varied concerns and put into conversation with quite different interlocutors. The American lectures begin with a reflection on Foucault's method in relation to recent philosophy. The lectures at Louvain begin and end with questions of jurisprudence. The Burlington seminar presentations adopt the later and larger scheme of the hermeneutic of the subject; they end with a public lecture about the self in modern philosophy. If Foucault constructs the various frames with an eye to diverse audiences, he reconsiders the role of Christian pastoral material in his genealogies as he reads further into antiquity. Attending mainly to the pieces of these lectures that describe Christian manifestations of truth, I reconstruct a few of their arguments rather than trace their sequences of presentation. I begin with the shared concern for truth showing or truth telling.

Alèthurgie is a neologism in French, as "alethurgy" is in English.[29] Foucault coined this "fictive word" by analogy to other Greek terms that have cast long shadows over European languages. One is *dramatourgia* (*dramaturgie*, dramaturgy), which meant in antiquity the composition of a drama or its main action. The other analogous term is *leitourgia*, literally "the work of the people." It referred in ancient civic life to various acts of public service, including sacrifices to the gods. Christians chose the word to describe their worship, so it became in French *liturgie*, in English *liturgy*. Alethurgy is the liturgy of truth.

At the beginning of the lectures on the government of the living, Foucault introduces the new term by describing the throne room of the Roman emperor Septimius Severus. Behind the throne, a mural depicts the emperor's natal constellations. The whims or judgments he pronounces from the throne are backed by the cosmic fate that decreed his elevation. It is hardly surprising that power should seek to give itself a natural, indeed, a religious foundation. What requires more thought is the excess in power's manifestation of truth: it is luxurious, spendthrift, even useless. This is Bataille's language. As if to amplify the echo, Foucault describes the "pure expenditure of truth." The astrological backdrop to Septimius Severus was a sort of "pure manifestation of truth," meant not to prove anything but to "unveil truth." Its truth must be distinguished from the sorts of technical expertise useful in governing. So Foucault offers his new word, "alethurgy," to mark the distinction. It names the "ensemble of possible procedures, verbal or not, by which one brings to light what is posited as true in opposition to the false, the hidden, the unsayable, the unforeseeable, the forgotten." More succinctly, alethurgy comprises "rituals and forms of the manifestation of truth."[30]

These forms of manifestation should not be neglected. Foucault says at first that "it is unlikely that there is any hegemony than can exercise itself without something like an alethurgy." A minute or two later he insists, "no hegemony without alethurgy." By the end of the lecture, the claim becomes still more vivid in a litany of rhetorical questions: "Can there be a power without its flashy rags [oripeaux]? . . . Can there be an exercise of power without a ring of truth, without an alethurgical circle that turns around it and accompanies it?"[31]

The questions call up two counter-examples from Foucault's earlier stories. In Discipline and Punish, penal reform fantasizes a power that can dispense with its oripeaux because it no longer needs the gruesome surplus of monarchical theater. Its acts of punishment will be calculated exactly as a rational pedagogy, without any dramatic supplement. Again, perhaps more strikingly, Septimius Severus must recall King Ubu. As Foucault tells it in Abnormals, Ubu power neglects appearances, no longer needing to make an impression. It can be slovenly or clumsily capricious because it doesn't depend on the qualities of the person exercising it. Do these counter-examples contradict Foucault's suggestions about power and its oripeaux? No. Penal reform actually replaces the extravagant performances of the public supplice with another theater—private, minimalist, but also much longer. Prison puts the delinquent at the center of a show that never ends.[32] This is a change of taste in drag, not its overcoming. As for King Ubu, whatever a reader learns from him about modern power comes from Jarry's theatrical excesses. That peculiar stagecraft suggests not so much an alternative world as a way of regarding this world. In our world, the slovenliness of the powerful bureaucrat is an aggressive drag. Bureaucratized tyrannies add to it more obvious *oripeaux*—tank parades, mass rallies, and other displays for boys. So the apparent counter-examples can be read into the new notion of alethurgy.

For all the care in its coining, "alethurgy" doesn't become a dominant term in Foucault's later lexicon. Even in the lectures on the government of the living, it drops mostly out of sight after the first few pages in favor of other notions, such as the "regime of truth." "Alethurgy" doesn't appear at all in the American lectures, and at Louvain only in the presentation of Greek material.[33] In English, Foucault speaks of truth obligations in relation to technologies of the self. At Louvain, the master term is *veridiction*, truth saying, and its particular form, the confession (*aveu*). Still the relative rarity of "alethurgy" doesn't imply that the impulse it names is important. Power is concerned with bodily drama. Its rags do flash. If the rise of modern governmentality required a final victory over the dramas of magical arts, it could never entirely do away with the need for bodying forth—as the last century's tyrannies knew. Studying Christianity before modernity, Foucault is certainly concerned with how bodies manifest truth or how they continue to conceal it under regimes of endless verbalization. He articulates his preoccupation with ritual expressions through a set of nested distinctions that recur in the lectures for Paris, America, and Louvain.

Foucault repeatedly distinguishes two meanings of "confession" in Christianity: the confession of faith and the confession of who one is, of one's state.[34] These two are relatively autonomous and sometimes opposed. To declare true doctrine is not the same as to discover and express the truth about oneself. The two imperatives play back and forth across Christian history. Foucault is more interested in subdividing the second form of confession.[35] One way to confess the truth of self is called in Greek *exomologêsis* or, in Tertullian's Latin, *publicatio*. In pre-Christian texts, *exomologêsis* means something like admission, confession, acknowledgment. In the Christian texts that preoccupy Foucault, it names the manifestation of public penance, especially in a culminating ritual event. The other form of confession of self is *exagoreusis*. In pre-Christian texts, this sometimes means telling of sins, sometimes the betrayal of a secret. Among Christians, it comes to mean the verbal declaration of a sin. Over centuries, and for some Christians only, it is legislated as an obligation of confession to the ear of a priest, auricular confession. What distinguishes Christianity, Foucault says several times, is not the invention of the fall but of its repetition.[36] Christianity is the religion of backsliders: it wants to fix transformation the second time around, yet in doing so it keeps showing the perils of change.

In this subdivision of Christian confession of self, *exomologêsis* is more clearly an alethurgy of bodily ritual. Foucault contrasts it with an early form of declaring one's sins by insisting that *exomologêsis* is not verbal. In it, "the word has the value of a cry, an expressive value."[37] Like the cry of the mad or the vivisected criminal, like the murmur of subterranean insects. *Exomologêsis* is also characterized by its "dramatization" or "dramaticity," the "dramatization of the drama," a "theatricalization." As Foucault says to his American audiences, *exomologêsis* requires "dramatic emphasis" and "maximum theatricality."[38] It refuses speech in order to express itself somatically and symbolically.

For his favorite example, Foucault returns to Jerome's description of the Roman matron Fabiola.[39] As part of a eulogy, Jerome recalls not only Fabiola's exemplary life but the very public repentance that was something like its pivot. Her grievous sin? She had abandoned a violent, vicious husband and married a second while the first still lived. After her second husband died, Jerome says, Fabiola recognized that she had violated the Gospel prohibition of remarriage. So she took up the state of public penance. In the days before Easter, at the Lateran basilica, she stood among the order of penitents. She beat the face with which she had lured her second husband to sinful union. Jerome blurs her sin with the marks she inflicts on her flesh: "she showed to all her wound and a weeping Rome saw the scar in her pale body." Sin is figured in bodily signs as a body atones for its sins. The signification is wordless. Fabiola sobs and laments; she does not speak. "She kept her limbs apart; her head, naked; her mouth, shut."[40] Fabiola is another convulsing body in Foucault. Unlike its predecessors, her suffering body does not register resistance so much as illustrate submission. She is not lacerated by her executioners. She is not twisted by demonic forces. She has instead chosen, repeatedly, to act in an extravagant theater of confession. Still a stress on Fabiola's choice is too simple. The sinner's body suffers the ravages of sin against its will. It must be submitted to penance as to a cure (remembering how harsh the cures of medicine can be). Moreover, if penance is chosen, it must also be assumed and carried out as a severe ritual. In all these ways, Fabiola's body too is a body submitting to other forces by convulsion.

Submission is less ambivalent in the second form of Christian confession, *exagoreusis*. Here the truth can be made manifest only with the subject's active compliance. Following the monastic author Cassian, Foucault emphasizes that *exagoreusis* requires not only the continuous scrutiny of thought but the effort to record mental motions before action, will, or desire. The subject must find the first flickerings of mental representation, the *logismoi* or *cogitationes*. Here Foucault likes to recall some of Cassian's favorite images for internal scrutiny: the mill that grinds all the grain, the tireless inspecting officer, the alert moneychanger who tests every coin to detect counterfeits.[41] The last two images emphasize vigilant agency. This sort of self-examination is only possible in confession to another, where the effort is not to recapitulate sins from the past but to report steadily on the deepest processes of one's present mind. The aim is to render into words the "flux of thinking," to achieve a practice of confession that "would perpetually *double* the flux of the soul" by rendering it into words.[42]

In the Louvain lectures especially, Foucault connects *exagoreusis* with the language of *Discipline and Punish*. He speaks of self-observation as surveillance, the key word for the prison as Panopticon.[43] The practice of surveillance establishes, he says, a vertical relationship of the self to itself, as if he were imagining a new penal architecture, with the observation tower suspended above roofless cells below. The most striking verbal recollection comes in this notion of doubling. In *Discipline and Punish*, the offender is doubled as the delinquent. Foucault recalls this explicitly at the Collège when summarizing his earlier books. As *Discipline and Punish* explored "the singular and fragile and contingent economy of relations of power," it showed particularly the doubling of the subject of law as *homo criminalis*.[44] There have been many other doublings in Foucault as well: of the poetic as the mad, of the unusual as the abnormal, of the sodomite as the homosexual, even of the body as the flesh. Explaining *exagoreusis* now, Foucault claims a Christian origin for the crucial link between doubling and verbalization. The most effective doubling requires the subject's constant cooperation to record itself in endless reports.

Sometimes doubling is justified as a cure, but it is accomplished in fact for the sake of exclusion or effacement. The double is an instrument both of control and of undoing. In Christian confession the undoing is particularly thorough. Foucault tells his American audiences that the verbalization of *exagoreusis* is permanent, exhaustive, and sacrificial. Sacrifice is demanded by both *exomologêsis* and *exagoreusis*, though they undo the self differently. The bodily showing of penance in *exomologêsis* is likened to martyrdom, to a refusal of self, to breaking off from the self. It chews the flesh to tear apart the sinful soul in hopes of rebirth. *Ego non sum ego*: I am not I, because I am no longer I.[45] There is a more particular sacrifice in the steady stream of verbal confession to one's director. The endless revelation of the truth of self is an unlimited renunciation. Truth about the self requires sacrifice: there is no knowledge of self without a sacrifice of self. It also ends in sacrifice: the endless revelation is for the sake of becoming someone else. This is the paradox that Foucault finds underneath the new forms of relation to self that Christianity establishes. I tell the truth of myself in order no longer to be myself; I speak myself to become something other than myself.[46]

Where does all this truth telling lead? In the American lectures, Foucault describes *exomologêsis* and *exagoreusis* as permanent poles in Christianity, one ontological (or physical), the other epistemological. After centuries, the epistemological, enacted as verbal reports of interior thoughts, comes to dominate within Christianity and so after it. The hermeneutics of self in the modern West is more rooted in Christian confession than in ancient philosophical practice, but it has also been formed as a positive reaction against the Christian paradox of self-sacrifice. At Louvain, Foucault tells a more interesting story. In the medieval West, he says, a centuries-long process mostly replaces the public penance known to Fabiola with the sacrament of private confession, itself a juridical successor to monastic practices of *exagoreusis*. The replacement is never complete. Particularly scandalous sins may still require public penance, which also returns in times of panic. Even within private confession, the confessor may need to see the face of the penitent to determine sincerity or candor. The penitent's tears, the penitent's blush—these are physical manifestations of truth under or around the requirement of verbalization. The flesh, a body double, has become a space of enacted transformation. Verbalization itself is the act of a body. Confession is a "speech act" to be sure (Foucault quotes J. L. Austin's English) but also a body's speaking.[47]

Sometimes a body writes out its confession. The most striking additions in the lectures at Louvain are the repeated mentions of writing. Foucault first contrasts the hermeneutics of the text and of the self. All of Christianity's techniques for textual interpretation would have been familiar to an ancient reader, but its techniques for interpreting the flux of the soul would not. They were new. Foucault then complicates the contrast of the two hermeneutics by tracing the verbalization of self back into written forms. He underlines a passage in which Chrysostom suggests that one should render an account of one's sins as if writing them down. What appears as a metaphor in Chrysostom Foucault finds as an actual practice of writing in Athanasius's account of the life of Anthony.[48]

During the years he wrote and lectured on Christian topics, Foucault was becoming more explicitly interested in practices of self-writing. By the time he speaks at Burlington, for example, he can describe at length and with pleasure ancient practices of writing in relation to daily self-examination—like the letters Marcus Aurelius wrote to his teacher, Fronto. Earlier that same year, he uses Athanasius on Anthony as springboard to a preliminary taxonomy of types of self-writing in antiquity.[49] Indeed, the topic would be the center of a new publication project to accompany or replace the *History of Sexuality*. If one believed in "literary periods," this would have to count as a new one for Foucault. Still the arc that connects the hermeneutic of the self with that of the text shouldn't obscure the puzzles around writing in relation to the wordless enactment of *exomologêsis* and the endless verbalization of *exagoreusis*—or the tension between those two.

PERMANENT DRAMA, ENDLESS SPEECH

For Foucault, Christianity sometimes means no more than the historically achieved forms of its pastoral power. That is the point of his perverse conclusion that Christianity is not ascetical, communal, mystical, scriptural, or eschatological. Foucault also stresses the persistent tensions and the alternative possibilities carried forward *within* Christian churches. The five counter-conducts that drive ecclesiastical history into modernity are intrinsic to the pastorate. More poignantly, if he judges that modernity marks the triumph of epistemological Christianity over ontological Christianity, of speech over bodily act, Foucault holds out the other possibility expressed in *exomologêsis*: bodily resistance that is the trace or anticipation of another regime of bodies and pleasures.

The lectures delivered at Dartmouth and Berkeley end, after all, with a tentative gesture toward an alternative. "Maybe our problem is now to discover that the self is nothing else than the historical correlation of the technology built in our history. Maybe the problem is to change those technologies." Foucault adds at Berkeley, "or maybe to get rid of those technologies, and then, to get rid of the sacrifice that is linked to those technologies."[50] The modern self is the epistemological Christian self without the paradox of sacrifice, which has been replaced by governmental management. To produce an alternative to the modern self for the future requires two motions: undoing the modern machinery, then evading what Foucault takes to be the Christian paradoxes of self-sacrifice.

The day after he presented the paper in Tokyo, Foucault sat for a conversation with an old acquaintance, Moriaki Watanabe. One of Foucault's Japanese translators, he is also an eminent scholar of European literature and theater. So it is perhaps not surprising that Watanabe asks Foucault at once about the importance of theater in his work. Foucault expresses pleasure at the question, then interprets his earlier work in theatrical terms: "I wanted to know how one staged sickness [*mis en scène la maladie*], how one staged madness, how one staged crime. . . . I want [now] to do a history of the *scene* on which one has then tried to distinguish the true and the false, but it's not this distinction that interests me; it's the constitution of the scene and of the theater."[51]

Foucault links this interest to Nietzsche, who is also fascinated by the transient event. It was Nietzsche who first defined philosophy as "the activity, which serves to know what happens and what happens now." The philosopher is the diagnostician of present actuality. Theater, Foucault continues, takes hold of the event and stages it. His own books should be understood as dramaturgies. His flaw as a writer—Foucault performs his own act of penance—is a "a sort of intensification, a dramatization of events about which one should speak less fervently."

Foucault is, in other words, rather prone to *exomologêsis*. Like Fabiola, he favors its "permanent drama," its "theatricalization."[52] He inherits a predisposition to the theater from Nietzsche, of course, but also from figures in his genealogy of literary ancestors, especially Artaud (for whom mise-en-scène is a central category). Perhaps he has other models too besides early Christian matrons.

In an infamous essay, Susan Sontag writes that camp is "the theatricalization of experience."[53] If Sontag generally misses the importance of religious camp, little imagination is required to add Fabiola, say, to her examples. Fabiola's performance of public penance at the Lateran basilica contains just the sort of excess one expects in camp movies or classic drag. It is not hard to imagine Fabiola played by Maria Montez or Justin Bond.

How does Foucault's notion of theatricalization differ, if it does, from Sontag's application of that notion to camp? Foucault evidently relishes the dramatic possibilities in the example of Fabiola, since he repeats it every time he talks about *exomologêsis*. Is there anything else to suggest that he sees in it a potential for camp? One way to pursue this question would be to stitch together evidence in Foucault of what would ordinarily count as camp sensibility. There is his confession to Watanabe of his own predilection for exaggeration, coupled with his evident nostalgia for Christianity's loss of grandly theatrical bodily penance. Nostalgia is a key ingredient in camp. So too is a taste for the too-gaudy costume: recall the *oripeaux* of power in the account of alethurgy. *Exomologêsis*, Foucault tells us, is Christian alethurgy.[54] Sackcloth, ashes, tears, lacerations—those are its *oripeaux*. I could go on. (One always can with camp.) More might be learned about camp in Foucault by reconsidering the compositional challenge of writing about it.

To write about camp with humorless literalism is to show oneself incompetent to appreciate it. Representing camp without losing it makes severe stylistic demands. As Sontag says, "To talk about Camp is therefore to betray it."[55] She records her own notes in numbered aphorisms, broken up into thematic sections by quotations from Oscar Wilde. The citations of Wilde are one sort of citation; the numbering, another. Sontag mocks the politico-artistic manifestos of her century by rewriting them in the self-consciously modern style of the collage or pastiche. She is also imitating Nietzsche—or Wittgenstein.

How does Foucault represent the *oripeaux* of power? He quotes from its cases. He reconstructs its terminologies. He parrots its regulations. Across his analyses, Foucault attends to power's creation of characters, whether for its agents or its victims. He exhausts whole repertoires of metaphors in describing its circuits. He strains to restage its innermost contests and to find in them the moments that allow his readers or hearers to imagine other histories of power.

What is the affect in these representations? Introducing the story of Fabiola at the Collège, Foucault says that "she was someone very wicked [*vilain*]: she had a first husband, she divorced, and she remarried before the death of her first husband." That *vilain* must be a small joke told at the expense of the audience. They would hardly consider such an action sinful at all. Reminding them of their judgment amplifies the theatricality of Fabiola's public penance—the disproportion of camp attachment. Such a small crime, such a magnificent repentance. As he reads excerpts of the account from Jerome, Foucault comments on some elements of the public performance that he takes to be characteristic. Only when he returns to Fabiola a little later does he note one more: Some of her actions are symbolic expressions of a class of sin. There is, he insists, "an expressive and symbolic relation" between "the body and the sin," considered now not as a particular historic event but as a type.[56] In short, *exomologêsis* is artifice all the way through. It is not the improvised release of the pressure of inward grief. It is the ritualized performance of a drama with set symbols. It is the convulsing body stylized as a capacity for accomplishing the Christian paradox of permanent change.

CHAPTER 6

THE ARTIST OF PLEASURES

A READER APPROACHING the later volumes of *History of Sexuality* immediately after the first may expect more of the same: more sources, more chronological range, further divisions of familiar topics, like biopower or disciplinarity or normalization. She finds instead what looks like an abrupt change of topic—or, at least, a broadening of the topic of sexuality beyond recognition. She is launched into an extended paraphrase of Greco-Roman texts on dietetics, household management, and erotic restraint, with excurses on dream interpretation and true love. As if Foucault had decided to write on something else entirely while keeping his series title (jokingly, perversely) unchanged. The reader's surprise needs attention. It is part of Foucault's pedagogy.

READERS' DISCONTINUITIES, WRITER'S CONTINUITIES

Surprised readers have felt many discontinuities, especially in Foucault's archive and in his framing of sexuality as topic. Amy Richlin famously chastises Foucault for producing an ancient world without women, Jews, Africans, children, babies, poor people, or slaves.[1] To which the opening pages of *History of Sexuality* 2 answer, Yes. Foucault concedes that he treats a small sliver of society through narrowly idealized texts. Yet Richlin's criticism points to a larger shift in the sources and the texture of Foucault's writing.

Foucault insists when beginning *History of Sexuality* 2 that his project never intended to be a social or even an intellectual history. He wanted to trace the constitution of sexuality as a category. Still, and however schematically, the first volume in the series alluded to a wide range of texts, from the most scientific or literary to the most concrete, particular, and domestic—from Freud and Proust or Lawrence to municipal court records and tabloid stories. That volume arranged archival items in constellation with items from other genres in ways that readers have come to call "Foucauldian." Foucault doesn't do this in *History of Sexuality* 2 and 3. He does not, because he cannot. He is, he promptly acknowledges, less expert in the ancient material. More important, there survive no comparable archives from Greco-Roman antiquity. The character of Foucault's reading and writing must change if he will pursue his questions further back.

The archives change in part by historical accident. Most legal, commercial, or domestic records from around the ancient Mediterranean have disappeared. The archival gaps also show a different way of writing about bodies. On Foucault's account, the techniques of discipline or the sciences of abnormality require new forms of composition and technologies for their filing. Bodies must be recorded meticulously, in their motions and changes, so that they can be sorted and diagnosed, trained and treated. They must be written down as never before, not in order to make heroes of them but in order to manage them at the scale of the nation-state.[2] So even if there were many more survivals from Mediterranean antiquity, they could never match the managerial detail of the modern archive. Foucault acknowledges that he now reads a handful of elite, prescriptive texts from the surviving ancient libraries. So he insists, even more than in *History of Sexuality* 1, that he is not offering a social history of sex or even a broad-gauge intellectual history of its concepts. He is trying only to study what he calls the "problematization" of sexuality—the sites or stages at which sexuality becomes an object of moral concern. Moral problematization is just the sort of thing that an inquirer *can* discover in an elite, prescriptive text. Reading such a text, she cannot tell what people of any class were doing with their genitals. Surely she can learn what earlier readers were being told about the moral problems posed by their genitals. That is what prescriptive texts do.

Of course, many readers have felt another discontinuity precisely with regard to the topic of sexuality. So much that appears in these two volumes doesn't seem to be about sex at all. To this complaint, the opening pages of *History of Sexuality* 2 again answer, Yes. The volume begins by marking a discontinuity in the very notion of sexuality. "One would have a very hard time finding among the Greeks (as later among the Latins) a notion like that of [modern] 'sexuality' and of [Christian] 'flesh.'" The word that figures in the title of the project is already our word, not theirs. Their words are so different that they cannot be translated. So, with apologies, Foucault announces that he will leave untranslated the Greek locution, *ta aphrodisia*, which seems to cover some of the same ground as our "sexuality." Even with the safeguard of that transliteration, he insists again that "our idea of 'sexuality' . . . concerns a reality of another sort; and it has, in our morality and our knowledge, entirely different functions."[3] There is no room in our systems of speech for translating *ta aphrodisia*. We have to make do, especially in book titles, with some mistranslation like "sexuality."

The complaints of discontinuity against Foucault are unwitting testimonies to his compositional purposes. They are applied to two books that mean to highlight various disruptions, not least in their central terms. One of the books' main tasks is to describe as precisely as possible, from a much later standpoint, an ambivalent discontinuity and the changes that led up to it. This is an effort to write across discontinuity without ignoring it. The continuity of that effort may help justify the persistence of Foucault's title. In *History of Sexuality* 2 and 3, Foucault pursues an inquiry that leads him away from his favorite kinds of sources and his characteristic ways of writing about them. He keeps on writing across a significant change in archive. The project's continuity is an effect of his persistence as a writer. Given Foucault's notorious (earlier) slogans about the disappearance of the author, this might seem another joke or a willful contradiction. It is rather a test of the reader's own continuities—which include, among other things, the set of expectations brought to these books.

How exactly did the reader think that Foucault would proceed with the series of books?

A first expectation: At the end of the first volume, and also in the Tokyo lecture, the contrast between *scientia sexualis* and *ars erotica* might lead a reader to predict that Foucault would turn from *scientia sexualis* to *ars erotica*, that he would seek an art of pleasure in contrast to the knowledge of sexuality—or seek bodies and pleasures rather than subjects and identities. Since this is a history of sexuality, Foucault might well return to some fork in the historical road, as it were, to consider what latent possibilities might remain for reconstituting an *ars erotica* in "the West." The focus on problematization in *History of Sexuality* 2 is something like this, only instead of describing a fork in the road that could lead toward a Western *ars erotica*, Foucault suggests instead a third possibility, an indigenous art of sexed bodies that he will describe by the word "stylization."

A second expectation in reading: Given Foucault's culminating indictment of biopower in *History of Sexuality* 1, a reader might expect that his main purpose in the rest of the series would be to expose the crushing management of living bodies and then to locate points of possible resistance. Instead, Foucault seems to turn away from the procreative aspects of sexuality toward precisely the nonprocreative, toward the asymmetrical stylization of sexuality within male-male relations.[4] Practices that he attacks under biopower, such as the medicalization of life or the demand to report the truth about oneself, seem to reappear in these later volumes without condemnation as Foucault evokes ancient medical and philosophical sources.

Foucault's odd acquiescence frustrates a third expectation, not so much of topic as of tone. *History of Sexuality* 1 was notable for its satire. It seems reasonable, after a wickedly ironic beginning, to expect that the rest of the series would be punctuated with humor. Yet a reader finds little laughter in the pages of *History of Sexuality* 2 and 3. There is no target like sexual liberation; no pompous prophet, like Lawrence. The reader finds instead a tone of careful attention. Has Foucault lost himself in adoration of antiquity? In the first volume, his laughter was provoked by modern sciences and directed at their improbable sequels in the liberation movements. *History of Sexuality* 2 and 3 are not about modern sciences or programs for liberating sexual desire. They want rather to tell backward the process of subjectivation by which individuals came to be subjects of sexuality. Why does that question require earnestness? What *is* the importance of being earnest?

I describe the tone, with a little joke, as if it were a moral attribute, but Foucault tells it sometimes as the consequence of an abrupt shift of style. In one of his last interviews, he is asked why he has turned to a "very different style" that is "clear, pure, smooth." Without contesting the question's assumptions, as he so often does, Foucault replies by admitting an abrupt "rupture" in his style just after *History of Sexuality* 1 (that is, in 1975–1976).[5] He links the change to his pursuit of a history of the subject that requires him to narrate a slow genesis and development. He means to tell a history that is not centered on anything like an event—a history in which the main story is the dance of continuity and discontinuity. What I called "earnestness" is a style required by a certain sort of storytelling. Or else it is a practice of attention required by slow mutations in power that the reigning power wants badly to conceal. Earnestness may be useful before very clever *oripeaux*.

SUBJECTS OF DESIRE

History of Sexuality 2 denies at once the constancy of sexual desire. Sexuality is not "an invariant" that is everywhere repressed. "Desire and the subject of desire" are not "outside the historical field."[6] A history of sexuality comprises the formation of the sciences and the constitution of regimes of power, but also—even more—an account of "the forms within which individuals can and should recognize themselves as subjects of this sexuality." Forms for recognition: these new subjects now see themselves, with the force of self-regard, as what they suppose themselves always to have been. Recognizing that I am a subject of a certain sort pins a prescribed history on me, even as it conceals the actual history that made me into that sort of subject. Behind the self-concealment that precedes self-recognition, Foucault must uncover the lost contingencies. His retelling has to recover my concealed history as it shakes my conviction that I now recognize the sort of self I truly am.

Where do satire or irony fit into this retelling? By a sharp irony at our expense, the prevailing regime makes us think that our liberation is possible only on its terms, while it prevents us from seeing that this "liberation" is the next step in our subjectivation. It closes our eyes to views of alternative selves. Satire directed against the external regime would be a mere distraction unless it could also alter the internal regime of recognition, the regime that has made the self and still resides within it. Is the best teaching rhetoric for this sort of situation irony or testimony? The question itself is an echo of ancient philosophy. Think of Socrates, but not only of Socrates.

To historicize the subject of desire, Foucault offers himself as the first counter-example. The stages of reformulating his project illustrate the possibility of interfering with the processes that produced recognition of sexual subjects. "As far as the motive that pushed me, it was very simple. . . . It is curiosity—the only kind of curiosity, in any case, that is worth the effort of being practiced with a little stubbornness: not [the kind] that tries to assimilate to itself what ought to be known but the [curiosity] that allows one to release the hold on oneself [se déprendre de soi-même]." Invoking the motive of curiosity (as he had in the "Masked Philosopher"), Foucault places his writing under the rubric of a present philosophy that attends continuously to its past. Mutations of power produce discontinuities in thinking. Philosophic curiosity steps over them. It is a way of detaching from oneself—where the self is not some true inner being so much as the artifact of particular regimes of power-knowledge. Curiosity resists the present regime by foreshadowing a changed self. "One may perhaps say to me that these games with myself should remain in the wings and that they are, at best, part of the preparatory works that are effaced as soon as they achieve their results. But what is philosophy today—I mean philosophic activity—if it is not the critical work of thought on itself?"[7]

The critical work of thought on itself can sound like pure abstraction. Some modern philosophy has certainly written it in that mode. The games that Foucault plays are experiments with the actual flow through time of his own thinking. They are written not as transcendental critique or as universal system but as essay. "The 'essay'—which must be understood as the modifying test of oneself in the game of truth . . . —is the living body of philosophy, at least if the latter is still what it once was, that is, an 'ascesis,' an exercise of the self, in thought."[8] The notion of the game qualifies the mention of ascesis: this is precisely not modern discipline of speech and body. This game retrieves ancient philosophical exercises—spiritual exercises, as Pierre Hadot would say, on analogy to gymnastic exercises, meant to make the body beautiful while giving order to the soul through the body. This is a game, but not of checkers or of animated slaughter. It is a game by which the self alters itself.

The body to be shaped, like the thinking, is eventually Foucault's own. The representation of that body, the "living body of philosophy," is an essay. Some texts play games in which the self that shapes the body is transformed. Models for these texts survive in the library of ancient philosophy. "These texts have as their role to be operators that allow individuals to question themselves about their proper conduct, to watch over it, to form it, and to fashion oneself as an ethical subject." Their function is "etho-poetic": to make or shape the *ethos*, the habits and tropisms of the self.[9] The essay, especially as inaugurated for French by Montaigne, may be the modern genre most like those ancient texts.

Foucault has claimed before that some kinds of writing transform the self through its body or create a new self to control the body. His study of modern discipline or the sciences of abnormality revealed them as regimes of writing. The modern archive is not a record or register only; it is an instrument for transformation. Nor is it new for Foucault to find a conceptual or linguistic surrogate for the body: the studies of normalization presented a series of body doubles, brought onstage by one new power or another as its required object. His challenge in *History of Sexuality* 2 and 3 is not to show that writing has effect or that bodies are shaped through linguistic representations. He means to discover how ancient etho-poetic writing differs from the disciplinary archive. Foucault must persuade the reader that an essay in curiosity is not another clinical dossier or a case before the court.

NARRATING A PROBLEMATIZATION

Foucault poses the question for *History of Sexuality* 2 and 3 in terms of moral problematization. What is the relation of the moralization of sex to retrieving ancient genres for reshaping selves?

The connection appears in two steps. The first distinguishes morality from prohibition or interdict, from the ideal of a code of rules. "Problematization" is precisely not prohibition. It is a kind of moral preoccupation that arises in the absence of codified obligation or penalty. How does a realm of activity become invested with the ethical concern that makes it into a moral domain? To see that the realm is not already and automatically moral is the first step. The second is to link the operation of an ethical concern that is not (yet) codified duty or prohibition to what Foucault calls "arts of existence." "By this one must understand reflective and voluntary practices by which men not only fix rules of conduct but seek to transform themselves, to modify themselves in their singular being, and to make of their life an oeuvre that carries certain aesthetic values and responds to certain criteria of style."[10] Ethical concern constitutes a moral domain for the practice of arts of self-fashioning. These arts treat a particular life as an aesthetic work that must answer to exigencies of style.

These exigencies can be felt only once a certain sort of domain has been traced out. In the lectures on abnormals, Foucault described a science that arose between the medical and the juridical. It was neither of them, because it found room between them. The space of the ancient stylization of a problematized sexuality is another *tertium quid*, placed this time between *scientia sexualis* and *ars erotica*. Ancient Mediterranean stylization is not an erotic art in the ordinary sense. It is not meant only to increase pleasure. Indeed, it is often marked by restraint, by austerity. Neither is it a science of sexuality in modern or early Christian senses (as Foucault will describe them). Stylization is an art of embodied existence—an *ars vivendi*, if not an *ars erotica*.

A domain opened by ethical concern for the practice of an art of life is not a domain that many modern readers would conceive as moral. Foucault invites his readers to revise their criteria for recognizing themselves as subjects of morality. He distinguishes three elements: the moral code prescribed through various prescriptive mechanisms; the actual behaviors that are to be measured against the code; and, most elusively, "the manner in which one ought to constitute oneself as a moral subject acting with reference to the prescriptive elements that constitute the code."[11] Foucault provides no short phrase to describe the third element of morality; he describes with some detail four points at which it can apply. They range from the ways in which a part of the subject is designated as the material for ethics to conceptions of the subject's teleology. A history of morality must thus include not only codes or behaviors but the means by which subjects are induced to constitute themselves. It must be a history of the forms of moral subjectivation. While Foucault concedes that every morality comprises elements both of code and of subjectivation, he distinguishes those that regularly emphasize codes from those that stress subjectivation. The former are code moralities; the latter, ethics-oriented moralities or ethics.

One function of this set of distinctions is to help the reader imagine continuities and discontinuities between ancient moralities and Christian ones. Foucault has already proposed, rather mischievously, that the continuities from pagan to Christian with regard to sex include at least four threads: a fear of unregulated expenditure, a schema of chaste comportment, a negative image of effeminacy, and a model of heroic abstention in pursuit of the truth. He adds immediately that these continuities can lead us to overlook the deeper change in the quality of moral prescription. We often look in the wrong places for moral continuity or discontinuity. When we ask whether certain prohibitions or obligations persist, we fail to understand that their functions change decisively whenever they are applied differently or to different sorts of subjects. In the change from antiquity to Christianity, the stability of some elements of code is engulfed by deeper changes in forms of subjectivation.[12]

Questions about the continuity and discontinuity of morality will preoccupy Foucault across these two volumes. They shouldn't eclipse a prior question about the possibility for conceiving an alternative mode of subjectivation around bodily desire. In describing ancient subject formation as an art, an aesthetic, a stylization, Foucault challenges the reader to imagine morality otherwise—to imagine a morality in which style is not the abdication of the ethical so much as its fulfillment. If he spends several hundred pages trying to shift the reader's habits for narrating moral continuity and discontinuity, he does so in order to open the reader's eyes to another way of conceiving the self. No easy task: it requires a kind of moral reeducation. So Foucault repeats his points across dozens of texts with a persistence that might seem only infatuated curiosity if it were not so necessary to his pedagogy. The reader is to be reeducated by recalling ancient educations. More precisely: while Foucault's text cannot recapitulate a Greek or Latin pedagogy in philosophy, it can provide a verbal image of it. This image prepares a reader to ask eventually, What educational alternative is open to me within the present regime of power?

History of Sexuality 2 and 3 were published, Foucault says, later than he intended and in a "an altogether different form." At one level, it is easy enough to describe the published form. Foucault reads selections from prescriptive texts that speak to four themes in sexual austerity: the life of the body, the institution of marriage, sexual relations between males, and wisdom. These can also be conceived as four relations of the (legally) free, male subject: to his body, to the other sex, to his own sex, and to the truth. Texts about these four relations are grouped according to "a simple chronological distribution": one set from the classical period of the fourth century BCE, another from the imperial period of the first and second centuries CE.[13] In short, Foucault imposes a grid of four topics at two chronological points. The chronology is simple in the sense that it is schematic. The periods are temporal foci rather than strictly defined segments; they are an idealized earlier-and-later in relation to the great before-and-after marked by the coming of Christianity. Still, the staging of historical change is less important here than the persuasive presentation of an alternative conception of moral subjectivation, one tied to the art of living as a demand for stylization.

A GENEALOGY OF STYLIZATION

In *History of Sexuality* 2 and 3, the conjoined words "style, stylize, stylization, stylistics" are at the center of the contrast between ancient sexual morality and its Christian replacement. To understand the force of those words is to understand what Foucault glimpses as an alternative to the codified regimes of the Christian pastorate and its modern successors.

Within *History of Sexuality*, the conjoined words begin to appear only with the second volume. They arrive almost hesitantly, as if Foucault were hunting still for the right words without quite finding them. Indeed, "stylize" (*stylizer*) appears for the first time in quotation marks that acknowledge its awkwardness.[14] In the third volume, its nominal form, "stylization" (*stylisation*), is replaced functionally by "stylistics" (*stylistique*). Foucault attributes his adoption of the terms to different sources in different places. In a late interview, he says, "The use that I make of 'style,' I borrow in large part from Peter Brown." This follows the interviewer's allusion to Brown's *The Making of Late Antiquity*.[15] But in two other pieces from 1984, an obituary and a subsequent interview, Foucault attributes the importance of style in historiography to Phillipe Ariès. Ariès "established the principle of a 'stylistics of existence'— I mean to say of a study of the forms by which man manifests himself, invents himself, forgets or denies himself in the fatality of being alive and mortal." Ariès may not have used the word "style," but Foucault judges that he was certainly concerned with it and that he was thus "an important precursor" to Brown and others.[16]

The mention of Ariès leads the reader to look further back than the appearance of Brown's book, in English or in French. Indeed, the reader must return to Foucault's earlier writings. If the notion of style recedes as an explanatory category in *History of Sexuality* 1 and other works immediately before it, it appears importantly in some works from the 1950s and 1960s.[17] In the introduction to Binswanger, for example, Foucault ascribes style to "an originary motion of the imagination" as it expresses itself through an image. "Expression is language, work of art, ethic." He writes or speaks repeatedly of style in relation to psychological science and its turn to research. It is only toward the end of the 1960s, when emphasizing the largest forces operating in fields of discourse, that Foucault sometimes denigrates literary style as an element on the surface of language. Even then the term moves around: if Foucault contrasts the desire for anonymity with the cultivation of idiosyncratic style, he also speaks of a style of anonymity.[18]

"Style" returns to prominence in Foucault's language along another route around 1980. In interviews about gay politics, Foucault begins to speak of *le style de vie*, perhaps under the influence of the contested English term "lifestyle." Foucault now speaks of style more resonantly. In 1981, he describes fighting to find a place for "the styles of homosexual life," which he then links to the notion of a "choice of existence." More strikingly, in an interview published in *Salmagundi*, Foucault refers to "the great problems, the great questions of style of life."[19] While he regrets that gay publications do not dedicate as much space as he would like to "questions of friendship among homosexuals or the signification of relations in the absence of codes or of established lines of conduct," gays have in fact begun to settle these questions for themselves. This has raised the level of political contestation, because what is most offensive to non-homosexuals is not particular sexual acts but "the gay style of life." Here style functions precisely as it will in *History of Sexuality* 2 and 3 to describe the elaboration of a conduct, a form of life, beyond codes.

None of the terms clustered around style are defined in the two volumes. They are contrasted with opposed modes of morality (like code);

they are linked with kindred notions (like aesthetics); they are depicted with nuanced and fugitive qualities (like increasing delicacy). In these volumes, Foucault ascribes style to a variety of things: to an activity or conduct, to a preoccupation or concern, to relations or relationships, and to ways of life or the whole of a life. If stylization or stylizing can be accomplished across a range of activities, Foucault is here concerned particularly with the stylistics of pleasures. Sometimes style seems to be an aspect of use rather than a synonym for it: "the conditions and the modalities of a 'use': the style of what the Greeks called the *chrêsis aphrodisiôn*." In other places, style is linked directly to aesthetics: "a stylization of attitude and an aesthetics of existence."[20]

For all of Foucault's care with translation, these conjoined terms have no Greek equivalent. The history of Western philosophy authorizes "art" or its cognates (after the Latin *ars*) as renderings for the Greek *technê*. Foucault relies on this convention, even if it seems increasingly improbable given the modern drift of the word "art." What is the Greek antecedent for "style" in the way Foucault is using it? He does not attempt to align it with locutions from the Greek literary tradition that are sometimes translated as "style." Nor does he reflect on its etymology—which is its own record of crossed and displaced meanings. Foucault's more abstract terms—like "stylization"—are products of nineteenth-century art criticism.[21] He relies on the current sense of a word prominent for his readers in order to teach them what is characteristic of Greek sexual morality under quite other terms.

Foucault acknowledges indirectly the modern and aesthetic origin of his key notions. Early in *History of Sexuality* 2, he explains that the moral problematization of sexual activity is linked in antiquity to certain arts of existence. These arts are reflective practices for turning one's life into "a work that carries certain aesthetic values and responds to certain criteria of style." The ancient arts lost both importance and autonomy, first under Christianity, then under modern techniques for education, medicine, and psychology. They did not disappear. Burckhardt (Nietzsche's teacher) long ago pointed out their importance in the Renaissance, but they can hardly be said to have stopped there. Foucault adds in a footnote: "It would be inexact to believe that since Burckhardt, the study of these arts and of this aesthetic of existence has been completely neglected. Let one recall Benjamin's study of Baudelaire."[22]

Foucault does not offer a citation. While a number of pieces in Benjamin's writings might be called a "study of Baudelaire," Foucault probably means two essays that had been published together in German since 1969 and recently translated into French: "The Paris of the Second Empire in Baudelaire" and "On Some Motifs in Baudelaire."[23] The essays overlap, but the first is most pertinent. In it, Benjamin ranges widely across Baudelaire's corpus, collating prose passages or fragments of the poems with passages from other literary writers and from political or economic histories. He wants to situate Baudelaire within a more accurate analysis of the dialectic of material forces in nineteenth-century Paris—to explicate him and then explain him.

Toward the end of the essay, Benjamin describes the heroism required to face modern life in a city. The latter-day hero appears in various improbable guises, as ragpicker and poet, scavenger of urban garbage and registrar of the city's sights or sounds. The modern hero's last guise, in Benjamin's reading of Baudelaire, is the dandy. With the dandy, the art of self-fashioning responds to modernity with bodily rigor. In the dandy's dress, even more in his deportment and daily regimen, a self is fashioned with splendid physical control. "So it is understandable that at certain times Baudelaire believed his flânerie [his city strolling] was clothed with the same worth as the exertion of his poetic power." Understandable, yet not accurate. For Benjamin, the dandy is the transposition into city streets of behaviors from the stock exchanges. Baudelaire's own pursuit of dandyism was in any case doomed to failure: "He did not have the gift of pleasing, which is such a significant element in the dandy's art of not pleasing."[24]

Benjamin here interprets Baudelaire's famous description of the dandy in "The Painter of Modern Life."[25] Foucault needs that description rather than Benjamin's critique of it. More precisely, he needs Benjamin only as a historiographer of a persistent preoccupation with shaping the self. Benjamin—like Burckhardt or Stephen Greenblatt in *Renaissance Self-Fashioning*—appears as a witness in Foucault to continuing historiographical interest. For the arts of existence themselves, Foucault's thought passes through Benjamin to Baudelaire—and to the dandy.

The dandy appears in Baudelaire as a figure, at once literary and historical, whose wealth and status permit him (the dandy is always male) to chase after his own happiness by self-making. "These beings have no other state than to cultivate the idea of the beautiful in their person, to satisfy their passions, to feel and to think." They have the means to translate fantasies into action. The fantasies are not especially erotic. The aim, the passion of dandyism is visible distinction. "It is above all the ardent need to make of oneself an originality, contained within the external limits of convention. It is a kind of cult of oneself."[26] Here is Foucault's theme, interestingly configured by contrast to (ordinary) erotic pursuits—and to women.

The dandy is like a late modern avatar of an ancient project, surviving despite Christianity and modern discipline. Baudelaire himself stresses the historical continuity with antiquity. He lists Caesar, Catiline, and Alcibiades as ancient examples of dandyism. He also describes it in terms astonishingly like those that Foucault will use for the problematization of ancient sexuality. For Baudelaire, dandyism is "an institution outside the laws"—as Foucault will say of male-male erotics within ancient Athens. It is, for Baudelaire, "an unwritten institution"—as Foucault will say when he contrasts self-fashioning with Christian codes. Benjamin's reading of Baudelaire equally emphasizes the historical reference: "Among all the relations that have involved modernity, it is the relation to classical antiquity that stands out. . . . Modernity signifies an epoch; it also signifies the force that is at work in this epoch to draw it close to antiquity."[27]

There are other resonances between this piece by Baudelaire and Foucault's justificatory preface. For example, Baudelaire announces the dandy as the quintessence of the moral character of the artistic observer of modernity, the observer who is characterized by insatiable curiosity and who is worthy to be called a philosopher.[28] Still I don't want to argue that Foucault has simply transposed Baudelaire's dandy from the streets of nineteenth-century Paris to the classical agora, or that the project of *History of Sexuality* 2 and 3 is only an extension of Baudelaire's meditation on the artist Constantin Guys. I do mean that Foucault finds in Baudelaire evidence for the mutating continuation of arts of existence once central to antiquity.

I rely not so much on a single footnote as on some remarks that Foucault inserted into a lecture mainly on Kant delivered at Berkeley in the fall of 1983. Foucault describes Baudelaire's notion of modernity: it is not mere attention to fugitive time but the heroic effort to detect the eternal through it. The painter of modern life "transfigures" daily life by entering into a "difficult game between the truth of the real and the exercise of liberty." Again: "Baudelairean modernity is an exercise in which extreme attention to the real is confronted by the practice of a liberty that at once respects the real and violates it."[29] A difficult game in a middle space; an attention modulated by freedom; an exercise that respects and transforms. These are elements in an art of existence. As if to confirm the reading, Foucault adds: "To be modern, this is not to accept oneself just as one is in the flux of moments that pass; it is to take oneself as the object of a complex and hard elaboration"—the elaboration of dandyism, to use the language of the nineteenth century. We have heard other names for it, more ancient. Foucault returns to one of them, with a modern sense, when he says that the space for self-fashioning in Baudelaire is to be found "in another place that Baudelaire calls art."[30]

Baudelaire is a figure from a punctuated genealogy. In *History of Sexuality* 2, Foucault says that there is certainly more to be done to recover the "long history of these aesthetics of existence and these technologies of self."[31] The problematization of sexual conduct in Mediterranean antiquity is one of the first chapters in it. Yet Foucault didn't set out to write the whole of that history, certainly not around Baudelaire. They are both after something larger. Baudelaire's modernity is characterized by a certain relation to antiquity (as Benjamin rightly says). It is also characterized by a transmutation of the real through a free play of attention (as Foucault insists). On Foucault's reading, Baudelaire's artist always seeks to discern behind the transient—behind the parade of Parisian fashions, say—some deeper form. So too Foucault in relation to the ancient arts of existence: his historiography, like the images rendered overnight by "the painter of modern life," means to reveal something more by rendering ancient texts. The same point could be made through the reference to Burckhardt: Renaissance self-fashioning depended on a sustained relation to antiquity in which, all conceits aside, there was no mere copying. In Baudelaire's modernity, in Burckhardt's Renaissance, self-fashioning turns historiography into an artistic instrument. One stylizes oneself by recalling and somehow transfiguring both the present and a classical past. Ancient stylization serves as template and as raw material. Here again the category of camp hovers nearby. After all, camp transmutes souvenirs from an adored and ambiguous past.

EROTIC STYLIZATION

In Foucault, as in Baudelaire, styles mutate as they circulate. They are ephemeral, even fugitive, but they also trace deeper patterns of change over centuries. One function of the notion of style in Foucault is to suggest this fleeting yet persistent circulation, especially of forms for pleasure.

In *History of Sexuality* 2, Foucault traces erotic stylization in all of the sections, not just in those labeled "Erotics." He uses prescriptive texts that stand in some relation to daily life, however schematic or hortatory. Consider the section titled "Economics," understood as the art of properly governing the household. The sexuality described here occurs in the densely regulated space of the home and family, the space in which male and female cohabit without merging—the space of gender segregation, gender definition. Their cohabitation is determined by custom but also by various kinds of law—civic, religious, and natural. Foucault asks, Why does ancient marriage become problematized if it is so heavily regulated? His answer is not to read this marital problematization as a precursor to Christian chastity in marriage. He notices instead that sex becomes problematic (in his sense) only in regard to the behavior of the male head of household. The fidelity recommended to the husband is quite different from the sexual exclusivity imposed upon the wife. He is invited to accept, voluntarily, a sexual symmetry, a "double sexual monopoly."[32] This is an invitation, not a universal ethical obligation (except perhaps in Plato's *Laws*). It is certainly not a New Law promulgated by God come in purified flesh.

During the classical period, Foucault finds a larger and more difficult realm of stylization in the relations between older and younger men. On his account, any sexual relation between men and "boys" is "an anxious theme" as a whole, not just a problematic area within another relation.[33] (I will follow Foucault's use of the term "boys," which he takes in turn from his Greek sources and just perhaps in sly allusion to gay slang. Since the term makes *me* anxious, I insist that he no more describes our "pedophilia" than our "homosexuality.") The relation of a man and a boy is problematic not because it constitutes a religious violation or signals a pathology but because it must preserve the boy's honor for future roles in the city. It is problematic because of civic maleness. So the moral problematization focuses on those issues, like perceived or enacted passivity, that could harm the boy in later political life. The risk is reflected in a persisting hesitation about the boy's role in sexual intercourse, about his pleasure. The "boy" must remain an object of pleasure for men without recognizing himself as an object—or taking his own pleasure in being one.

Describing this space for sexual problematization, Foucault returns to the notion of a game. He draws contrasts with marriage: male-male relationships are an open game both spatially (played in the open) and metaphorically (played beyond law). They are a game so far as they are a test.[34] As in sports, the aim is to learn how to take care of oneself, how to carry oneself, what attitude to have, how not to get bested or else to lose honorably. As in sports too, there are lessons for all participants, on both sides, since stylized demands apply both to the pursued and the pursuer.

The notion of the game allows Foucault to describe how the stylization of erotics can be taken up into Greek philosophy, where it becomes the privileged game of truth. There is no more striking example of the scope of sexuality as Foucault conceives it. His point is not that some Greek speakers used erotic metaphors to describe philosophy. He insists rather that the relation to truth is an erotic site. The title, "True Love," coming after the section on erotics, may lead the reader to expect that Foucault is (at last!) entering the realm of romance. He is interested rather in the philosophic transformation by which bodily love becomes love of the true, redirecting erotics toward truth. This redirection has many consequences, especially in Plato (as Foucault reads him). In Platonic erotics, for example, the problem of the boy's status is resolved by reversing pursuer and pursued. Again, since the object of passion is most of all truth, desire rather than fulfillment is the stuff of true love. Most interestingly, philosophy pushes stylization of free erotic relations toward the strictest austerity, an indefinite abstention. In true love, you stylize bodily erotics by *not* acting out, by intensifying desire through its endless restraint.[35]

For Foucault, Plato's "true love" is a culminating classical prescription. Still the Platonic dialogues are evidently dramatizations of a style. "One must keep in mind that this 'asceticism' was not a manner of disqualifying the love of boys; it was on the contrary a fashion of stylizing it and so, in giving it form and figure, of valorizing it."[36] Giving it form and figure: representations of abstention are both commendations of a style and its imaginative figuration. Styles circulate in prescriptive moral texts and in what we would call their literary elements or in literature simply.

Foucault juxtaposes the Platonic valorization at the end of the second volume of *History of Sexuality* with a curious text at the beginning of the third: an ancient book of dream interpretation by Artemidorus. He uses Artemidorus to mark the chronological transition from classical to imperial on the claim that the text gives evidence of widespread attitudes in the later period.[37] It also illustrates a practical art so shows a technique that was being brought to bear on the interpretation of the self, on the reconstitution of the inward experience of a self. Artemidorus offers as well a taxonomy of the elements of erotic relations that can be combined into significant styles. If he is a charming ancestor to Freud, he is another sort of painter of the most current life, a caricaturist of the nightly flow of dreams.

According to Foucault's Artemidorus, the dreamer's particular sexual acts are not so important as their stylization. "The principal question appears to bear much less on the conformity of acts to a natural structure or a positive regulation than on what one might call the subject's 'style of activity.'" Sexual acts are evaluated not by their conformity to a rule but "from the actor, from his manner of being, from his own situation, from his relation to others, and from the position that he occupies with regard to them."[38] Indeed, the first thing to consider for Artemidorus in a sexual dream is "the personage" (*personnage*)—of the dreamer, certainly, but also of other sexual actors. Here the *personnage* is not the projection of a clinical entity (like the pervert) or of a criminological one (like the delinquent). The *personnage* is the subject of styles of acting, the subject being styled, and the subject styling. Like Baudelaire's dandy, the dreamer in Artemidorus is obliged to be preoccupied with styles, their combination and their anticipation.

THE DIFFERENCES THAT CHRISTIANITY MAKES

At the end of *History of Sexuality* 2, Foucault confirms what the reader has regretfully observed: he is not going to supply even the indirect titillation of a catalogue of ancient sexual prohibitions. If a certain suspicion of sexuality among the Greeks is quite old, the resulting sexual interdictions are both sparse and monotonous. There is no point in writing their history.

Two other things are more interesting for Foucault and apparently more useful in the reeducation of his readers. The first is the distinction between a universal law and a principle of stylization, which he has attempted to describe throughout this volume and which he again relates to a difference between a history of codes and a history of ethics understood as self-cultivation. The second point to attract his interest is the shift across European history in the relations that are the main focus for thinking sex. He has noted, for example, that Greek "boys" are curiously like later European women in the concerns they elicit. Both Christian and modern cultures take up the problem of love in relations between men and women rather than in relations to young men. In a sufficiently historical view, the problematization of European sex moves from boys to women to children.[39]

These teasing remarks on the long duration of sexuality are connected to Foucault's coyness over historical beginnings and his fascination with the endless mutations of power. They also show his effort both to imagine forms of life before Christian sexuality and to write Christianity's impact on the history of sexual morality. He has explained the distribution of his material over two volumes as a simple chronological sequence. It is more significantly a gradual approach to the cultural dominance of Christianity. Foucault gives the two volumes subtitles that mark a change in ancient prescriptive texts from "the use of pleasures" to "the care of self." He is at pains to distinguish both of them from Christian asceticism and self-scrutiny. Whenever Foucault summarizes his narrative of change in antiquity, he immediately qualifies it to prevent any confusion with what comes next in Christianity.

Foucault must write a change of style carefully to show both that it is (only) a style (thus neither law nor nature) and that a sequence of styles traces an epochal shift. He thus deploys terms usually applied to language when describing antiquity's change from classical to imperial. It is a "displacement, inflection, and difference of accentuation." It sees the introduction of a "new stylistics of existence." The later moral texts about marriage, for example, present a new "exigency," a word that Foucault has used before to describe the demands of style. After several hundred pages of always revised efforts to describe the change, Foucault ends by insisting on the difficulty of writing it except as the millennial "elaboration of a rigorous morality. And in a certain fashion, the sexual austerity that one encounters among the philosophers of the first centuries of our era roots itself in this [more] ancient tradition, at least so far as it announces a future morality."[40]

The future has been present throughout *History of Sexuality* 2 and 3 in at least two forms. Our present appears in the volumes as a future, because misunderstandings arising from our current regimes of sexuality guide Foucault's exegesis. There has also been a constant presence of antiquity's immediate future, of Christendom. Contrasts with Christianity recur, often page after page, from the beginning of the second volume to the very end of the third. Foucault's narrative form is never a simple before and after. It repeats temporal juxtaposition. However eager Foucault is to stress the difference between ancient sexual stylizations and Christian sexual codes, he never attempts to describe the former except by contrast with the latter. If there is no hope of retrieving the ancient practices directly into our present, there is also no hope of depicting them without the multiple presents that have occurred since antiquity, in Christianity and its modern descendants.

One effect of Foucault's narrative juxtapositions is to obscure ancient religions. He mentions at some points the role of ancient religious precepts or rituals. In these asides, a reader might glimpse the possibility of imagining a lost relation of sexual morality to divinity or a forgotten way of placing divinity within and around the desiring body. Concerns like these animated Foucault's essay on Klossowski. But there is no attempt, in these later volumes, to cultivate that alternative imagination. (How would it change Foucault's reading of Platonic "true love" to dwell on the carefully staged contest of divinities in the *Symposium*? Or on Socrates's display of mythographic expertise and his concluding prayer in the *Phaedrus*?) A relatively weak religious motivation for ancient morals helps Foucault contrast them with Christianity. It also makes space in the narrative of ancient texts for Christianity as an impending religious future. The reading of antiquity is both driven and limited by later religious concerns.

The refusal of simple sequence in Foucault's narrative multiplies the roles of time in relation to style. Style implies mutability, and the practice of stylization depends on it. Styles change, and stylization is a change. The narration of a succession of ancient styles in the constant presence of Christianity attaches the study of style as style to a temporal contrast. This is part of what Foucault understands by "transfiguration" in Baudelaire. The present must be seen attentively and yet only as the present—as one, transient iteration of processes operating along another scale of time. Perhaps this is what Baudelaire recognizes in the artistic imperative to show that style is always temporal. The study of styles past cannot be a full retrieval. It can prepare, by juxtaposition, for the discovery of means of transfiguring the present. Styles unroll in time, and the representation of style as style requires temporal juxtaposition. Self-fashioning takes the time of an individual life; it seems to require a relation over historical time to a lost and classical past.

THE PERSISTENCE OF POWER

In their first edition, the back covers of both *History of Sexuality* 2 and 3 are mostly empty. They contain neither blurbs nor summaries. The only text, identical on both covers, is a quotation from René Char: "Human history is the long succession of synonyms for a single word [*vocable*]. It is an obligation to contradict it."[41]

The quotation comes from "L'âge cassant," a work that looks on the page like a sequence of aphorisms. Foucault takes the quotation from the middle of the text. It is preceded by an aphorism that denies any sense of fixity in this life for those who are truly alive. It is followed by a Nietzschean aphorism on the labyrinth of the present, between the past that is not and the is-not that is to come. The aphorism that Foucault quotes describes history as repetitive speaking. The repetition is not exact; it is the succession of synonyms for a single word. *Vocable*, not *mot*: a sounding word, a word in the mouth. Confronted with this repetition, one is obliged to a contrary speech, not mere denial or the negation of silence.

Foucault's placement of the quotation suggests that he has written these two volumes out of the obligation to contradict. He is tracing some part of the succession of synonyms. Which is the underlying word, the insistent *vocable*? Not "sexuality" surely, since Foucault insists on tracking its origins. "Sexuality" is merely one of the synonyms. So too are its

Greek antecedents like "erotics" or complementary terms like "dietetics" and "economics." Closer to the underlying *vocable* might be the set of words we English speakers now translate and condense as "power." Still no single word can stand in for the persisting *vocable*. It is spoken only in their succession.

If the underlying *vocable* is supposed to be something related to power, the reader may suddenly remember how little prominence power or its synonyms actually have in these two volumes. The word *pouvoir* occurs dozens of times, but most often in describing concrete relations to oneself or to particular others. There are none of the lyrical evocations of the machinery of power that appeared in earlier texts. Some of the key technical terms are simply absent. For example, *dispositif* doesn't figure in these two volumes. The description of power in antiquity seems to require different words. "Power" itself may be one of the synonyms for some other *vocable*, deeper still. Or it may be that the evocation of power in antiquity requires a turn away from the spatial analysis emphasized by a term like *dispositif*.

Foucault's spatial analogies for power are much better known than his temporal ones. I have noted these spaces frequently in my reading: the great confinement of *History of Madness*, the Panopticon in *Discipline and Punish*, the convent in *Abnormals*. I have remarked on some of the technical words Foucault borrows or bends to classify the spatial operations of power, beginning with *dispositif* and *quadrillage*. I have insisted on the recurring image of the appearance of a new form of power in the interstices of the old. Given Foucault's spatial imagination of power, a reader begins of course to think of resistance as a matter of *getting outside*.

The imaginative habit carries over when Foucault describes the operation of power on the internal spatialization of subjects. He points to the various faculty maps of the modern soul; the spatialized internal economies of psychoanalysis; the "doubling" of the modern self or soul as the point of application for a new form of power. He searches in monastic practice for the innermost space in which the first deviant desires flicker into view. So it is also easy for a reader to hunt for the source of resistance or the prospect of resubjectivation as an internal outside, as a quasi-spatial surplus or excess inside the subject, as something left over on which resubjectivation can work.

What if the more useful language for describing ancient alternatives to present power, the more hopeful way of imagining their resistance or resubjectivation, were in relation to time? The reader has already encountered this possibility. Recall the evocation of the Fourierist vision at end of *Discipline and Punish*, which is quite literally time on another calendar, after the great social change that establishes the harmonious dance of human differences. Recall the famous alternative spoken at end of *History of Sexuality* 1: "And we should consider that one day, perhaps, in another economy of bodies and pleasures, one will no longer understand very well how the ruses of sexuality . . . succeeded in submitting us to the austere monarchy of sex."[42] One day: this is a time marker for alternative subjectivation. So far as spaces occur in history, they are colored and conditioned by time. That has been Foucault's teaching over decades, not least in one of his most famous texts, the lecture titled "On Other Spaces." The lecture was delivered in 1967, a year after his essay on Blanchot; it was published only in 1984. It is almost always read for what it says about space. I rehearse the parts of it that tell time.

The lecture begins by contrasting the imagination of time and of space. It announces that while the mythology of the nineteenth century (Baudelaire's century) was preoccupied with history, "our" preoccupation is with space. The contrast is subtler than it sounds. A contrast between two epochs is a temporal contrast. Moreover, what Foucault means by history in the nineteenth century is very specific: "themes of development and of standstill, themes of crisis and cycle, themes of the accumulation of the past, the great surplus of deaths, the menacing cooling down of the world."[43] In short, "history" here means not time so much as a particular plot for it—the plot implicit in disciplinarity, which understands bodily life as development and arrest, crisis and cycle, so tries to outwit death by managing life. In this lecture, "space" also takes a particular meaning: a network of possible connections and especially of possible actions. Space is conceived as simultaneity. This conception comes with its own history. What we understand by space differs from earlier understandings; representations of space happen in time. So Foucault is evidently interested in the interaction for our epoch of notions of history and of space.

The most familiar part of the lecture presents what sounds like a spatial contrast between utopia and heterotopia. A utopia is a setting (*emplacement*) with no real place (*lieu*) that has direct or inverted analogies with the real space (*espace*) of a society. Here Foucault emphasizes the Greek etymology *u-topia*, no place. By contrast, a heterotopia is a real place, traced out within an existing society, in which larger social settings are represented, contested, and inverted. A heterotopia is a sort of outside that is permitted on the margin of the inside.

Foucault lists five characteristics of heterotopias. The first two are the most familiar. Foucault argues that heterotopias probably occur in every society, though not in the same way. For example, he distinguishes older heterotopias of crisis or liminality from recent heterotopias of deviance. He then declares that societies can change the function of a given heterotopia. He gives as an example the (European) cemetery. The other three characteristics show better the relations of time and space. Foucault claims that a heterotopia can juxtapose a series of settings that are incompatible. His example is the succession of scenes in a theater. From this notion of punctuated succession he argues that a heterotopia is often linked to cuts in time. Heterotopias open up "heterochronies," other times.[44] They also suppose a system for regulating their function in the times of human lives: they control entrances and exits, either by coercion or by rituals and purifications. A heterotopia has a boundary in time, and this boundary is a ritualized sequence or event.

Turn from the lecture on other places back to *History of Sexuality* 2 and 3. In Western thinking, pre-Christian antiquity is one of the great heterochronies. It marks time in so many ways, most of all with regard to Western sexual morality. Originally pagan antiquity served as the surpassed or suppressed type of sexual depravity, as in Paul's infamous fresco of the excesses of idolaters (Romans 1) or Augustine's evocation of Carthage as a clanging "cauldron of shameful loves" (*Confessions* 3.1.1). It has also supplied Christian authors with arguments and examples of sexual virtue—of restraint, fidelity, even virginity. Early in *History of Sexuality* 2, while enumerating some of the continuities between antiquity and Christianity, Foucault refers to Francis de Sales's argument from the chastity of elephants.[45] While the argument reaches the seventeenth-century Christian text through a long genealogy of other Christian writers, it derives originally from Pliny's *Natural History*. Foucault's instance could be multiplied by a thousand: it is characteristic of a whole line of Christian sexual morality, which finds in antiquity the scientific and philosophic proofs for its own precepts. In these volumes, Foucault changes the temporal function of antiquity once again—to the Other that it was originally in Christian rhetoric. Of course, for Foucault antiquity differs from Christianity not as darkness from light, not as demonic from angelic, but as before and after in the consolidation of power over sexuality.

In Foucault, antiquity becomes once again the other time within the asserted continuity of Western civilization. It is no longer the authorizing origin. It is the forgotten boundary of the Other. We are defined by it. We are drawn to write across it.

CHAPTER 7

THE VIOLATED MOTHER AND THE
NAKED PHILOSOPHER

THERE ARE REASONS TO SUSPECT any reading of Foucault's last lectures (1982–1984), especially when they are taken as conclusions spoken in anticipation of his death. When it came, the death was the result of unpredictable contests in a body. If Foucault knew his health to be failing, he still wrote these series of lectures with a curiosity that ignores mortality.

There are other reasons to be wary of these lectures, precisely because of that unrestrained curiosity. The lectures record Foucault's new reading of ancient sources, for good and for ill. Sometimes he gains by seeing them with fresh eyes. At other moments, he seems only to read familiar texts predictably. While Foucault regularly warns that his readings are schematic and selective, he still discovers in his favorite passages the origins of the largest patterns in Western philosophy. His old dialectic of the beginning-less beginning is now exaggerated, every refusal of a beginning accompanied more closely by a grand declaration of novelty. Foucault sometimes ventures claims for startling discoveries by himself or his colleagues. He reports a reading by Georges Dumézil of Socrates's dying words—the famous reminder to offer a cock in sacrifice to Asclepius. He repeats that no one has understood this foundational teaching of Western philosophy for two millennia—until Dumézil. The reading he then offers doesn't differ from readings found in other sources or in undergraduate seminars. Even if the claims for Dumézil's originality are excused as the exaggerations of friendship, Foucault's readings of this and other texts aren't always fresh or compelling. Sometimes he is so busy arranging the texts taxonomically—extracting from them what serves his stories—that he doesn't step back far enough from them to reflect on them as writing. Foucault isn't always an astute reader of ancient philosophy. He is not always a particularly Foucauldian reader.

I find myself impatient on some of these pages, wishing that Foucault had done better. Then, a page later, I come upon a passage in which he discovers by reading old texts new versions of his best questions. He reformulates the project of a history of sexuality once again. He no longer wants to find an origin for the modern hermeneutic, conceived as an offshoot of the epistemological temptation in Christianity. He searches instead for alternatives to the modern development of Western rationality. He wants to find a new "old" art for making human lives beautiful.

I see the last three lecture series, especially the last two, as a continuous report of this search and as an ongoing reading performed publicly. The lectures are connected thematically. They are laced together by cross-references. They run together in Foucault's mind. Though he describes them jokingly as a long excursion, a "Greco-Latin trip" lasting several years, Foucault returns through them to questions about thinking and language, about the ritual transformation of bodies and their souls, that animated his writing from the 1960s on.[1] The side trip is a trip home.

LECTURES FROM 1982:
AN ANCIENT ART FOR MAKING SUBJECTS

Foucault delivered a series of lectures under the title "Hermeneutic of the Subject" from January through March 1982 at the Collège. He had used a version of this title fourteen months earlier at Dartmouth: "About the Beginning of the Hermeneutic of the Self." In America, the title described an effort to locate an origin for the Western subject in Christian monastic practices. Now, in Paris, it leads Foucault back to the Greco-Roman schools of philosophy. There is no longer any programmatic mention of sex or sexuality. Foucault announces his theme synoptically: "In what form of history were there knitted together in the West the relations between the elements 'subject' and 'truth,' elements that do not usually fall within the practice, the habitual analysis of the historian?"[2] The word "form" may seem to be a casual synonym for "kind" or "sort," but I underline it. This will be a formally deliberate history in pursuit of a form.

Foucault distinguishes two modes of relation between the subject and truth. Philosophy is "the form of thought that asks itself what it is that permits the subject to have access to the truth, the form of thought that tries to determine the conditions and limits of the subject's access to the truth." Spirituality by contrast is "the ensemble of those investigations, practices, and experiences, which may be purifications, ascetical acts, renunciations, control of gazing, modifications of existence, and so on, which constitute, not for knowledge but for the subject, for the subject's very being, the price to pay for having access to the truth."[3] If form appears again in defining both these notions, the startling term is "spirituality." "Philosophy" is, of course, simply the modern descendant of a word that the Greeks themselves used. "Spirituality" is not. It has no clear Greek antecedent—unless it too is a part of philosophy. So why speak of spirituality?

A quick answer is that Foucault is following Pierre Hadot, whom he cites at the start of *History of Sexuality* 2 as his guide through ancient philosophy. Hadot uses "spiritual exercises" to describe a tradition that runs from the ancient schools forward. That answer only pushes the question back one step: Why does Hadot describe these as "spiritual exercises"? He is thinking of that influential, early modern Christian pattern for changing the self, the *Spiritual Exercises* of Ignatius of Loyola, founder of the Jesuits. These exercises are not only the means for training Jesuits; they are the pattern behind most Catholic "retreats" for the laity. So the phrase has in our ears a specifically Christian meaning. Hadot relies on the Ignatian analogy because it is so well known. He regards the Ignatian exercises as "only a Christian version of a Greco-Roman tradition."[4] He insists that the term *exercitium spirituale* is attested in early Latin Christianity and that it was nothing more than a translation of the Greek *askêsis*, which Foucault emphasizes in describing spirituality.

Even if Hadot is right about the continuity from antiquity to Ignatius, there is still the risk of misunderstanding because of a shift in meanings attached to "spirituality." In the medieval Latin that authorizes the English "spirituality," *spiritualitas* can mean technically the quality of being a spirit as opposed to being matter. The technical meaning multiplies symbolically and metaphorically. In various early and medieval Christian authors, spirituality is contrasted with animality, carnality, bodiliness. This range of meaning is transferred into Middle French. In the early modern period the French term begins to shift in tandem with "mysticism." Spirituality becomes a dangerous excess of devotion, a figment of devout imagination, often tethered by claims of extraordinary experience. The term is used to name a particular mystical heresy, the views of Madame Guyon espoused by Fénelon. Our own notions of it descend from this pejorative sense. We tend to mean a noninstitutional practice or attitude that is somehow religious without being religious, that brings one close to God without implicating one in all the messiness of ongoing religious communities.

For Hadot, and for Foucault after him, the word's accent falls differently. Hadot writes, "The word 'spiritual' may well lead one to understand that these exercises are the work not merely of thought but of the individual's entire psychism"—reason, passions, body, everything that a human being is.[5] For Foucault, we might speak instead of the individual's entire somatism: the body in all of its capacities over the span of its life. The emphasis on body is not unique to Foucault. It is interesting to remember that "spirituality" was widely used by San Francisco leather communities in the 1970s and 1980s to describe the aims and effects of rigorous bodily practices.[6]

Whatever his lexical inspirations or confirmations, Foucault's use of "spirituality" makes a double reference to bodies. The practices it prescribes involve the body, and their aim is a change of subject through the body. The bodily reference is clear enough even in the basic description already quoted: spirituality involves "purifications, ascetical acts, renunciations, conversions of looking, modifications of existence." The importance of body in resubjectivation, "for the subject's very being," is almost as clear. Spirituality presupposes that the subject, having no possession of truth by right, must be changed in order to teach truth, "must modify itself, transform itself, displace itself." The subject's "being" must be put in play. A particular subjectivation is opened to change, but the being that receives or undergoes subjectivation is also converted or transformed. That being is embodied. The two main motions accomplished by ancient spirituality, *erôs* and *askêsis*, refer to bodies and depend on their powers. The effect of ancient spirituality is less a cognitive act than a transfiguring illumination. An act of knowing can never give access to the truth unless it is "prepared, accompanied, doubled, achieved" by a "transformation of the subject, not the individual but the subject itself in its being as subject."[7]

For Foucault, ancient teaching develops from lessons in self-care for the aristocratic young to a general pedagogy. No longer confined to youth, it is lifelong care for adults. The teaching must become more critical since it needs to uproot bad habits. It becomes more and more like medicine. The school of philosophy, hospital for souls, strips away the vices of childhood, undoes the malformed lessons of earlier pedagogies. Foucault describes the extended teaching practice with a startling phrase: "To become again what one never was, that is, I think, one of the elements, one of the most fundamental themes of this practice of the self."[8]

To become again, by remaking what has already been made. On Foucault's reading, the ancient teachers didn't expect a clean slate for writing a new subject. Even the young Alcibiades approaches Socrates already deformed by family and civic training, by passions, by so-called virtues and all-too-real vices. If Socrates is going to change him, he has to find in an already-formed subject some room for change. In the later authors to whom Foucault goes for the generalized form of self-care, this room allows the teacher, over many years, to convert the subject in various ways. Yet this conversion is somehow also a return: to become again what we never were.

A reader may suddenly suspect a sort of turn in Foucault himself, as if the notion of liberation, so sardonically mocked in *History of Sexuality* 1, were now staging a belated revenge. Wasn't liberation supposed to be bad? The liberation promised by the practices of Greek self-care is precisely not the liberation of snuggling into an identity manufactured by biopower. Ancient self-care begins as a decentering of the received self and becomes a constant cultivation of whatever it is that allows one to stand in a relationship of remaking to oneself. In the later ancient writers, this active self-remaking can take place even in the midst of political life. Conversion or turning demands no abandonment of the world. Its achievement of freedom is immanent. This only restates the paradox: to find in an already-formed subject the makings of a future self that is a return to self. How did Greek self-care undo this temporal knot? What in the student could it address?

Certainly the pedagogies of self-care address reason. This is the function as much of Socratic dialectic as of Stoic and Epicurean doctrines. The physiological speech of the Epicureans, for example, reformulates cosmology so that it can aid in shaping the soul. Then again, as Foucault shows in meticulous detail, self-care rearranges the bodily habits of daily life: what you eat and wear, how you sleep, how you help or don't help your friends, when you speak or don't. Self-care prescribes various ascetical exercises in which the body is alternately agent and patient. It is the body that bears the subject, that can be subjected. The body is a reservoir of alternate lives.

Foucault dwells on a description of the "Hellenistic" version of the turn toward oneself, the *epistrophê*, which is certainly not Christian but also not exactly Platonic. The word *epistrophê* carries more than physical meanings in ordinary speech: it can be a political reaction (like a counter-coup), a vehement confrontation with someone, or a change of opinion. It is associated with love: 'H *Epistrophía*, the turner, is the goddess Aphrodite, who spins hearts. Foucault mentions the "ritual gesture" of turning in place used both to show and to accomplish the liberation of a slave. Reading of the ritual in Seneca, Foucault concludes, "So a rupture for the self, a rupture all around the self, a rupture for the benefit of the self, but not a rupture within the self."[9]

The ritual emancipation of self described by Seneca requires that one keep oneself in view. More important is to "go toward the self as one goes toward a goal." We become again what we never were. In this iteration of the paradox of self-formation, Foucault summarizes what he calls "one of the elements of the fundamental uncertainty, or the fundamental oscillation."[10] Is the self a point to which you return or an object toward which you strive? Is the time of philosophic learning a long circle or a long line? Or both? A Nietzschean time, in short, that resists representation, that cannot be narrated straightforwardly. Foucault captures this by distinguishing conversion as break (trans-subjectivation) from conversion without caesura, in a continuous process (auto-subjectivation).

What distinguishes this practice of time from the obsession with timed action in modern discipline, described so chillingly in *Discipline and Punish*? What is the difference between Stoic "teleological concentration" and modern military drill or the modern classroom? It is not enough to say that the Stoic *chooses* to concentrate on the end, because one effect of skilled discipline is that it colonizes desires. Discipline's subjects want it. The reader might rather say that the difference between discipline and Stoic training lies perhaps in the Stoic's lack of confidence in predictable results. Perhaps in ancient philosophy's requirement for long trust in a single teacher, who is precisely not the interchangeable observer in the Panopticon. Or perhaps the difference between discipline and philosophic training lies in the very oscillation of philosophic time within the body, in its not being a plot of progress or of managed expenditure for the sake of a greater profit.

Against discipline, ancient philosophic teaching ran out the measure of time to the individual's end, then condensed it. It set lessons about fortifying oneself against calamities by going through all the evils that could befall, about living each day as if it were the last. Here the whole task is a sort of temporal therapy. One wants to avoid being terrorized by the future, seized by it in advance. The fool who is preoccupied with the future cannot grasp the present or retain the past. So the goal of the prescribed meditation on future evils is actually to seal off the future as future, nullifying its specificity by removing its futurity, by "presentifying" it, by treating it as already done.[11] One aims to become again what one never was by changing one's relation to the future in such a way that it becomes present. This is not the reiterated sequence of timed motions for the group's profit but the stretching and shrinking of time until the individual's present becomes an image of a divine eternity, of a perfect intensity, the opposite of sequence.

There is another echo here. Meditating on Klossowski, Foucault described a principle for reading religious signs—a principle of Christian typological interpretation. The tree in the Garden of Eden, the lure of our fall, "has become one day what it always was," the cross of redemption.[12] The tree of the fall "always was" the saving cross under a divine providence, which expresses itself in an authorship possible only to eternity. Without providence, without an eternal author of a typological scripture, transformations are much more uncertain. In the regime of events here below, you cannot become one day the type that you always were. You can only turn your body back toward a "true" subject that you never were.

In January 1983, Foucault resumes his lectures as if after a brief pause. He recapitulates "the themes I have cut across or evoked over the last years, I would say even over the ten or maybe twelve years I have been teaching here." He has not been pursuing a history of mentalities or a history of representations. He has wanted instead a history of thought, "an analysis of what one might call homes [or centers, *foyers*] of experience in which there are mutually articulated, first, forms of a possible knowledge; second, normative frameworks of behavior for individuals; and finally the virtual modes of existence for possible subjects."[13] A history of thought retells the connections made in charmed or charged moments of experience.

Attending to experience requires three "theoretical shifts" or "displacements" in Foucault's attention and his writing. He narrates these shifts twice—at the very beginning of the lectures and then again after an "exergue" drawn from Kant. I mostly pass over the remarks on Kant, but I do want to note Foucault's expressed relation to them. He turns to the Kantian text at first topically, to consider "this relationship between the government of self and that of others." He is in fact more fascinated by the *way* in which Kant treats the topic. Foucault associates this to himself as a heraldic blazon or fetish.[14]

Foucault multiplies oddly such technical descriptions for his relation to Kant. The Kantian text is an exergue, a preliminary inscription in a text or a line on a coin that gives the date and place of its minting. Kant's essay is both a motto and a specific occasion. So Foucault stresses the occasion on which Kant originally wrote. Foucault next calls the essay a *blason*, a formulaic paraphrase of a coat of arms. Foucault has toyed with heraldic devices or emblems before, as when he described Diderot's chatting genitals as one of our society's emblems.[15] Here he claims an occasional essay by Kant as his emblem, his heraldic device. Finally, Foucault declares or confesses that Kant's essay is a fetish for him—that is, to speak simplistically, an object invested with (displaced?) desires. An inscription, a heraldic design, a fetish: three ways of conceiving commentary materially, they are also three figurations of a relation to an inherited past.

Kant's essay, published in a learned journal, describes and enacts a relationship between an author and a public. The relationship is "concrete, institutional, or in any case instituted."[16] As Foucault reads it, the function of Kant's piece isn't to inaugurate the relationship of learned writer to interested reader so much as to explain it. There are various other topics on the Kantian table, including the relation of Christianity to Judaism. The topic that most attracts Foucault is this rhetorical address, especially as it emphasizes or draws attention to the present within which it unfolds. "What is this 'now' inside of which all of us are, and which is the site, the point [from which] I write?"[17] The editors supply the missing words in order to render the last phrase grammatical. It is more interesting to read its juxtaposition ungrammatically: "the site, the point I write." The now *that* Foucault writes—like the now that Baudelaire's painter of modern life rendered so rapidly, so endlessly, going every day to render anew.

A bit later, with his customary disclaimers about beginnings, Foucault notes that in Kant philosophy becomes "the surface of emergence of its own discursive actuality, an actuality that it questions as an event of which it has to say the philosophical meaning, value, and singularity." Surface of emergence, event—these are charged words for Foucault, especially in regard to (his own) writing. He finds in Kant (again) some of his own preoccupations with writing the present, not least as modernity: "philosophy as a discourse of modernity, as a discourse about modernity." This is for Foucault the other and perhaps more interesting meaning of critique. It isn't a search to secure the grounds of true knowledge against skepticism so much as an effort to provide "an ontology of the present, an ontology of actuality, an ontology of modernity, an ontology of ourselves."[18]

All of this colors what Foucault means when he speaks before and after the Kantian exergue about the "theoretical shifts" or "displacements" that have constituted his own writing. There are three of them. The first shift moves from "*connaissance* to *savoir*, and [then] from *savoir* to discursive practices and rules of truth telling." Foucault will say, while summarizing this point after a week, that the study of the "formation of *savoirs* . . . should be done not as the history of the development of *connaissances* but from the point of view of the analysis of discursive practices and the history of forms of truth telling."[19] The distinction between the contrasted words is notoriously difficult for English readers. It cannot be settled by appealing to a fixed Foucauldian vocabulary, since he uses the terms in various ways. Sometimes he intermingles them. More clarity is possible in these particular texts. Distinguishing between the content of knowledge and its form, Foucault is not separating fact knowledge from art knowledge or the accumulation of facts from the knowing that comes in discursive practices that produce truth. Especially in this context, *savoir* can be better understood as artisanal or compositional knowledge. Like the enacted preoccupation of Kant's emblematic essay, *savoir* means here the knowledge of how speech can be made in the relation of author to reading public. *Savoir* is the knowledge of an author who knows from long practice the scene for engaging readers.

Foucault's second "theoretical" shift is to pay attention to "the normative matrices of behavior," a phrase liable to misunderstanding. Foucault insists here, in a passage I have already mentioned, that he is not interested in providing a theory of Power with a capital "P" or even a general analysis of institutions of domination. He wants instead to present "the techniques and procedures by which one undertakes to conduct the conduct of others," the exercise of procedures within the field of governmentality. When he summarizes the description a week later, he says that he sets aside a Theory of Power or Domination to present "the history and analysis of procedures and technologies of governmentality."[20] The normative matrices of behavior are then the techniques, procedures, technologies that constitute governmentality.

Foucault turns, third, from an account of the subject to the "different forms by which the individual is led to constitute himself [or herself] as subject." When he repeats the word "form" in this paragraph, he means to emphasize above all the concrete activities by which the subject gives form to itself, the "pragmatics of self" by which the self is shaped. Form is here both an artifact and the arrangement of the practices that produce it.[21]

I describe the three displacements in the present tense; Foucault narrates them as both past and future. He speaks in retrospect about the writing he has done for more than a decade, and he sets an agenda for the lectures he is about to begin. If the three displacements are points of method or procedure, they are also demands on Foucault's own writing, even the writing of scripts that he will read out in a lecture hall. A text on the formation of the truth-telling subject must draw attention to the person of its author. In these opening lectures, Foucault reiterates his persisting concerns with the origins and boundaries of speech. He negotiates the impulse to continue speaking with, against, and about historical formations of speech. Speech doesn't unfold in the alleged eternity of decontextualized propositions but in the historical present of a regime of power and its speaking subjects. Foucault's last lecture series are a single speech after the fashion of Proust's torrent of a novel. They register their own writing.

Foucault shows his awareness of the demands on his composition in a passage of the lecture script that he didn't actually read. He raises against himself a triple charge of historicism, nominalism, and nihilism—as if quoting the standard objections against Foucauldianism by academic gossip columnists. He sketches a way to step around these objections while refusing to accept their judgment on the three -isms. The best response is to examine the judgment behind each of these "reproaches" that rules out historicism, nominalism, and nihilism beforehand. The examination conducts a historicist, nominalist, and nihilist analysis of the prejudgment in order to follow "the *development* of this critical game, this form of thought."[22] The reply to reproaches against Foucault's way of writing enrolls them in its narratives.

The lectures from 1983 and 1984 are truth telling about telling truth. They perform reflection over time. They tell truth in the present about a different truth telling in the past. The writing hovers over its own origin. It also hovers, as Kant did, around its relation to its readers. The relation is both displayed and parodied in the situation of Foucault's lecture hall at the Collège. He reads (selectively, with improvisations) from a script to an anonymous crowd over a thicket of recorders. In the very last sentence of the lecture series, Foucault will name the relation of the teacher to student in ancient spiritual direction as an erotics. In the situation of his own lecturing, the erotic must appear chiefly in anonymous distance, as endlessly deferred desire. A few weeks into the series, in a prefatory aside, he refers to "the ritual of the alethurgy of the lectures," and he invites students to a separate discussion in an effort to "detheatricalize all this a little."[23] That is a gesture in a theater of redirection. The minimalist staging of the lecture hall and its famous voice points always offstage. The auditors bring desires of various kinds when they come to hear Foucault—or to catch a glimpse of the body behind the voice. Foucault himself seems to desire some contact in the anonymous crowd. The frustration of each of those desires is part of his history lesson. It draws the contrast with ancient pedagogies while directing desire to a future in which they would have successors.

In these lectures, Foucault speaks (or reads what he has written) about the origin of spiritual direction, understood as a form of truth telling in a more intimate space between teacher and student. The space was hardly free from perils. Moreover, ancient pedagogical erotics became Christian spiritual direction at the end of its long life.[24] (Hadot's claim of continuity from ancient exercises to Christian ones gives grounds for suspecting something dangerous in the former.) The transit into Christianity marks the sad conclusion and constant boundary of Foucault's speech. Christianity is both the term of contrast and the point of a transformation. On that (other) side of Christianity, before Christianity, Foucault still wants to trace the Greek notion of *parrhesia* through its significant mutations, especially from its politico-rhetorical form into philosophy.

The protagonists of his stories are Pericles and Socrates. His chief concern is to contrast rhetorical *parrhesia* with the philosophical, its "daughter," its successor, and its opposite.[25] On the way to describing politico-rhetorical *parrhesia*, Foucault performs a reading of Euripides's *Ion*, a play within which he finds its multiple forms. His reading of Euripides is theatrical in several robust senses, not least because it is the most vivid and embodied reading of the whole series of lectures.

Foucault attends to the scene of *parrhesia* and to its characters. He applies the notion of scene to a variety of texts, from Plato's letters to the performances of the sophists. He does not stress the scripting or codification of performance. He means something like the opposite: the scene that most interests him is an open situation of risk with an unknowable outcome. Like the space of male-male erotics in *History of Sexuality 2*, some acts of truth telling are marked by an absence of codification. More strongly even than the scenes of Athenian *erôs*, they are "irruptive"; they create "a fracture"; they are fields of "an undefined eventuality." Watching them, a viewer should attend to confrontations between speaking bodies, to their "dramatics."[26] So Foucault is already thinking about scenes, characters, dramas before he turns to Euripides. For him, Euripides is not, as for Nietzsche, an example of deceptive spectacle. He is the tragedian of the embodiment of dangerous speech.

Euripides's plot in *Ion* is sufficiently complicated to resist quick summary. Fortunately, a grasp on the plot is not so important for following Foucault, who treats *Ion* as a gallery of kinds of truth telling arranged around the secret of the eponymous hero's birth. Foucault distinguishes four kinds. The first is the truth telling of the oracle at Delphi. The truth uttered in the name of the "oblique god" is "always reticent, enigmatic, difficult to understand."[27] It is especially so in this case, since the god who speaks has a criminal secret: he is Ion's father by rape. The second truth telling takes the form of violent accusation against the concealing god. It is performed by a bereaved and implicated woman, Creusa—Ion's mother, Apollo's victim. She also performs the third kind of true speech: confession. The fourth truth, the last, is spoken by the goddess Athena, who concludes the play with a consecration that dedicates her city to frankness.

Foucault's reading of the play is remarkably detailed. He treats the text more integrally and, I would suggest, more imaginatively than he does the Platonic dialogues or letters. He is a more responsive reader of this tragedy than of some philosophy. Foucault's declared interest is what the play implies for rhetorical or political *parrhesia*, yet some of his most vivid analyses concern the second and third kinds of truth telling, Creusa's accusation and confession. His guide in reading them is Dumézil's book, *Apollon sonore*. Foucault paraphrases Dumézil's interpretation of Apollo in terms of the (hypothesized) functions of Indo-European mythology. He ends with the pairing of oracle and song. The oracle is "the form of the voice" through which the god speaks truth to human beings. The song is the form by which humans praise gods. These are the two directions or exchanges "in this administration of the sacred, in this game of the sacred."[28]

Foucault applies Dumézil's analysis carefully—one might say, pedantically—to features in *Ion*. He is most taken by the relation of oracle and song, particularly Apollo's deceiving oracle and the speech of the violated Creusa that is more cry than hymn. Creusa responds not in the well-ordered cadences of liturgy but with "the cry [*cri*] against the oracle that refuses to tell the truth." A cry of pain, tears, groans, an angry chant— elements of "an organized cry, a ritual cry: the cry of complaint, the cry of recrimination." Foucault refers repeatedly to ritual as he emphasizes that human societies do sometimes recognize the cry of the weak against the strong. They recognize it as the indispensable invocation for another kind of speech, for the more confident citizen speech of frank declaration. Creusa passes from crying against the god to the steadier confession of her own history so sets the stage for the consecrating speech of Athena. The goddess will found democracy as a regime of human truth telling. Still, "the cry of humans [was needed to] pull from the silent god [Apollo] the discourse that will justly establish the power to speak."[29]

A woman cries out against Apollo and establishes the possibility for democracy, which becomes the possibility for philosophy. Foucault's reading of Creusa in *Ion* might as well be Nietzsche's frightening rehearsal of the cry of Ariadne against Apollo—the cry that Nietzsche impersonates in "Ariadne's Lament." Most of this text appears for the first time in his new gospel, *Zarathustra*, where it is spoken by the Magician. Nietzsche later extracted the poem, gave it a new ending, and marked it for inclusion in his *Dionysus Dithyrambs*, a book on his table when he ceased to want to write.

"Ariadne's Lament" is a brutal scene of desire, abandonment, and surrender. In its final version, it is the midnight voice of Ariadne, "splayed out, shuddering," as she hears her lover move near, then retreat. At last Ariadne calls out:

> No!
> come back!
> *With* all your torments!
> All my tears course
> their course to you!
> and my last heart-flame,
> it burns up to you.
> Oh come back,

my unknown god! my *pain*!
  my last happiness! . . .

A flash of lightning. Dionysus becomes visible in emerald beauty.

Dionysus:
Be wise, Ariadne! . . .
You have little ears, you have my ears:
stick a wise word inside!—
Must one not first hate oneself, if one is to love oneself?
I am your labyrinth.[30]

A brutal scene, even by Nietzschean standards: the transcript of rape. Is it any easier to read it after remembering that Nietzsche wanted to be the favorite of Dionysus so envied Ariadne? Or is it harder to read once it becomes the scene of Nietzsche's own desire?

Although Foucault doesn't speak often of Ariadne, he does allude to this passage.[31] Perhaps he didn't know this particular transposition of the Nietzschean verses. He obviously knew her appearance at the end of *Beyond Good and Evil*, where she accompanies Apollo. There she is silent, perhaps because she has learned (with Creusa) that a cry extorted from a convulsing human body is the only proper speech for getting a god's attention. Foucault himself wrote of those convulsing bodies at Loudun—or in the asylums—as the price paid for resisting certain powers. So now, at the (mythical) origin of the truth telling that will become politics, then philosophy, Foucault locates another female body—convulsed first in rape, then in childbirth, and finally in chanted recrimination. The origin of truth telling is a female accusation against the mendacious silence of a male god.

I underscore the repeated genders to raise again difficult questions that have run alongside my reading. To begin: Who is Foucault to write such things? Or who is Foucault when he writes them? Creusa is one of a line of female bodies in Foucault. Sometimes he speaks their names, as with Fabiola. More often he omits the names, either because of gaps in his sources or because he wishes to stress the defacements accomplished by power. Foucault has portrayed certain crucial episodes of resistance to power as violence done to women's bodies by powerful men or by power itself portrayed as male. He writes about these episodes with a body that has male genitals (or so we assume).

Readers understandably raise sharp questions: Does Foucault condemn gendered violence sharply enough? Does he perpetuate stereotypes about it? Does he encourage voyeurism by the very repetition of these stories?

I find myself anxious before such questions. I don't want Foucault to be dismissed before reading on a charge of misogyny. So I feel the urge to say that I didn't know the man in circumstances that would allow me to render what is, after all, a particular moral judgment about a many-faced prejudice. Or I want to add that Foucault's texts do sometimes complicate the relations of violence to gender. Male bodies also convulse. Foucault's most gruesome depiction of violence must be the opening of *Discipline and Punish*, with its narratives about the torture of Damiens the regicide. Again, Foucault often writes through or against gender expectations, as when he generalizes the power of the magical ring in *The Indiscreet Jewels* over both men and women. Elsewhere, in the much-criticized and poorly read preface to the memoirs of Herculine Barbin, Foucault explicitly contests the imperative of the sociobiological binary Male *or* Female.[32] All of these defensive impulses matter less to me than other questions that get lost when skirmishing over whether to cast Foucault aside as a misogynist.

One set of lost questions centers on authorization: Which bodies do we consider authorized to write the cries of other resisting bodies? Describing Fabiola or Creusa, Foucault emphasizes the cry beyond articulate speech—the cry of true repentance before a forgiving god, the cry of accusation against a violent and shameless god. He is trying once again to bring the cry beyond language into language, precisely so that it will have effects on the systems of power that live in languages. *How far* does it matter that his body is presumed to have the genitals that make him a man or that link him (through complex cultural symbols) to the fictive gender of the god that demands Fabiola's repentance or the god that raped Creusa? If we want to prohibit Foucault from writing about these women, much less on their behalf, is that because we presume that his genitals do the writing—just as in Diderot's satire, where the speaking jewels produce volumes for an eager readership? And isn't that prohibition itself part of the mythology of biopower, which assures us that nothing about a body matters as much as the sex to which it is assigned? *Your sex determines what you must say and the truths you must* hold. *Sex dictates whatever you write.* Those are precepts of biopower. Who enunciates them to prohibit Foucault's speech? Are they authorized to enforce them by their bodies? And what kinds of bodies are those?

Just here another set of questions can be lost. What kind of relation do we assume between the legibility of a body and its writing? Are bodies so legible that we can read them off beforehand and then calculate the kinds of writing that they are allowed to perform? Or is the legibility of bodies a constantly contested effect of power, in which writing, like convulsions, performs all kinds of roles, confirming and denying, repeating and displacing? When I read Foucault struggling to register Creusa's cry, I want the possibility of an embodied authorship that can contest power by writing across assigned identities, their privileges and inhibitions. As a reader of many identifications, I want to hold open the risk of *parrhesia* in writing, the indeterminacy of writing not only as signifying text but as bodily artifact. I leave censorship to the systems of governmentality, which will do it zealously in any case.

If a reader will permit Foucault to write about Creusa and then read the writing, there may yet be things to learn from him.[33] Creusa herself makes the crucial transit from cry to confession, from the truth of convulsed accusation to the truth of historical narration. The movement from the second to the third of the enumerated types of truth is decisive, as Foucault tells it, for politics and philosophy. It is also an enactment of a spirituality—indeed, of a turning that accomplishes a change in the subject. What is most interesting, Creusa's transit from cry to confession, anticipates Foucault's effort to write her cry. When writing, Foucault uses his body to produce an artifact that imitates or continues Creusa's bodily performance of a spirituality that finds speech. He becomes a writer by registering through his body the representation of her bodily transit from cry to speech.

It is indeed a *representation*. Nietzsche writes his scene as a play, with stage directions and special effects. Foucault is rendering not Creusa, some historical figure, but Creusa the character in a play by Euripides. Foucault may write so forcefully or so freely because he never forgets the difference between words and bodies.

In the (dramatic) history retold by these lectures, Creusa's cry gives way to the (Platonic) voice of the polity or regime.[34] The continuing story tells the passage from the political truth telling of established democracy (call it Pericles) to the philosophical truth telling of spiritual direction that is also an erotics (call it Socrates). Philosophy is, Foucault repeats, the *daughter* of political truth telling. That is a striking image after the reading of *Ion*. Who, after all, is philosophy's mother? And what is her cry? How does her chanted imprecation persist in the intimate correction of a philosophic master, especially one who describes himself as a midwife and reverses the erotic roles he is given? Philosophy comes out of Creusa's cry and never loses its echo. The echo returns as a final character in Foucault's lectures on philosophy.

LECTURES FROM 1984:
THE PHILOSOPHER'S SCANDALOUS BODY

The final series continues, as if without interruption, in the consideration of *parrhesia*. Foucault twice emphasizes the continuity—once before giving an enriched summary of the previous year, once after it.[35] The series continues under the same title, as if the interruption of eleven months (March 9 to February 1) were a mere accident. While he stresses continuity, Foucault emphasizes as well the "disjointed" character of his considerations. I take him to mean that they are episodic. He jumps from text to text without pretending to give a coherent history any more than he had elsewhere.

The previous series ventured through dramatic and political forms of truth telling in order to reach Plato. This series turns to the ancient Cynics as another form of truth telling and another line of descent from Socrates. The difference between two Platonic dialogues, *Alcibiades* and *Laches*, becomes two more modes of truth telling that pull philosophy in opposite directions, before splitting much of Western civilization. Foucault uses the retrospect of his summary to enumerate four basic modes of truth telling: the prophetic, the ontological, the technical, and the parrhesiastic. Each runs through Western history, and each has its modern successors—though the parrhesiastic survives among us, late descendants, only in combination with other forms (say, in certain lectures performed as history of thought). All the more reason to attend to ancient *parrhesia* as a missing element. So Foucault describes the four modes of truth telling again, now as four standpoints within philosophy, each of which combines consideration of the conditions of truth telling, the structures and rules of government, and the modalities for forming the moral subject (*alêtheia, politeia, êthos*). He turns with special interest to the last, the parrhesiastic standpoint in philosophy. It tries "justly, stubbornly and always beginning again" to interconnect questions of truth, power, and ethical formation; recognizing the irreducibility of these three, it insists on the impossibility of thinking truth, power, and ethics except in their essential, fundamental relation.[36] It seems, in other words, very much like Foucault's own speech in these years.

Foucault goes first to the Platonic telling of Socrates's death and then to the Cynics, who are the other students of Socrates. His reading of the *Phaedo* is marred, as I've suggested, by his claims for the originality of Dumézil's reading of the dialogue's famous ending: Socrates's injunction to Crito to sacrifice the cock to Asclepius. If the claim of originality is odd, its purpose is not: Foucault means to save Socrates from the charge of hating life, a charge that Nietzsche famously considers.[37] This is connected to another contribution by Dumézil, more interesting if also more fantastic. Foucault reports conversations with both Dumézil and Veyne about tracing the Greek word for care (*epimeleia*) back to a root that would associate it with music or singing. The word that has preoccupied Foucault is now seen to carry a sort of "musical secret, a secret of musical appeal."[38]

The musical sense of care—a Nietzschean spirit of music—is the implicit link as Foucault turns from *Phaedo* to *Laches*. If the former dialogue risks losing bodily life to disease, the latter emphasizes the body in its setting and its imagery. It is, on Foucault's reading, a dialogue about both the conditions of truth telling and the relation of speech to deeds. The relation can be dissonant, as it is in the case of the showman Stesilaus, who preaches military skills that he does not possess. It can also be consonant, as it is in Socrates, whose embodied life harmonizes or symphonizes with his words, making them credible. This happy relation of *logos* to *bios*, of speech or argument to life, turns attention to the study of one's existence, to "the form" of the "style of existence."[39]

Enter the Cynics. In them, despite all the difficulties of historical reconstruction, Foucault finds the least-mediated relation between form of life and truth telling. In them, the Socratic harmonization of life is made the great precept. *Bios* becomes alethurgy: life is the declaration

of truth.[40] The Cynics are much less concerned with doctrinal elabora-
tions than with passing down forms of life. They are less interested in
metaphysical treatises or technical disputes than in finding the genres
in which to make manifest the style of life that shows forth truth. So
when Foucault sketches the continuation of Cynicism in Western culture, it cannot surprise that he identifies the artistic life as one of its
modern forms—and Baudelaire as one of its exemplars.[41] Cynicism
stylizes life, then seeks ways in which to broadcast and record its stylizations. In this sense, Foucault writes not only as a philosophical par-
rhesiast but as a Cynic.

Foucault finds in the Cynics an embodiment of truth telling, of the
truth itself. He paraphrases a description of one Cynic who "has suffered, has endured, has deprived himself so that truth could, in some
way, take body in his own life, in his own existence, take body in his
body." The description, interestingly enough, comes from a Christian
author, Gregory of Nyssa, who is describing a Christian Cynic (and
who relies on the incarnational tropes of Christianity). Foucault reads
it as evidence of the persistence of Cynicism even under Christianity.
He appropriates its incarnational language to describe the essence of
Cynicism as a persistent possibility in the West. "The very body of the
truth is rendered visible, and laughable, in a certain style of life."[42] The
Cynic's way of life, which bares the body, renders visible the body of
truth. The truth must have a body.

The Cynic's body: notorious for its nakedness, its inappropriate vis-
ibility—its public ingestion, copulation, secretion, excretion. Cynics
flout decorum, refusing tasteful privacy. They will do anything in public, just like the dogs from which they get their name. Their excesses are
not only a declaration of fierce allegiance to truth; they are an exaggerated reflection, a scandalously consistent application, of four widely
held philosophical values: the conviction that true life ought to be
unconcealed, unmixed, straightforward, and incorruptible. Cynicism
accomplishes a "transvaluation" of these values. It dramatizes and de-
forms them, rendering them scandalously extreme, ugly, disgraceful,
repellent. Cynicism is the grimace of philosophy staring back at itself in
a curved mirror. Cynicism presents a series of breaking points at which
philosophy must confront its own inconsistencies. It is a carnival but
also a race to the limit.[43]

The transvaluation of philosophic values materializes them, embodies them without any prettifying qualifications. The Cynic's unconcealed life is "really, materially, physically public." The Cynic cultivates "actual, material, physical poverty." Cynicism performs a "material, physical, bodily dramatization" of independent life. The Cynic stages a "visible theater of truth." Yet the result is hardly artistic in any ordinary sense. It seems animal or bestial, the inversion of human convention.[44] Among many other things, Cynic life inverts gender expectations—though Foucault alludes to this only indirectly. If the Cynic body as he describes it is mostly male, ancient Cynicism was notorious for including women as equal members. Foucault tells the story of Crates stripping himself before his suitor, Hipparchia, as a challenge to her desire. He doesn't stress the sequel: Hipparchia accepts the challenge. She marries Crates and takes up his version of philosophic life.[45] Her body is also exposed—not least by men, including philosophic rivals, who seek to shame her for pursuing philosophy.

The Cynic is the last in a series of Foucauldian bodies that testify to a truth that cannot be recognized within the rules of human convention, within the proprieties of human speech. Speech meets another limit in the ability to teach the form of life to distracted players of social games. Foucault tells the story of Diogenes trying to speak in public about serious things.[46] No one pays any attention. So he stops talking and begins to imitate birdcalls. Immediately a crowd gathers to listen. While they won't listen to his words, they relish a human body making bird noises. The Cynic's body speaks in a register that might be scandalous enough to be heard.

Where does the Cynic fit in the line of scandalous bodies that appear in Foucault's writing? Outrageous buffoonery would seem to link the Cynic to King Ubu, whose gross bodiliness provoked laughter. That is not the only or the most helpful connection. It overlooks the Cynic's willed endurance of public suffering—which would link him (or her) to Fabiola. It understates as well the Cynic's negotiation at the edge of speech or reason: the birdcalls of Diogenes are like insect murmurs of the mad. Public copulations—that recalls the chattering genitals. But most striking may be the Cynic's transmutation of social ostracism and physical suffering into philosophic teaching. That is the terror and the deed of Creusa.

The terror and deed of Creusa belong to a play. The Cynics' copulations are also so many public performances, as much artifice as the
imitation of birdcalls.[47] Here Foucault may show most clearly how
he reads Artaud against the judgment of Blanchot. Artaud sometimes hoped that "the body and the cry" could undo language so
that the subject would become wholly "material energy, the suffering of flesh." He knew that mise-en-scène required bodily discipline,
ritual, artful self-fashioning. The Cynic's capacity for suffering is an
education, and Creusa's cry belongs to literature. Both are theater.
The line of convulsing bodies: they are alike not because they are
identical bodies suffering identical convulsions but because each of
them repeats the challenge of a mise-en-scène.[48] Philosophical theater
is the space for disarticulating bodies in order to speak them again
and otherwise.

FOUCAULT'S SONG

Foucault has argued that the Cynics performed a transvaluation of
four ancient values. "Transvaluation" is a Nietzschean word, one of the
most famous. The "transvaluation of all values" is Zarathustra's slo-
gan. There may be other allusions to him here—as with the grimace
as distorting mirror. A reader might conclude that Nietzsche too is a
Cynic, a notion that Foucault mentions in passing.[49] She could also conclude that Foucault is evoking Nietzsche's *Zarathustra* in order to align
the Cynics with the alternative to Christian morality, with the road not
taken by loud promoters of the tablets of law. Yet Foucault ends this
last series of lectures by sketching the persistence of *parrhesia* within
Christianity. He divides the religion once again into two "poles"; only
this time, instead of the ontological (or bodily) and the epistemological, it is the mystical and the ascetical. Here mysticism is a parrhesiastic confidence in an "eternal face-to-face with God." Asceticism, at the
opposite pole, is an anti-parrhesiastic suspicion of the self that takes
refuge in "fearful and reverential obedience before God." Christian
pastoral care is institutionalized around the second pole. The other
pole, the ascetical, must correspond in some sense to what Foucault
had earlier called the epistemological. The survival of mysticism, even
under institutional pressure, is the survival of an alternative confidence

in ontological or bodily manifestation, a confidence not unlike the Cynics' direct approach to speaking and living.[50]

The lectures as Foucault read them end with these remarks on Christianity. He had prepared some additional things to say "about the general framework of these analyses." Their outline is found in the lecture script. There Foucault considers the charge that he has made the Cynics inappropriately central in his story of ancient philosophy. He replies that he wanted with Cynicism "solely to explore a limit, one of two limits between which the themes of care of self and courage of truth are deployed."[51] The other limit is the Platonic. At the end of his teaching Foucault finds himself once again tracing a limit—or rather two. They seem to be not so much the extremity of experience or its representation as paired-and-opposed ways of linking the care for the soul with the courage of truth—of linking human subjects to their "games of truth." The contrast between Platonists and Cynics becomes a contrast between self-care that emphasizes knowledge (the epistemological?) and self-care that abandons metaphysical knowledge in favor of the cultivation of a way of life best described as "stripped off animal truth" (the ontological?). Platonism is identified with *psychê*, soul; Cynicism with *bios*, at once life and (animal) body. Or Platonism is "the other world" and Cynicism "the other life."

The other life is represented through a bodily drama set in the heterotopia of Mediterranean antiquity. Foucault has gestured forward to the echoes of Cynicism in modernity—to Baudelaire and to Nietzsche among others. Perhaps even to himself, in the congruence of his practice of writing with the provocations of the ancient school. He has then reminded the reader, in the course of the lectures, how close the Cynics' truth telling stands to the edge of the tolerable, of the audibly human. If Creusa's agonized transit from cry to confession was required for the founding of philosophy, the continuance of philosophy requires a series of performances at the edge of sight or of hearing. Truth telling will always demand that someone cry out—and that someone register the cry.

What if philosophic writing—or philosophic writing so far as it is resistance—is more like a convulsed cry than voluntary speech? The Cynics write in many ways, most of all with their disobedient bodies. They speak; they also cry out. Their teaching is recorded not in textbooks but in shocking stories. Foucault has prepared to write on the

Cynics by struggling to represent the body's murmurs and cries. He has also prepared by turning his writing toward the essay as what he calls the "living body of philosophy."[52] Since Montaigne, the essay has transcribed the experiences of a particular body—with all its passions and pains, its ecstasies and convulsions. Also its curiosities: in his last books and his last lectures, Foucault writes out the wandering course of his late reading on bodies in an aging body.

EMBODIED WRITING, *OR* AMONG THE MOURNERS

IN THE END, so many fans and enemies fixed on a convulsing body they imagined as Foucault's own. Some were fascinated by his rumored tastes in sex; many more, by his secretive death from AIDS— or rather, as we used to say, from its "complications."

Once in class, an undergraduate assured me that "Foucault denied AIDS and then he died from it." He gave voice to a common view. Some have gone further to say that Foucault wanted such a death. For them, as for Miller, it was the punishing conclusion to a dark hunt for pleasure.[1] Or the triumph of the death drive. Or final anonymity.

I am not interested in staging an alternative drama based on Foucault's biography. Being the kind of fan I am, I disdain those morality plays. A reader as well of religious ethics, I discourage easy lessons. The formula for such dramas is so stultifyingly simple: Apply a sentimental certainty your readers already profess about Life to the biographical remains left by a notorious death. All that archival labor—all those footnoted pages—to pronounce upon one corpse a judgment fixed long in advance!

Why *do* readers desire to secure the truth of writing in a judgment on an author's body? If the didactic dramas don't interest me, I am drawn by that question. Foucault was too, not least because that readerly desire is often the creature and conduit of modern power.

■

One of the most controversial narratives about Foucault is a book by Hervé Guibert, *To the Friend Who Did Not Save My Life*. A book, I say vaguely, because its genre is part of the controversy. It is most often called, in a French phrase we can never quite get over into English, a *roman à clef*, a novel that discloses scandalous truths about the famous or fashionable once it is properly unlocked. Given Guibert's habits of writing, it might be truer to say that the book protests the distinction between memoir and fiction—not so much blurring it as confounding it. The account in *To the Friend* is refracted or contradicted by some of Guibert's other pieces, including an earlier story and what presents itself as a contemporary journal.[2]

In *To the Friend*, Guibert introduces "Muzil" as a famous, older intimate of the narratorial "I." Muzil had "the strength, the senseless pride, also the generosity" not to tell his friends that he was dying of AIDS.[3] By writing the book, Guibert (or at least his narrator—irremediable confusion of memoir and fiction) has failed in that reticence. This is a book about Guibert's AIDS that discloses the cause and circumstances of Muzil's death.

In a famous scene dated to 1981, the narrator reports to Muzil over dinner some mysterious news just in from America: a new "cancer" is killing gay men. Muzil falls out of his chair seized by "a fit of mad laugher" (*une quinte de fou rire*). A *quinte* is typically a fit of coughing, and it will be Muzil's endless coughing that gives away his own defeat by the disease. His laughter here is *fou*, mad, because Foucault— I mean, Muzil—was made famous by a book that strains to hear the voiceless voices of the mad. Somewhat recovered from the fit, Muzil says, "A cancer that would touch only homosexuals; no, that would be too beautiful to be true; that's enough to make one die laughing."[4] Disease, madness, death, laughter: so many of Foucault's famous words. As if he were now going to fall victim to the lethal buffoonery of biopower he had so long criticized.

Guibert's narrator continues: Muzil never had so many fits of mad laughter as while he was dying. One of them was provoked by a proposal from a doctor who wanted to establish a chain of boutique hospices for the terminally ill. Muzil proposes instead clinics where one would go to *pretend* to die. Surrounded by tasteful furnishings, buoyed up by ambient music, a client would make the motions of dying but would then slip out the back of the building by a concealed door, ready to begin another life, "without baggage, with nothing in one's hands, without a name, needing to invent one's new identity."[5] Another life, like that of a masked philosopher.

There is no such clinic for Muzil. There is only a dermatological unit run by a doctor whom he knows through charity work and who persuades him to undergo tests. When Muzil recounts the morning of humiliation to Guibert's narrator, he describes how "the body . . . thrown into medical circuits, loses all identity, remains nothing more than a packet of involuntary flesh," stripped of identity not for the sake a new one but to be pushed here and there, affixed to a chart.[6] Muzil's chart is falsified to conceal the diagnosis, to separate a famous name from the stigma of AIDS in this flesh.

The supervising doctor later tells Muzil's assistant—who recalls it for "Guibert"—that Muzil cut through the doctor's efforts to buffer the diagnosis with a single question: "How much time?"[7] Which means, how much time left to write. Muzil wanted to finish a book or series of books in which he had become trapped. Muzil's project much resembles Foucault's *History of Sexuality*.

In Guibert's book, Muzil collapses in his kitchen before the holiday weekend of Pentecost, the feast of fluent speaking. He is found, unconscious, in his own blood. Taken to the hospital, he continues to be racked by pneumocystis. He begins to suffer mental confusion. Guibert's narrator confesses: "From my first visit to the hospital, I'd noted it all down in my journal, point by point, gesture by gesture, and without omitting the least word. . . . This daily activity comforted me and disgusted me. I knew that Muzil would have so much pain if he knew that I reported all of this like a spy, like an adversary."[8]

Muzil is moved to another hospital. He deteriorates. Inoperable lesions are found on his brain, but they must be kept secret. So must Muzil's rapid approach to death. Sitting vigil the next day, Guibert's narrator kisses Muzil's hand. Back home, he washes up as if after a disgusting sexual escapade. Then the narrator goes to write it all down. He is seized by remorse. Suddenly a sort of vision (or vertigo) gives him untroubled possession of the "ignoble transcriptions" he is making, because the agony they register is not Muzil's but his own. "Beyond friendship, we would be linked by a sort of common thanatological luck."[9]

Sometime later—days, weeks—the narrator arrives at the hospital for a visit. Muzil has died. The corpse is already tagged.

Later still, a brief ceremony is announced for the hospital courtyard to mark the moving of the coffin. There are so many people milling in the nearby streets, jammed into the courtyard. A crowd to watch the single body carried away for burial far from Paris in the hometown of Muzil's family.

What does Foucault's death do to the interpretation of his works? Does it close a system? Pass a moral judgment? Make us sigh with relief that there will be no more changes of view, no more subtleties? Or relief that he can no longer object to our readings?

Why need it do anything decisive at all? What unexamined creed about bodily agency and writing makes death so decisive? And how would our view of the writer's death change if we regarded resistant writing as a cry or a murmur rather than an act?

■

On some versions of Christianity, death marks the end of probation and the moment of individual judgment. While that judgment is held to happen out of sight, records are kept of some visible signs of progress toward it. Imagine some entries from a parish register, one that may perhaps exist in Poitiers. The man later known as Michel Foucault was born into a Catholic family. They were "Catholic" at least in one common meaning of the term: they were likely to appear at a parish church for life-stage rituals. So Foucault was baptized, under the names "Paul-Michel," an apostle and an archangel. He was taken to Mass and eventually made his first communion. He even sang as a choirboy. After time in nonreligious schools, he spent the last three years of secondary education at a prep school run by the Christian Brothers. His mother is reported to have chosen this school over its Jesuit competitor because the Brothers made fewer religious demands on their students.[10] Unfortunately for the parish register, Foucault's interest had already fixed on philosophy and his passions on other young men. By the time he was twenty and newly enrolled in the elite national institution that was to serve as his university (the ENS), he had apparently stopped going to Mass. Four years later, if only for a brief time, he joined the French Communist Party. In the decades following, his politics and cultural sensibilities remained on the antireligious left. Foucault practiced and occasionally espoused homosexuality. He never married. There would be no entry in the register for that but also no corresponding dossier from a marriage tribunal granting an annulment on psychological grounds.

When Foucault died, aged fifty-seven, his mother wanted a full funeral Mass. A Dominican priest who knew his religious views proposed a compromise: a service of memory and blessing—perhaps of absolution.[11] If Foucault had written nothing, if he had spent his life selling stock or managing crops, he might well have been reabsorbed into this archival Catholicism. Another lapsed Catholic reconciled at last. Or so this archival record would say. Christianity overwrites bodies in many ways, not least by recording only some of the rituals they perform.

■

Foucault would sometimes laugh about his fascination with Catholic topics. In a series of recorded conversations with a young hitchhiker in 1976, he recalled nostalgically what church power used to be.[12] Foucault helped the young man, Thierry Voeltzel, to plan and publish the book of conversations. At the public memorial service, Thierry would figure among the inner circle of mourners, alongside Hervé Guibert.

Eight years earlier, talking to Thierry for the tape recorder, Foucault is just an anonymous "older friend." He jokes that he is the only one who remains interested in the daily operation of the Catholic Church in France. Thierry ends a comment by saying, "I don't think that there are a lot of people interested in that." Foucault replies, "No, no, certainly not. There's no one but me," and then he laughs.[13]

It is a joke, of course, but the laughter is not mad. Is Foucault's point that the church remains a formidable machinery, whether many take an interest in it or not? Or is it that theology can be, for an unbeliever, a fascinating branch of the literature of fantasy? Or does the "older friend" here avow a curiosity that crosses identities and their periods to pull old configurations of power words into a present?

A body might give its time by curiosity to reperform old structures of power—or to continue performing them long after childhood.

■

Before his "novel" or his "journal" about Foucault, Guibert wrote a short story titled "The Secrets of a Man." It begins with the question of removing three lesions from the brain of a philosopher. Though un-named, the philosopher is Foucault.

Once the skull is opened, the reluctant surgeon is overwhelmed by beauties within: instead of the usual swirls of opaque tissue, a glow-ing land divided into fiefdoms. If a few towers have already collapsed, much of its life continues. In place after place, there appear the things Foucault studied and wrote. Deeper down, memories of childhood are shielded from the stupidities of interpretation by the shimmering veil of all that writing. The most hidden vessels contain two or three im-ages as terrible dioramas. In the first, the boy-philosopher is taken to a hospital by his father, a surgeon, in order to witness the amputation of a man's leg. The sight is supposed to make a man out of him.

If this was in fact one of Foucault's early memories, we should still shield it. I am only reading Guibert's story, not the cerebral folds them-selves. I am reminded of the interview in which Foucault described writing as his version of surgery, resistance to his father's profession and repetition of it. "I'm a physician; let's say I'm a diagnostician. I want to make a diagnosis, and my work consists of revealing by the very incision of writing something that might be the truth of what is dead." In this image, writing removes what covers the hidden truth. Then Foucault says, "Really, writing tries to make the whole sub-stance—not only of existence but of the body—pour itself out, through the mysterious channels of pen and letters, in the minute traces that one deposits on paper." The effort cannot succeed. "The heavy volume of the body never manages to deploy itself on the surface of the paper."[14]

Guibert's story retells the cerebral anatomy from the *Birth of the Clinic* with a magical variation. This magic cannot alter the fundamental restriction of writing. Guibert cannot get Foucault's brain onto paper.

■

My reading has followed a line of scandalous bodies in Foucault. Many of them lack speech. They reply to the endless loquacity of power with inarticulate sounds: the insect murmurs of the excluded mad, the groaning prayers of a dismembered regicide, the cries of convuls-ing nuns, genitals that remain silent as we fantasize their enchanted speech, the groans of the Lenten penitent Fabiola, the cries of Creusa to the rapist Apollo, the animal noises or public love cries of the ancient Cynics trying to lure crowds back toward divinity. Foucault's longing to record these sounds—he crouches again and again to hear them—is always checked by his conviction that they occur at the limit of language. They resound in the place he sometimes associates with the poetic but also with the holy.

A reader might conclude that Foucault is pious about those convulsing bodies. He is. His piety urges him to find a form for registering their sounds. The urge is ethical in at least two senses. It is the imperative for any writer who wants to avoid becoming another accomplice of reigning power. It also engages in *ethopoiêsis*, in the making and unmaking of ethical subjects. The scandalous bodies resist being turned into certain subjects, but they also enact, in resistance, the hope of alternative subjectivation, of ethical transformation.

The forms that Foucault creates by writing are not intended for cataloguing bodies. They serve instead to open a curious time in which the sounds of unaccomplished subjectivation can become audible. In the original preface to *History of Madness*, this time was likened to dawn. The lyrical image disappears in later works, but not the sense of a time before.

For Foucault, the most arduous writing recalls scenes of bodily resistance at the edges of language. The scenes are often religious in superficial ways. They are more deeply religious in structure, so far as they evoke the ritual or liturgical time of transformation. Religious writing isn't defined by its subject matter so much as by its liturgical alteration of bodies in time. Religious language attracts Foucault by its ritual processes, not its table of topics.

■

At the memorial service before Foucault's body was taken from Paris for its burial, a card on the coffin carried three names: Matthieu, Hervé, Daniel. Daniel Defert, his longtime companion. Hervé Guibert. Matthieu Lindon.

Lindon was introduced into Foucault's circle of friends by Thierry Voeltzel, the hitchhiker. Invited to a performance by a Japanese dancer at Foucault's apartment, Lindon there met Hervé Guibert.[15]

Some years on, Lindon read the manuscript of Guibert's *To the Friend*. He loved it.[16] More than twenty years later, he wrote his own memoir of his time with Foucault. It is a story of love, not of sex—at least, not between the two of them.

Lindon recalls Foucault's reaction to finishing *History of Sexuality* 2 and 3 after so many years of self-doubting revision. The completion gave him pleasure. "But on rising from the table where he had inwardly decreed this end [to the writing], he knocked over a glass that broke, and just then it seemed to him that the time of satisfaction was ended; it had not lasted but a few seconds."[17] Seconds of satisfaction at the completion of a book—that's not the time that matters; that's not the bodily effect to notice. Foucault was right to move on.

Sometimes, Foucault would say that every author writes to produce the last book ever.[18] He confessed to the delirious impulse. Then he used his body to write against it, knowing all too vividly that every mortal body is an event.

ACKNOWLEDGMENTS

This book grew out of a number of classes. Two stand out in my memory. In the fall of 2007, I was lucky enough to co-teach a seminar on Foucault with Lynne Huffer at Emory University. Three years later, I was bold enough to offer a lecture course on Foucault and religion at Harvard's Divinity School. I am grateful to each member of those classes—for hearing me out, but even more for challenging my reading at many points. I also give thanks for the obligations of a teaching life. Having to say something about Foucault, week after week, supplied me with the foolish courage to write about him.

A number of friends read the book or parts of it in draft. I am grateful to comments and exhortations from Ellen Armour, Tom Beaudoin, James Bernauer, Kent Brintnall, Hannah Hofheinz, Amy Hollywood, Lynne Huffer, Suzanna Krivulskaya, Jana Sawicki, and Shannon Winnubst.

I finished this book during two years at the Danforth Center on Religion and Politics of Washington University, St. Louis. I am grateful for conversations with many colleagues there, not least those who welcomed a stranger into their *collegium*.

INTRODUCTION: EMBODIED READING *OR* THE MASKED PHILOSOPHER

1. I think especially of two alluring books: Halperin, *Saint Foucault*, and Huffer, *Mad for Foucault*. I'll return to both of them in what follows, sometimes explicitly, more often implicitly. Huffer in particular will be an invisible interlocutor on many pages. All translations are my own.

2. James, "Death of the Lion," 375–376.

3. Ibid., 364, 367.

4. Halperin remarks, "All of us who write about the life or thought of Michel Foucault are embarrassed—though evidently not sufficiently embarrassed—by the implicit contradiction between Foucault's critical practice and our own" (*Saint Foucault*, 127). The remark is either charmingly optimistic or wickedly ironic. Certainly no one *should* write about Foucault without suffering this embarrassment from page to page.

5. Gracq, *En lisant en écrivant*, in *Oeuvres complètes*, 2:674.

6. Foucault, "Le philosophe masqué," *Dits et écrits* (hereafter *DE*), 4:104–110. Memories differ about how widely Foucault's authorship was assumed when the interview first appeared.

7. To take the most obvious example, Nietzsche, *Jenseits von Gut und Böse*, no. 40, in *Sämtliche Werke*, 5:57, line 26. For Foucault on Nietzsche on preserving masks, see *Leçons sur la volonté de savoir*, 198. There are many other references to masks in the Foucault texts. In 1965, for example, Foucault told an interviewer that he would teach psychology to a prep school class in philosophy only after putting on a perfect mask—and then altering his voice, like Anthony Perkins in *Psycho* ("Philosophie et psychologie," *DE*, 1:448). At other times, there is masking without mention of a mask. In an interview with a gay magazine, Foucault plays coy until the very end when—like a French drag performer—he rips off

his wig by letting his name be spoken. See "De l'amitié comme mode de vie," with the disclosure in *DE*, 4:167. Again, in a roundtable on prisons, Foucault adopts a pseudonym with historical resonance—and without relinquishing it ("Luttes autour des prisons"). Finally, Foucault avows a desire for "anonymous writing"; see especially "Le sujet et le livre," 77, 79–80.

8. I insist on this, partly to draw attention to one immediate effect: Foucault's putting on masks excited—still excites—impulses to rip them off, to expose. Consider the published accounts of Guibert and their use in de Villiers, *Opacity and the Closet*, 37–61.

9. Foucault, "Le philosophe masqué," *DE*, 4:104.

10. I have in mind the mention of the play between anonymity and "a morality of civil identity" in Foucault, *Archéologie de savoir*, 28. Elsewhere Foucault associates anonymity with intense collaboration or immersion in a community of thinkers—by analogy to the group of mathematicians known as "Bourbaki." See the remarks in a 1967 interview, Foucault, "Sur les façons d'écrire l'histoire," *DE*, 1:597. For a more thorough collation of Foucault's remarks on anonymity and an interpretation of their relation to resistance, see Bordeleau, *Foucault anonymat*.

11. For another obvious example, see Nietzsche, *Fröhliche Wissenschaft*, preface to the second edition, no. 4, in *Sämtliche Werke*, 3:352, lines 20–24; comparing Foucault in *Leçons sur la volonté de savoir*, 198, 200–201, 208.

12. This occurs in the retrospective preface in *Histoire de la folie*, 9.

13. Chevallier points to Foucault's recollection, when writing about Deleuze, of the Stoic doctrine of the "incorporeals" emitted by bodies through contacts with other bodies around them. Foucault knows the doctrine, he thinks, through Bréhier's account of ancient Stoicism (Chevallier, *Foucault et le christianisme*, 23–24). Perhaps so, but naming a source that Foucault read doesn't yet explain either how he read it or how he used it in his own writing.

14. Foucault, "Le philosophe masqué," *DE*, 4:106.

15. Nietzsche, *Jenseits von Gut und Böse*, prologue and no. 295, in *Sämtliche Werke*, 5:12, especially lines 9–12, and 5:238–239.

16. Foucault, *Le beau danger*, 39 (anti-Christian), 44 (conversion), 55 (absolution), 56 (benediction).

17. Chevallier is preoccupied with the unity of Christianity in Foucault. He tries to capture its stages in a chronology of views and methods. See, for summaries, Chevallier, *Foucault et le christianisme*, 17, 55.

18. One consequence is that my book differs in purpose, form, and tone from a number of influential studies with which it shares topics. I think immediately of Bernauer, *Michel Foucault's Force of Flight*; Carrette, *Foucault and Religion*; and Chevallier, *Foucault et le christianisme*—to name three projects that differ significantly among themselves. In what follows, I will sometimes correlate what I write with what is said in these books. But I insist that these are at best correlations. Our projects diverge too much to admit a direct comparison.

CHAPTER 1: HUNTER OF THE SACRED

1. In English, we regularly mistake or misremember the title of Foucault's book. We call it *History of Madness*, but that is only a part of its subtitle. The main title is *Folie et déraison*—difficult to translate, but for that reason worth reflection. *Folie* may be madness, but it is also folly. *Déraison* is both the unreasonable and the antirational. It is important for Foucault's purposes to have an allusion to reason in the main title: important too, I suspect, to put the ambivalent *histoire* into the subtitle.

2. Foucault, *Folie et déraison*, viii.

3. For the language of illusion and approving narratives of how Foucault moved beyond literature, see Dreyfus and Rabinow, *Michel Foucault*, especially viii, 1–103; Rajchman, *Michel Foucault*, especially 6; Megill, *Prophets of Extremity*, especially 221–222. For a more nuanced account, see O'Leary, *Foucault and Fiction*, 39–59.

4. See the retrospective remarks in Foucault, *Le beau danger*, 50–53; "La folie, l'absence d'oeuvre," *DE*, 1:419; "Folie, littérature, société," *DE*, 2:109.

5. For example, Foucault, *Folie et déraison*, 35, 299, 416–417, 424–426, 439, 456, 612, 636, 641–643. Compare Foucault's 1962 review of Laplanche on Hölderlin, "Le 'non' du père," *DE*, 1:200, for limit, law, and language. There are other associations as well, of course. In a later conversation, Foucault will link Nietzsche, Bataille, and Blanchot as antisystematic writers of an experience of the limit in which the subject is detached from itself. See "Entretien avec Michel Foucault," *DE*, 4:43.

6. From the conversation with Watanabe, "La scène de la philosophie," *DE*, 3:588–589. More prosaically, Foucault will associate Blanchot and Bataille with "the religious problem" that also drew him to Dumézil and Lévi-Strauss ("Qui êtes-vous, professeur Foucault?," *DE*, 1:614).

7. Pinguet, "Les années d'apprentissage," 130–131. In the interview with Claude Bonnefoy from 1968, Foucault "invokes" his relation to Nietzsche as a crushing pedigree (*Le beau danger*, 41). The feeling of weight, like so much else in Foucault's intellectual autobiography, may be a useful fiction. It conceals questions about the order both of Foucault's attractions (was Nietzsche really first?) and of his independence (how far did he read Nietzsche before consulting Nietzsche's other French readers?). Here as elsewhere, I repeat Foucault's story just as his story.

8. I agree emphatically with Carrette on the importance of these early essays for reading Foucault (*Foucault and Religion*, 1–3, 143). I can't agree that religion disappears after them only to reappear around 1976 (20–21). Nor do I think that Foucault's later writing misses theology in favor of religion as a social practice (110–111). Finally, I will try to show that there is much more in Foucault's relation to religion or Christianity than critique. There are many other pieces— essays, lectures, prefaces—from the 1960s in which Foucault takes up related issues. I omit them with regret but with a clear conscience. Here and on all the

pages that follow, I don't pretend to give a comprehensive review of Foucault's writing, much less a survey or synthesis of his thinking on the topics I broach. I am only trying to record my reading of particular texts under the prompting of my guiding questions.

9. Foucault, *Folie et déraison*, i.

10. Ibid.

11. Ibid., ii.

12. Ibid., iii.

13. Ibid., v (emphasis added). Compare "La folie, l'absence d'oeuvre."

14. Foucault, *Folie et déraison*, vi. Compare *Les mots et les choses*, 398.

15. Foucault, *Folie et déraison*, vii. Elsewhere Foucault recalls Kafka's story of the burrow-empire pervaded by sound ("Le langage à l'infini," *DE*, 1:255).

16. Foucault, *Folie et déraison*, ix.

17. Ibid., x. Compare Char, *Oeuvres complètes*, 260–261.

18. Foucault, "Introduction," in Binswanger, *Le rêve et l'existence*, where Char's "Partage formel" occurs quite prominently at the beginning and end (*DE*, 1:65, 118–119). For a helpful collation of Char's texts, see Kelly, "Passages beyond Resistance," 121–127. Foucault is reported to have delighted in discovering that he shared his passion for Char with Pierre Boulez (Macey, *Lives*, 50). Years later, Foucault will quote Char again on the back of his last two books.

19. Foucault, *Folie et déraison*, xi; Char, "Partage formel," in *Oeuvres complètes*, 155–169, to which I will refer by the more precise section numbers.

20. Char, "Partage formel," nos. 9 and 17 (Heraclitus), 14 (lustration in the fountain), 15 (initiates—ironically), 17 (abyss, echoing Genesis 1:1), 20 (the burning of a heretic), 36 (transcendent presences), 45 (fantastic gods), 48 (the poet's recommendation).

21. Derrida, "Cogito et histoire de la folie," especially 55–69.

22. Foucault, *Histoire de la folie à l'âge classique*, 9–11.

23. The best-known example occurs in his inaugural lecture at the Collège de France, where Foucault imagines himself slipping into speech behind or inside another voice. It turns out to be the voice of his predecessor, Jean Hyppolite. See Foucault, *L'ordre du discours*, 7–8, 81–82.

24. Foucault, "Préface à la transgression," *DE*, 1:234–235, 242, 244–245, 246, 249–250.

25. Bataille, *Oeuvres complètes*, 3:491–494 (*Madame Edwarda*), 3:239–251 (*L'Abbé C*).

26. Foucault, "Préface à la transgression," *DE*, 1:234.

27. A few years later, Foucault explicitly announces a circular structure for his appreciation of Deleuze ("Theatrum philosophicum," *DE*, 2:76). He also notes Deleuze's objection to it.

28. Foucault, "Préface à la transgression," *DE*, 1:236.

29. Ibid., 1:239, 240.

30. Much later, Foucault will claim in an interview to have been attracted in

Nietzsche to *The Birth of Tragedy* and the *Genealogy of Morals* rather than *Zarathustra* ("Les problèmes de la culture," *DE*, 2:372). The claim has a role in the play of the particular interview, but it clearly doesn't characterize all of Foucault's writing on or around Nietzsche.

31. Foucault, "Préface à la transgression," *DE*, 1:247.

32. Ibid., 1:248. Chevallier concludes that in the 1960s Foucault meant by the divine "what man experiences when he disappears as the subject of his language and his thought" (*Michel Foucault et le christianisme*, 288). That may be part of the meaning, but it can't be all. It overlooks Foucault's preoccupation in these essays with bodies, before and after sexuality.

33. Foucault, "Préface à la transgression," *DE*, 1:250. Foucault quotes the "new version" of Bataille's novel, in which this passage (among many others) has been revised—perhaps by Bataille, perhaps by the editor-publisher, Alain Gheerbrant, with Bataille's approval. See Gheerbrant and Aichelbaum, *K éditeur*, 28–29, with the bibliographic notes on 44 (which gives the printing date as 1945), 75–76. The earlier and later versions are printed in Bataille, *Oeuvres complètes*, 1:9–78, 1:569–608, respectively.

34. Bataille, untitled prefatory note, *Acéphale*, no. 1 (June 1936), [3]. I follow the reproduction in *Acéphale: Religion, sociologie, philosophie* (1995) for which there is no separate pagination. The text is also reprinted in Bataille, *Oeuvres complètes*, 1:442–446, with the quotation on 445. Masson, a sometime patient of Foucault's father, had provided illustrations for the 1928 edition of Bataille's *History of the Eye*. In the 1960s, Foucault kept a drawing by Masson, given to his father, on his writing desk. See Macey, *Lives*, 16, 92, 239.

35. I translate Kierkegaard from the French, which carries no citation. For an English version in context, see *Søren Kierkegaard's Journals and Papers*, 6:60, entry 6256. For the analysis of fascism, see Bataille, "Propositions sur le fascisme," *Acéphale*, no. 2 (January 1937), 18–20 (reprinted in *Oeuvres complètes*, 1:467–470); "Propositions sur la mort de Dieu," *Acéphale*, no. 2 (January 1937), 21, no. 15 (*Oeuvres complètes*, 1:473); "Une 'religion hygiénique et pédagogique': Le néo-paganisme allemand," *Acéphale*, no. 2 (January 1937), 8–9 (*Oeuvres complètes*, 1:458–459). It is worth remembering how fully Foucault also shared these political convictions. See Bernauer, "Michel Foucault's Philosophy of Religion."

36. For example, Surya, *Georges Bataille*, 251; Sweedler, *The Dismembered Community*, 89. It is important to remember that the testimonies to these forest rites are still marked by ironic evasion, comic invention, and simple refusal. Compare, for example, the interviews with Klossowski and Leiris in Henri-Lévy, *Les aventures de la liberté*, 171–172 (Klossowski contradicting Surya), 174 (Leiris contradicting Klossowski).

37. "Note sur la fondation d'un Collège de sociologie," *Acéphale*, nos. 3–4: *Dionysos* (July 1937), 26; reprinted in Hollier, *Collège*, 25–27, and in Bataille, *Oeuvres complètes*, 1:491–492. A footnote in the original explains that the statement had been drafted in March 1937.

38. The lecture-essay "Le corps du néant" was first delivered as a lecture to the Dominican community at Saint-Maximin in 1941 (Arnaud, *Pierre Klossowski*, 204). It was originally published in Klossowski, *Sade, mon prochain*, 155–183, then suppressed in the revised edition twenty years later.

39. I follow the chronology in Arnaud, *Pierre Klossowski*, 186–187.

40. These themes—unholy twins, demonic mirrors, entrapping spectacles—are emphasized in Foucault's contemporary afterword to a German translation of Flaubert's *The Temptation of St. Anthony* (*DE*, 1:299, 305).

41. Foucault, "La prose d'Actéon," *DE*, 1:327. Compare *Fröhliche Wissenschaft*, no. 342, in Nietzsche, *Sämtliche Werke*, 3:571.

42. Foucault, "La prose d'Actéon," 328, quoting Klossowski's version of Nietzsche, *Fröhliche Wissenschaft*, no. 341, in *Sämtliche Werke*, 3:570, from Klossowski, *Un si funeste désir*, 21–22. Klossowski renders the passage somewhat differently in Nietzsche, *Le gai savoir*, 232.

43. Foucault, "La prose d'Actéon," *DE*, 1:329.

44. Ibid., 1:330.

45. For Klossowski elsewhere, Christianity's early encounter with the linguistic possibilities of myth are absorbed within it as aversion. See, for example, the discussions of the young Augustine in Klossowski, *Origines cultuelles et mythiques*, 12, and the appended note.

46. Foucault, "La prose d'Actéon," *DE*, 1:332.

47. Ibid., 1:336.

48. I note these limits of Foucault's reading while acknowledging that Klossowski is reported to have said that Foucault was his best commentator (Arnaud, *Pierre Klossowski*, 190).

49. In the afterword to Flaubert's *St. Anthony*, Foucault also emphasizes the book's theatrical techniques without copying them—though he spends more time describing them than he does with Klossowski.

50. Foucault, "La prose d'Actéon," *DE*, 1:329.

51. Klossowski, *Le bain de Diane*, 28, 44, 49, 50. Other notions that invite theological exegesis include vocation (25); spiritual genealogy (33, with reference to notions of sacramental kinship); ecstasy (34); liturgy (34); mystical (35); heresy (35); and, of course, Demon (throughout, but perhaps especially 46–50).

52. Klossowski, "Diane et Actéon" (1955), between 8 and 9 in *Le bain de Diane*. For the drawing's date, see Klossowski, *Pierre Klossowski*, 19.

53. Klossowski, *Le bain de Diane*, 9 (for the quoted phrase), 106–108 (for the threat of rape). Foucault cites the original edition by Jean-Jacques Pauvert from 1956.

54. Klossowski, "L'hommage à la vierge," in *Sade, mon prochain*, 105–117. This essay is deleted from the later edition and specifically criticized in its preface. It remains an interesting doublet for the reading of Diana not least because it links the destruction of virginity to the denial of immortality. It concludes with a quotation from Augustine on that denial's frantic consequences.

55. For example, Carrette, *Foucault and Religion*, 74, 83–84. It is even more implausible to tender these reductive charges against Klossowski, for whom, as I've suggested, sexual difference is a central enigma. In Chapter 7, I return to the question of Foucault's misogyny.

56. Foucault, "La prose d'Actéon," *DE*, 1:328–329.

57. See the 1956 edition of Klossowski, *Le bain de Diane*, with the plates inserted after 8, 24, 104, 120. They are black-and-white photographs reprinted on light blue paper. The statue is not identified in the text, but it would have been familiar to many Parisians: the Diana of Versailles, now housed in the Louvre.

58. Foucault, "La prose d'Actéon," *DE*, 1:329, 336.

59. Foucault, "La pensée du dehors," *DE*, 1:519, 522–523.

60. Ibid., 1:520.

61. Here it may be important to repeat that I am reading Foucault on Blanchot rather than Blanchot himself. For an attentive and perceptive study of Blanchot's complex relation to religious topics and texts, see Hart, *The Dark Gaze*.

62. Blanchot, *Celui qui ne m'accompagnait pas*, 125, quoted in Foucault, "La pensée du dehors," *DE*, 1:523–524.

63. Foucault, "La pensée du dehors," *DE*, 1:520.

64. Ibid., 1:521–523.

65. Ibid., 1:523. In the afterword to Flaubert's *St. Anthony*, Foucault describes the book as the first "literary work that has its proper place only in the space of books" (*DE*, 1:298). Others that follow in this canon are Mallarmé, Joyce, Roussel, Kafka, Pound, and Borges—but not (yet) Blanchot.

66. Foucault, "La pensée du dehors," *DE*, 1:521, 537, 531. I report Foucault's characterization of negative theology without endorsing it. To my mind, he is importantly mistaken about a number of Christian texts. How far might the mistake be motivated by the impulse to make Blanchot's analysis appear inevitable?

67. Ibid., 1:529 (transgression), 524 (mask, theater), 537 (the fold), 518 and 539 (the liar's paradox).

68. Ibid., 1:522 (Artaud), 539 (voice, recoil). The judgment on Artaud here is certainly mimetic fidelity to Blanchot. In his own writing during later years, Foucault continues to be fascinated by "the body and the cry," as I show later.

69. Blanchot, "Le roman pur," in *Chroniques littéraires*, 508.

70. Macey, *Lives*, 55, whose source is unclear.

71. Foucault, "De l'archéologie à la dynastie," *DE*, 2:412.

72. Foucault, "Theatrum philosophicum," *DE*, 2:76, 99.

73. Ibid., 2:80, 99; compare Artaud, "Sur le théâtre Balinais," in *Le théâtre et son double*, 64–81, perhaps especially 65–68. One obvious motive for Foucault's turn to Artaud here is the importance that Deleuze gives him.

74. O'Leary describes this ambivalent moment differently, saying that Foucault "prematurely cut off an intense investigation of the powers that certain

forms of language—which we call literature—possess" (*Foucault and Fiction*, 58). I suggest that he did not so much cut them off as relocate them—away from his investment in Blanchot.

75. Blanchot, *Michel Foucault tel que je l'imagine*, 11 (baroque style), 17 (pomps of interiority), 49 (power from below), 26 (negative theology).

CHAPTER 2: THE DISMEMBERED ASSASSIN AND
THE WELL-SCRUBBED DELINQUENTS

1. Foucault, *Surveiller et punir*, 9–11 (for the accounts of Damiens), 12–13 (for Faucher's rules).

2. Foucault, *Naissance de la clinique*, v.

3. Ibid., vi, vii, ix.

4. Foucault, *Surveiller et punir*, 19.

5. Ibid., 34.

6. Ibid., 28. In contrast, Davidson finds that a "preoccupation with genealogy" forced Foucault "to articulate some general rules for the study of power, providing not so much a new theory of power as a new approach to the problems of power in modern societies" ("Archaeology, Genealogy, Ethics," 225). If this were true without qualification, then Foucault would be the successor (rather than the opponent) of penal rule writers, who prided themselves precisely on discovering "a new approach to the problems of power in modern societies."

7. Foucault, *Surveiller et punir*, 31.

8. Ibid., 27.

9. Ibid., 12–13, 19 and 27 (Faucher's rules).

10. Bataille, *Oeuvres complètes*, 5:43–76. *Supplicium* also referred in classical Latin to various forms of legal punishment. So *supplicium supremum* meant both the extremities of suffering and the death penalty.

11. For example, Foucault, *Surveiller et punir*, 14, 49, 53, 54, 61, 69–70.

12. I am not making a terminological remark about the use of *supplice* in early twentieth-century French Catholicism—say, in the catechisms from which Foucault might have been taught. The word seems to have been applied more often to the punishment of the damned than to Christ's Crucifixion, which tended to draw its own, dedicated terminology (passion, sacrifice). I'm only suggesting that Bataille makes explicit what any reflection will show—the sacrifice on Calvary, which is cited in every Catholic Eucharist, was accomplished as a *supplice* in the multiple senses of that term.

13. The notion of a transit or transfer from the church to the clinic recurs in Foucault. He doesn't claim to have invented it. In the 1968 interview with Bonnefoy, he attributes to "a nineteenth-century physician" the remark that "health has replaced salvation" (*Le beau danger*, 32). Despite Foucault's constant care to undo the beginnings and endings of historical narrative, he seems to agree there with the physician in a strong sense of replacement—as if there were no

churches after the triumph of medicine, as if all churches had to conform to the new system of power. At other times, of course, Foucault will speak of contemporary Christian churches as uncanny survivals of much older power.

14. Foucault, *Surveiller et punir*, 80.

15. Ibid., 145 (basic function); Foucault, *Les anormaux*, 45, 47 (elementary form). For the rhetorical effect of juxtaposing this and other technical terms with the vivid descriptions of suffering, see Farge, "Un récit violent," especially 191–192.

16. In Foucault's writing, a terminological succession is not an absolute break. He still uses *partage* in *Surveiller et punir* and does so, indeed, to describe some of the divisions also described by *quadrillage*. See, for example, the discussion of *partage binaire* on p. 201. Agamben argues that Foucault uses *dispositif* as a successor for *positivité*, which term he had learned from Hyppolite on Hegel (*Che cos'è un dispositivo*, 8–12). I'm not sure that there is a simple succession. Even if there were, the reference to Hyppolite hardly helps explain Foucault's choice of *dispositif*. While I agree with Agamben on the interest of the theological resonances of the Latin *dispositio* (18–20), I doubt that Foucault heard them.

17. Foucault, *Folie et déraison*, 207; compare 203–204.

18. Foucault, "Le jeu de Michel Foucault," *DE*, 3:299.

19. Foucault, *Surveiller et punir*, 105.

20. Ibid., 112.

21. Ibid., 114.

22. Ibid., 131–132, 125.

23. Ibid., 171 (military dream), 139 (generalizing monastic techniques), 143 and 145 (monastic cloister and cell), 151 (monastic *horarium*), 163 (asceticism become exercise).

24. Ibid., 172.

25. Ibid., 191, 193.

26. Ibid., 185.

27. Ibid.

28. Ibid., 186 (power of the norm), 217 (discipline).

29. Ibid., 203. I will come back to this point later, in discussing the *oripeaux* that Foucault ascribes to power in *Du gouvernement des vivants*.

30. Foucault, *Surveiller et punir*, 202.

31. Ibid., 233, 238.

32. The doubling of the body recurs in Foucault, as I hope to show, and it is applied to many topics. For example, a reader can obviously compare this doubling of the criminal body with what Foucault says about "Man and His Doubles" in *Les mots et les choses* (314–354), but also with the doubling produced by the early modern doctrine of signatures (ibid., 43–45). The notion of the double body is authorized above all by Artaud in *Le théâtre et son double*, perhaps most clearly in "Un athlétisme affectif," 156.

33. Foucault, *Surveiller et punir*, 248, 255.

34. Ibid., 258.

35. Ibid., 282.

36. Ibid., 300.

37. Ibid., 295–299, 313–314. On 295, the second superscript callout "2" ought to be corrected to "3."

38. Ibid., 207, 252.

39. For Benjamin, the most succinct statement may be in the sketch "Paris, die Hauptstadt des XIX Jahrhunderts," in *Die Passagen-Werk*, 1:45–47. A more detailed engagement can be inferred from Convolute W, in ibid., 2:764–799. Recall as well Klossowski, "Sade et Fourier."

40. Barthes, *Oeuvres complètes*, 3:701.

41. Foucault, *Surveiller et punir*, 296. Foucault's own relation to anarchy is neither simple nor settled. In 1980, he will both claim anarchy and keep it at a distance by proposing "anarcheology" as a new name for his manner of proceeding (*Du gouvernement des vivants*, 76–77).

42. Foucault, *Surveiller et punir*, 314. I distinguish between war or battle in this text and the Marxist language of struggle (*lutte* in French). Foucault is always suspicious of Marxist jargon, and he expresses his scruples about the implications of this particular term ("Non au sexe roi," *DE*, 3:268; "Michel Foucault et le zen," *DE*, 3:606). For Foucault's much fuller consideration of the image of racial warfare, "la lutte des races," see *"Il faut défendre la société,"* 57–73.

43. Foucault, *Surveiller et punir*, 315.

44. See Farge, "Un récit violent," 195.

45. Something of this notion will return a few years later when Foucault begins to speak of "alethurgy" (as in *Du gouvernement des vivants*, 8–10). I return to this notion later.

CHAPTER 3: THE BUFFOON-KING AND THE POSSESSED NUNS

1. For the circumstances around Foucault's lecturing, and his pleasure in teaching despite them, see the recollections of Ewald, "Au Collège de France," especially 50–51.

2. Foucault, *"Il faut défendre la société,"* 3–4.

3. Foucault slips once—or else once deliberately gives the full name: "Algarron" (*Les anormaux*, 4).

4. Ibid. "Personify" is my word, not Foucault's. I use it to name the processes that produce what he calls both a *personnage* and a *caractère*. "Characterize" might be a slightly more precise word, but it has other, less appropriate meanings in English.

5. Ibid., 6.

6. Ibid., 7.

7. Ibid., 12–13.

8. Brotchie, *Alfred Jarry*, 11. Jarry offered more fanciful explanations, including this from a series of notes published just before the first stage performance:

"I do not know what is meant by the name Ubu, which is the more eternal deformation of the name of his still-living accidental prototype: *Ybex*, perhaps, or Vulture. But this is only one of the scenes of his role" ("Les paralipomènes d'Ubu," in Jarry, *Oeuvres complètes*, 1:467).

9. For a reconstruction, and a description of the first performances, see Brotchie, *Alfred Jarry*, 156–164.

10. Consider again the careful notes about stage setting in Jarry's letter to Lugné-Poë, head of the theater at which it would premiere, in Jarry, *Oeuvres complètes*, 1:1042–1044. Still Jarry seems to me more interested in disrupting the conventions for staging bodies than in fixing new ones. Peter Brook rightly contrasts two productions of *Ubu roi*. The first, while ingeniously imitating Jarry's drawings of the play's characters, failed to capture the "life" in them. The second production "invented an up-to-the-minute pop-art style of its own" so convinced its audience (*The Empty Space*, 69). The second sort of performance and its disruption of bodily convention matter most to Jarry, however exactly achieved.

11. Foucault, "Un si cruel savoir," *DE*, 1:215; compare Jarry, "Discours," in his *Oeuvres complètes*, 1:401. Beyond the obvious allusion to Jarry in the opening line, Foucault refers later in the essay to a scene in Jarry's novel, *Surmâle* (*DE*, 1:225).

12. Foucault, "Un si cruel savoir," *DE*, 1:217–218.

13. Brotchie, *Alfred Jarry*, 179–181.

14. Foucault, *Les anormaux*, 24.

15. Ibid., 46.

16. Foucault took his Hegel more from Hyppolite than from Kojève. He acknowledges this debt of affection in many places, but famously and at length in the concluding section of his inaugural lecture at the Collège de France (*L'ordre du discours*, 74–82). Even so, I am talking here not about how Foucault learned Hegel but about his relation to widely circulated Hegelian languages for power.

17. Kojève, *Introduction à la lecture de Hegel*, 28.

18. Nietzsche, *Jenseits von Gut und Böse*, no. 13, in *Sämtliche Werke*, 5:27, line 30.

19. The question of Freud's transmission in French is differently vexed than it is in English. If the problem in English is the tyranny of a single version, the problem in French is the multiplicity of versions. See, as two instances of a growing bibliography, Dufresne, "Pour introduire la lecture française de Freud"; and Quinodoz, "How Translations of Freud's Writings Have Influenced French Psychoanalytic Thinking."

20. Foucault, *Les anormaux*, 122.

21. Ibid., 124.

22. Read in another way, these mechanical and geometrico-logical descriptions of power have striking resonances with what Foucault says about the early modern notion of *convenientia* in *Les mots et les choses*, 32–40. Power is de-

scribed using images much like those once applied to the intelligible coherence of creation. This remark is not so much about Foucault as about the persistence of theological languages in modern regimes of power.

23. This mistake seems to arise almost inevitably from the established genres of academic commentary. In an essay centrally concerned with the representation of power, someone as astute as Stuart Hall paraphrases Foucault into theories, (fixed) approaches, positions, (original) conceptions, models, and propositions, without seeming to ask whether Foucault's interest in representation might extend to representations of his representations of power. See Hall, "The Work of Representation," in his *Representation*, 13–74.

24. Gracq, *Le rivage des Syrtes*, in his *Oeuvres complètes*, 1:553–839. Originally published in 1951, the novel appeared in English as *The Opposing Shore* in 1986. "Julien Gracq" is the pseudonym that Louis Poirier adopted on the publication of his first novel, *Au château d'Argol* (1938). For the report, see Daniel, *La blessure*, 184, in an entry for April 25, 1968. Foucault associated the novel with Porto Farina, Tunisia. For the interview, see Foucault, "La fête de l'écriture," *DE*, 2:734. He mentions two other novels: Malcolm Lowry's *Under the Volcano* and Jean Demelier's *Le rêve de Job* (which he misremembers as *Le livre de Job*). The interview was occasioned by his pleasure in a fourth, Jacques Almira's *Voyage à Naucratis*.

25. Gracq, *Le rivage des Syrtes*, 1:555 (nobleman), 557 (decrepitude), 558 (mummified).

26. Ibid., 1:568 (mold), 566 (Marino).

27. Ibid., 1:557 (clownish), 569 (smile).

28. Ibid., 1:810.

29. Ibid., 1:822.

30. Ibid., 1:826–827.

31. Ibid., 1:562.

32. On writing fiction, see Foucault, "Les rapports de pouvoir," *DE*, 3:236; on writing novels, "Sur les façons d'écrire l'histoire," *DE*, 1:588–589, 593.

33. Mauriac, *Mauriac et fils*, 244, in a journal entry dated July 7, 1976. Mauriac hesitates in recalling the phrase "fictive construction" but then reaffirms it. A few years earlier, Foucault had described as a "fictive description" his collation of various texts into the composite portrait of a psychiatrist (*Le pouvoir psychiatrique*, 5).

34. Foucault, "Les rapports de pouvoir," *DE*, 3:236.

35. Foucault, *Les anormaux*, 47–48.

36. Let me take two examples from a single page (ibid., 156). In citing a psychiatric report in the case of a pederast, Foucault writes that "this is doubtless not the first case, but it seems to me one of the clearest and most significant." He chooses the case not for strict priority (which it is impossible ever to prove) but for clarity and significance. A few lines later, in commenting on "the first speculative article . . . on homosexuality" by Westphal, Foucault remarks that

it represents "the date of birth, in any case the date of breaking forth, of the opening of the field of anomaly." The date of birth is a date of hatching or opening—that is, of a display.

37. Ibid., 134.

38. Foucault, *Folie et déraison*, 153, 158. For other references to Zacchia (whom Foucault knows as "Zacchias"), see 153–154, 158–159, 260, 282–283, 291–293.

39. Foucault, *Les anormaux*, 158, for the insistence that the history or survey is sketchy, vague, and schematic.

40. Ibid., 163 (penance), 168 (confessional).

41. The awkwardness leads some readers to dismiss or underestimate what follows. Elden, for example, describes the ensuing discussion as a "digression" and reduces some sixty pages of the lecture's printed text to two paragraphs. See Elden, "The Constitution of the Normal," 99–100.

42. Foucault, *Les anormaux*, 155.

43. Ibid., 157.

44. Ibid., 187.

45. Ibid., 189.

46. Certeau, *La possession de Loudun* (1970), though I follow the revised edition (2005). Foucault mentions Certeau's book when he begins to quote the trial proceedings (*Les anormaux*, 194).

47. Foucault, *Les anormaux*, 191.

48. Ibid., 197.

49. Ibid. According to Certeau, even the devils play on the distinction between body and flesh, which they call "flesh-God" (*La possession de Loudun*, 92–93).

50. Foucault, *Les anormaux*, 198.

51. Certeau, *La possession de Loudun*, 175–181 (map of bodily locations), 182–183 (facial expressions), 200–201 (kicking), 202 (taking up positions).

52. Certeau quotes Jarry's *L'amour absolu*: "the possession of the Holy Spirit and of the demon is notoriously symmetrical" (*La possession de Loudun*, 20–21). For Certeau on tragicomedy, 197.

53. Foucault, *Les anormaux*, 202.

54. Ibid., 206, 198. Certeau comments at length on the role of attending physicians at Loudun and on the eagerness of church authorities to adduce medical judgment in corroboration of church findings.

55. Foucault, *Les anormaux*, 300; Certeau, *La possession de Loudun*, 206–207.

CHAPTER 4: CHATTING GENITALS

1. Recall, for example, the political tones in Bouchard's introduction to Foucault, *Language, Counter-Memory, Practice*, especially 17 (transgressive history), 18 (counterculture, the sixties), 21 (the sixties), 25 (the relation of theory to practice).

2. Foucault's irony in this book has been emphasized by some readers and notably in relation to queer theory by Huffer, *Mad for Foucault*, perhaps especially 127–134. Beer undertakes a sustained reading of Foucault's rhetorical

and linguistic devices but then falls back into claims about Foucault's theory of power. See his *Michel Foucault*, for example, 80 ("a comprehensive theory"), 85 (theory in contrast with examples), 90, 95, 97, 101–102, 116. A similar slip from emphasizing irony to desiring useful analyses occurs in Downing, *Cambridge Introduction to Foucault*, 87, 91–92, 95. White not only emphasizes Foucault's style in *History of Sexuality* 1, he reduces Foucault's thought to the trope of catachresis (*The Content of the Form*, 105–106, 128–134).

3. I choose "mocking" deliberately to name the intensification of Foucault's irony, and I stand by it despite his later insistence that he never meant to deny the importance of movements for homosexual emancipation or gay liberation. For example, in talking to Jean Le Bitoux in 1978, he says, "So when I show the historical character of this notion of homosexuality, it's not to say that you were wrong to fight against this notion. I say the contrary, that it was indeed necessary to fight against it. . . . [But] I think that at present the very notion of sexuality . . . it seems necessary to reevaluate it or, rather, to make a new evaluation of it. . . . In other words, we have to liberate ourselves even from this notion of sexuality" ("Le gay savoir," 47). I am ready to subscribe to these remarks, but not before noting how much they differ in tone from *History of Sexuality* 1. For the complex history of this interview's text, see Halperin, "Michel Foucault, Jean Le Bitoux."

4. Foucault, *Histoire de la sexualité*, 1:105.

5. Ibid., 1:211. Here, as more generally, I do my best to use "we" following Foucault's variable and sometimes indefinite recourse to the pronoun. In *History of Sexuality* 1, "we" means to include the reader as representative subject of the modern regime of sexuality.

6. Foucault, "Le gay savoir," 49.

7. For Jouy, see Foucault, *Histoire de la sexualité*, 1:43–45. The more detailed discussion of the case is in *Les anormaux*, 275–290. The narrative rhetoric in the condensed version is still rather complicated; see Beer, *Michel Foucault*, 103–111. For the remarks on method, see Foucault, *Histoire de la sexualité*, 1:123–129 (propositions), 129 (rules as prescriptions).

8. Foucault, *Histoire de la sexualité*, 1:11. The interest of the punctuation is lost in Hurley's English version, which reads "We Other Victorians."

9. Foucault, *Histoire de la sexualité*, 1:9, 10.

10. Foucault makes these remarks in his preface to a French collection of excerpts from *My Secret Life*, DE, 3:131–132. Compare *Histoire de la sexualité*, 1:31.

11. Foucault, "Préface," DE, 3:132.

12. Foucault, *Histoire de la sexualité*, 1:104.

13. For the anatomical impossibility of penises speaking, Diderot, *Les bijoux indiscrets*, 53; for the way in which the ring does by magic what male lovers do by casual habit, 52; for an episode of male chatter, 149–154.

14. Foucault, *Histoire de la sexualité*, 1:101.

15. In the lectures, Foucault uses some of Nietzsche's remarks from *Gay Science* to construct a picture of interested knowledge. But a better parallel for

the subtitle to *Histoire de la sexualité* 1 is found in Foucault, "Nietzsche, la généalogie, l'histoire," *DE*, 2:152–156.

16. Foucault, *Histoire de la sexualité*, 1:104–105, "the *histoire* of this will to truth."

17. Foucault is quite deliberate in displaying specific configurations of the will to know, so I resist the claim that he is haplessly overpowered by them. Compare Beer, *Michel Foucault*, 87, who elsewhere defends Foucault against charges of self-contradiction from Baudrillard and Derrida.

18. Foucault, *Histoire de la sexualité*, 1:16.

19. Ibid., 1:30n1 ("the following volume, *The Flesh and the Body* [*La chair et le corps*]"); 79n1 ("These questions will be taken up again in the *Power of Truth* [*Pouvoir de la vérité*]," which is not listed among the titles of the series). For the summary, 150.

20. For Foucault's description of one topical circle, see ibid., 1:119.

21. The words occur together in the first sentence of the book as the episodes of an alleged continuity (*Histoire de la sexualité*, 1:9). They appear widely spaced in the final section as the terms of a contrast of forms of sovereign power (177).

22. Foucault, *Surveiller et punir*, 27.

23. Foucault, *Histoire de la sexualité*, 1:91–92.

24. Ibid., 1:133–134.

25. Ibid., 1:27–29, 51. Compare 1:77–82 on the confessional as the origin of the distinctive speech of *scientia sexualis*.

26. Ibid., 1:13 (transgression), 14 (prophecy, garden), 15 (theologians and exhorters), 17 (sin against sex).

27. Dinshaw describes this aptly in the "Coda" to her *Getting Medieval*, 198–200.

28. Foucault, *Histoire de la sexualité*, 1:59.

29. For the mathematical sense, ibid., 1:121; for an ironic quotation, 206.

30. Foucault, *Surveiller et punir*, 248, 255, 258 (dangerousness).

31. Foucault, *Les anormaux*, 18 (juridical subject), 22 (double). In *Folie et déraison*, Foucault contrasts the experience of the person as a subject of the law with the experience of the person as a social being (159).

32. For example, Norton, *The Myth of the Modern Homosexual*, 8–10; or Paglia, *Vamps and Tramps*, 99.

33. Halperin, *How to Do the History*, 135.

34. Foucault is not fair to some liberationist discourse, which was well aware that both its language and its erotic roles were transitory. I think especially of Carl Wittman's "Gay Manifesto," which describes gayness itself as a transitional phase on the way to a bisexuality or omnisexuality after the undoing of patriarchal gender categories.

35. Foucault, *Histoire de la sexualité*, 1:109. On other pages, Foucault uses "theory" to describe medico-scientific formulations he means to resist, such as the "theory of repression" (170) or "the armature of a general theory of sex" (204).

36. Foucault, *Le gouvernement de soi*, 41. Compare Foucault, *Sécurité, territoire,*

population, 1–6. For "our" need of theory, see his preface to the American edition of Deleuze and Guattari, *Anti-Oedipus*, *DE*, 3:133–134; compare the interview from the same year, "Le jeu de Michel Foucault," *DE*, 3:302.

37. For logical examples, see *Histoire de la sexualité*, 1:103 ("a logic of concupiscence and of desire"), 129 ("the logic of a global strategy"), or 102 (a "Logic of sex" in contrast with a "Physics," both phrases italicized). For a mathematical example, 125 (power relations are intelligible so far as they are traversed by a calculation or arithmetic or even calculus [*un calcul*]).

38. For example, in Foucault, *Histoire de la sexualité*, 1:122, "the condition of possibility of power" becomes, in the next clause, "the point of view that allows its exercise to be rendered intelligible"—where the reference is always to a particular form of power.

39. For one argument about the importance of Bachelard to Foucault's writings about power, see Privitera, *Problems of Style*, especially 67–98.

40. Bachelard, *La psychanalyse du feu*, 11–12.

41. Foucault, *Histoire de la sexualité*, 1:113–114.

42. Recall, as one obvious example from Barthes, the first twelve sections of Barthes, *S/Z*, in *Oeuvres complètes*, 3:121–135. For code rather than law in Foucault, see *Histoire de la sexualité*, 1:119. In volumes 2 and 3, "code" will almost always appear in connection with law and, indeed, with Christianity. Elsewhere it ranges more widely. Like so many other contrast terms in Foucault, the sense of the opposition matters more than the particular term.

43. Foucault, *Histoire de la sexualité*, 1:127.

44. Foucault applies this triplet to Deleuze and Guattari in the preface to *Anti-Oedipus*, *DE*, 3:134.

45. Consider the long series of negations in Foucault, *Histoire de la sexualité*, 1:110–112. Compare Blanchot, *Michel Foucault tel que je l'imagine*, 26.

46. Foucault, *Histoire de la sexualité*, 1:121–122.

47. Ibid., 1:136. Compare the description of instinct in *Les anormaux*, 128–129.

48. Foucault, *Histoire de la sexualité*, 1:183 (anatomo-politics and biopolitics), 184 (biopower), 188 (biohistory). For the newness of biopower, 187 ("for the first time without doubt in history"), 188 ("no need to insist here on the rupture that was then produced").

49. Ibid., 1:200.

50. From Lawrence, "*A propos* of Lady Chatterley's Lover," 308, lines 23–24.

51. Foucault, *Histoire de la sexualité*, 1:209. Compare 103, sex as the explanation (*raison*) for everything.

52. Ibid., 1:211.

53. Foucault, *Surveiller et punir*, 233 (in the title), 238 (with the reference to Baltard).

54. Recall Foucault's interview with O'Higgins, "Sexual Choice, Sexual Act," 20, with the corresponding French text in *DE*, 4: 331–332.

55. Foucault, *Histoire de la sexualité*, 1:60.

56. Ibid., 1:120, where Foucault remarks on conceiving "sex without the law, and power without the king." The challenge—or resistance—in each case is the same, and getting past it requires the same sort of imaginative reversal.

57. Indeed, he used it as early as "La folie, l'absence d'oeuvre," with regard to madness (*DE*, 1:412).

58. Foucault, "Le gay savoir," 51.

CHAPTER 5: THE SOBBING MATRON AND THE LOQUACIOUS MONK

1. A first draft of *Histoire de la sexualité* 2 undertaken in 1977–1978 included material on modern confessional practice. (For this manuscript, see Chevallier, *Michel Foucault et le christianisme*, 8, 62, and especially 149–154.) But already in January 1979, Foucault had started on a second version of the text that focused on Mediterranean antiquity. See Defert, "Chronologie," *DE*, 1:56.

2. See again Chevallier, *Michel Foucault et le christianisme*, especially 8.

3. Lindon, *Ce qu'aimer veut dire*, 114, quoting Hervé Guibert; compare Guibert, "Les secrets d'un homme," 108.

4. Foucault, *Du gouvernement des vivants*, 74–75.

5. Bellon, "'Je crois au temps . . . ,'" 4–5.

6. Compare Rabinow, "Foucault's Untimely Struggle," especially 26.

7. There are also argumentative resemblances among the lectures, of course, and it seems clear that Foucault adapted some pages of his script from the Collège for use in the States and in Belgium. It is equally clear that he adds other material to the core texts from Tertullian, Cassian, or John Chrysostom. I mention these variations, but I do not intend to catalogue them. I am not trying to reconstruct the redactional history of these lectures, much less to use them to reconstitute *Histoire de la sexualité* 4. For these lectures particularly, there are significant differences between the order of composition and the order of publication or translation—as Foucault insists ("Le retour de la morale," *DE*, 4:697). The 1980 lectures at the Collège were published in French only in 2012 (*Du gouvernement des vivants*). The 1980 Dartmouth lectures appeared first in English in 1993 ("About the Beginning"). A collation of their texts with the texts read at Berkeley followed in 1998 (in *Religion and Culture*). The 1981 lectures were printed in French in 2012 (*Mal faire*). The 1982 lectures from Vermont, the last to be delivered, arrived first in English in 1988 (*Technologies of the Self*). Their publication preceded that of the French lectures that supply their context by almost twenty-five years.

8. Nietzsche, "Schopenhauer als Erzieher," section 8, in his *Sämtliche Werke*, 1:417, lines 14–16.

9. Foucault, "Sexualité et pouvoir," *DE*, 3:552.

10. Ibid., 3:556–557. Chevallier writes at length about Foucault's deployment of "the Orient" within what he regards as the suppressed binary, Dionysus against Christ (e.g., *Michel Foucault et le christianisme*, 241). In the Tokyo lecture, "the Orient" is used more familiarly and more colloquially.

11. Foucault, "Sexualité et pouvoir," 3:560.

· 12. With the notion of condensation, I am trying to describe an elusive textual relation. What Foucault reads in Tokyo is sometimes very close to what he had read some weeks before in Paris. The clearest place to see this is in the enumeration of the properties of pastoral power. The account given in Tokyo follows the sense and some of the phrasing of a lecture given at the Collège on February 8, 1978 ("Sexualité et pouvoir," 3:561–562; *Sécurité, territoire, population,* 129–133). But it is as if Foucault had done an outline or sketch *after* having done a series of oil studies.

13. Foucault, *Sécurité, territoire, population,* 3–4.

14. Ibid., 10.

15. Ibid., 111. On Foucault's habit of shifting from the announced title to what actually interested him, see Ewald, "Au Collège de France," 51.

16. Foucault, *Sécurité, territoire, population,* 349, 365.

17. Ibid., 123–124.

18. Ibid., 155. The argument about the historical distinctiveness of Christian pastoral power is made again in the first of the Tanner Lectures on October 10, 1979, and published in English as part of the lecture series in 1981 ("*Omnes et Singulatim*").

19. Foucault, *Sécurité, territoire, population,* 169. For Foucault's denials of any intention to write history, see, for example, 139, 154, 169, 197.

20. Ibid., 176. I return to Foucault's use of "style" in the next chapter.

21. Ibid., 183, 187.

22. Ibid., 198, 204–205, 199.

23. Foucault also changes his analysis of some of these counter-conducts. In the Stanford lectures, for example, mysticism becomes one of the persisting expressions of pastoral government rather than a counter-conduct against it ("*Omnes et singulatim,*" 241).

24. Foucault, "Sexualité et pouvoir," *DE,* 3:559 (Veyne), 560 (Plato), 561 (David), 562 (Good Shepherd).

25. A number of the intermediate sources are named in the notes to the edition of the lectures. These and others are discussed by Chevallier, *Michel Foucault et le christianisme,* 113–114, 188–194.

26. Foucault, *Sécurité, territoire, population,* 156.

27. See especially the editorial notes for the lectures of February 15 and 22, in ibid., 160–165, 188–193.

28. Foucault, "About the Beginning," passim. Carrette helpfully republishes two lectures from Dartmouth, adding in the notes the most significant passages from the longer series given at Berkeley the month before. A comparison of the tapes from Berkeley with the text from Dartmouth will show innumerable small differences not noted by Carrette. Another lecture given at NYU, "Sexuality and Solitude," overlaps in part with these two but also includes new material, especially from Augustine.

29. Foucault refers to a close precedent in ancient Greek: *alêthourgês* is attested in the *Allegoriae* of Heraclitus, a later belle-lettrist not to be confused with the gnomic philosopher. The term means something like acting truly. Here I rely on the musty authority of Lidell and Scott, *Greek-English Lexicon*, 64a; compare Foucault, *Du gouvernement des vivants*, 8.

30. Foucault, *Du gouvernement des vivants*, 10, 7, 8–9.

31. Ibid., 8, 9, 18. Elsewhere Foucault describes the mimicry of courtly rhetoric by plain petitioners seeking royal intervention: They must "dress up in tatters of fabric . . . if they want to be noticed on the scene of power. . . . [They are like] a poor troupe of buffoons, who would deck themselves out however they can in a few flashy rags [*oripeaux*] that were once sumptuous" ("La vie des hommes infâmes," *DE*, 3:250).

32. Foucault, *Surveiller et punir*, 255.

33. Foucault, *Du gouvernement des vivants*, 91. Alethurgy does reappear in this lecture series at a key moment in the description of Christian texts. See Foucault's remarks on *exomologêsis* as an alethurgy of the sinner as sinner (301) and on the "alethurgy of myself" (303). For alethurgy in the lectures at Louvain, see Foucault, *Mal faire*, 28, 33, 54, 59, 68 (where it is a synonym for veridiction). The term returns with some frequency in the last lecture series at the Collège. In *Le gouvernement de soi*, it is applied to decisive revelations in Greek tragedies (77–78, 80, 82–83, 108, 126). In *Le courage de la vérité*, it figures in the culminating description of the Cynic way of life as a manifestation of truth (159, 200).

34. Foucault, *Du gouvernement des vivants*, 82–83; "About the Beginning," 169–170; *Mal faire*, 90. Here and in what follows, I translate *aveu* as "confession," but always with the awareness that I risk several misunderstandings. In modern French, an *aveu* can be a confession to a priest or to the police, but it also has resonances closer to its antiquated English cousin, "avowal." At the same time, the French also use *confession* to mean sacramental confession and the confession of faith.

35. For the reiteration of the basic distinction, see Foucault, *Du gouvernement des vivants*, 301; "About the Beginning," 179; *Mal faire*, 161.

36. Foucault, *Du gouvernement des vivants*, 175, 222.

37. Ibid., 207.

38. Ibid., 205; "About the Beginning," 172.

39. For Fabiola, Foucault, *Du gouvernement des vivants*, 202; "About the Beginning," 171–172; *Mal faire*, 106.

40. Foucault combines and amplifies Jerome, Letter 77, nos. 4–5, as in his *Epistulae*, 55:40–42. I translate these passages a bit differently than Foucault does, adding other emphases.

41. For the pursuit of *logismoi* or *cogitationes*, Foucault, *Du gouvernement des vivants*, 293; "About the Beginning," 175; *Mal faire*, 144–145. For Cassian's images, Foucault, *Du gouvernement des vivants*, 294–297; "About the Beginning," 175–176; *Mal faire*, 147–148.

42. Foucault, *Du gouvernement des vivants*, 295, 300 (emphasis added).

43. Foucault, *Mal faire*, 145–146, 162.

44. Foucault, *Du gouvernement des vivants*, 78–79.

45. For the argument, see Foucault, "About the Beginning," 175–179. For this motto, see *Du gouvernement des vivants*, 222; "About the Beginning," 173.

46. Here I combine Foucault, *Du gouvernement des vivants*, 303; "About the Beginning," 168–169, 173, 179–180; "Sexuality and Solitude," 184; and *Mal faire*, 182.

47. Foucault, *Mal faire*, 188.

48. Ibid., 165, 142. The text by John Chrysostom is probably from the homily on Psalm 5, Migne, *PG* 50:581. For the practice of writing, see Athanasius, *Vita Antonii*, sect. 55, Migne, *PG* 26:924.

49. For the epistles of Marcus Aurelius, see Foucault, *Technologies of the Self*, 28–30; for the use of Athanasius, "L'écriture de soi," *DE*, 4:415–416.

50. Foucault, "About the Beginning," 181.

51. Foucault, "La scène de la philosophie," *DE*, 3:571–572.

52. Ibid., 3:573 (Nietzsche's definition), 574 (Foucault's flaw); for both "permanent drama" and "theatricalization," *Du gouvernement des vivants*, 205.

53. Sontag, "Notes on Camp," in her *Against Interpretation*, 287, no. 36. I am not arguing for direct influence. I cannot find reference in Foucault's published work to Sontag on camp. Certainly Sontag knew some of Foucault's early work. Indeed, she was among the first to introduce him to American readers. See *Against Interpretation*, 104, 172.

54. Foucault, *Du gouvernement des vivants*, 301.

55. Sontag, "Notes on Camp," 275, before the numbered sections.

56. Foucault, *Du gouvernement des vivants*, 202, 207.

CHAPTER 6: THE ARTIST OF PLEASURES

1. Richlin, "Foucault's *History of Sexuality*," 139. There have been many criticisms of Foucault's exclusions. I don't mean to reduce them all to Richlin's or, indeed, to caricature hers. For an astute review of some of the salient issues, see O'Leary, *Foucault and the Art of Ethics*, 58–68.

2. Foucault, *Surveiller et punir*, 193, on unheroic or antiheroic writing of lives.

3. Foucault, *Histoire de la sexualité*, 2:43–44.

4. Foucault is quite clear about how limited his ancient sources are with respect to gender. To take one caution early in the text: "one must always remember that this is a man's morality, made by and for men" (ibid., 2:56).

5. Foucault, "Le retour de la morale," *DE*, 4:696–697. Neither the title nor the final form of the interview can be attributed to Foucault.

6. Foucault, *Histoire de la sexualité*, 2:10.

7. Ibid., 2:14.

8. Ibid., 2:15.

9. Ibid., 2:18–19.

10. Ibid., 2:16–17.

11. Ibid., 2:33.

12. Even in saying that much, I may have tipped the balance of continuity and discontinuity that Foucault struggles to arrange. For a helpful reminder of that balance, see Clark, "Foucault, the Fathers and Sex."

13. Foucault, *Histoire de la sexualité*, 2:9, 18.

14. Ibid., 2:107: "not to codify sexual conduct precisely, but rather to 'stylize' it."

15. Foucault, "Le retour de la morale," *DE*, 4:698. In his biography of Augustine, Brown frequently refers to style in the literary or rhetorical sense (e.g., *Augustine of Hippo*, 71, 134, 255–256), but he also speaks of "style of life" (9). "Style of life" figures more prominently in *The Making of Late Antiquity* (e.g., 29, 34, but especially 97). In an introduction to the French translation of that work, Brown emphasizes the question of style (*Genèse de l'antiquité tardive*, 15n1, 16–19). In an accompanying preface, Paul Veyne associates himself (and Foucault) with Brown's use of the term (ibid., xi–xii, xix–xxii). But these last two pieces could not have influenced Foucault's use, since Veyne writes that he has on his desk the completed manuscript of Foucault's study of ancient love (xix–xx). He calls the terminological convergence one of those "coincidences that are delightful strokes of luck" (xix).

16. Foucault, "Le souci de la vérité," *DE*, 4:648; for the phrase, "Le style de l'histoire," *DE*, 4:650.

17. To say that the notion of style recedes is not to say that it vanishes. For example, each of the opening passages in *Surveiller et punir* is said to define a "penal style" (13).

18. For the quotation, see Foucault, "Introduction," *DE*, 1:118. For other positive mentions of style, see "La psychologie de 1850 à 1950," *DE*, 1:121; "La recherche scientifique et la psychologie," 1:152, 155; "Sur l'archéologie des sciences," 1:712. For a negative mention, see Foucault, "Réponse à une question," *DE*, 1:685. For the style of anonymity, see Foucault, "Sur les façons d'écrire l'histoire," *DE*, 1:597. Gerald Bruns points to the "interesting question" of the relationship between Foucault's early inquiries into "modernist themes" and his later studies, where "the idea is to constitute oneself, in a strong modernist sense, as a 'work of art.'" See Bruns, "Foucault's Modernism," 350.

19. Foucault, "Le triomphe social du plaisir sexuel," *DE*, 4:309. For the *Salmagundi* interview, Foucault, "Choix sexuel, acte sexuel," *DE*, 4:333. The corresponding passage in English reads "the major issues and questions of lifestyle" ("Social Choice, Sexual Act," 21).

20. See *Histoire de la sexualité*, 2:63 (*chrêsis aphrodisiôn*) and 2:106 (esthetics of existence). Compare to these 2:67–68 (art or practice of using pleasures), 2:251 (stylization of *aphrodisia*), and 3:251 (stylizing one's pleasure generally).

21. O'Leary provides a sort of Heideggerian etymology for "stylize" that reinforces Foucault's use, but it blurs two ancient facts. First, "stylus" actually

descends from a Latin word, though it looks like and was sometimes anciently taken for a Greek word. Second, the use of *stilus* to mean what we now call style was a metaphorical extension, as if I were to say that "Walter Pater writes with a gemlike pen." Compare O'Leary, *Foucault and the Art of Ethics*, 2–3. A passage sometimes cited as the first attestation of the French *stylisation* is Natanson, "Estampes d'Outamaro et de Hiroshigé," 139. The piece is an interesting example not only of *Japonisme* but of saturated prose.

22. Foucault, *Histoire de la sexualité*, 2:17n1. In Burckhardt, the state itself is a work of art (*Kunstwerk*). See *Die Kultur der Renaissance*, 13.

23. Benjamin, *Charles Baudelaire: Ein Lyriker*, which appeared in 1982 in French as *Charles Baudelaire, un poète lyrique à l'apogée du capitalisme*. The first essay was unpublished during Benjamin's lifetime. The second appeared as a journal article in 1939.

24. Benjamin, "Das Paris des Second Empire bei Baudelaire," in *Charles Baudelaire: Ein Lyriker*, 104, 105.

25. Baudelaire, *Le peintre de la vie moderne*, in *Baudelaire: Écrits sur l'art*, 535–539.

26. Ibid., 535, 536.

27. Ibid.; compare Benjamin, "Das Paris des Second Empire bei Baudelaire," 88.

28. Baudelaire, *Le peintre*, 509, 513.

29. Foucault, "Qu'est-ce que les Lumières," *DE*, 4:570. For the lecture's circumstances, see Sluga, "Foucault à Berkeley," 840–841.

30. Foucault, "Qu'est-ce que les Lumières," *DE*, 4:571.

31. Foucault, *Histoire de la sexualité*, 2:17.

32. Ibid., 2:184.

33. Ibid., 2:207. According to Lindon, it was also the favored term in Foucault's private speech ("Rue de Vaugirard," 67).

34. Foucault, *Histoire de la sexualité*, 2:228.

35. Ibid., 2:266–268.

36. Ibid., 2:269.

37. Ibid., 3:22.

38. Ibid., 3:49.

39. Ibid., 2:235, 251–252, 277.

40. Ibid., 3:84, 89; for "exigency," 99, 199, 213; for the millennial "elaboration," 271. Compare the use of the analogy to accentuation in describing even much larger changes across European history in 2:277.

41. Char, *Oeuvres complètes*, 766.

42. Foucault, *Histoire de la sexualité*, 1:211.

43. Foucault, "Des espaces autres," *DE*, 4:752. Foucault had used the notion of heterotopia before this lecture, notably in the preface to *Les mots et les choses*, 9.

44. Foucault, "Des espaces autres," *DE*, 4:759.

45. Foucault, *Histoire de la sexualité*, 2:23.

CHAPTER 7: THE VIOLATED MOTHER AND THE NAKED PHILOSOPHER

1. Foucault, *Le courage de la vérité*, 2.

2. Foucault, *L'herméneutique du sujet*, 4.

3. For both of these characterizations, ibid., 16–17.

4. Hadot, *Exercises spirituels et philosophie antique*, 21.

5. Ibid.

6. Printed evidence exactly contemporary with one of Foucault's lecture series can be found in Mains, *Urban Aboriginals*. The book is filled with references to spiritual experiences or contacts, spiritual forces and yearnings, spiritual arts or rituals. See especially 27, 45, 100, 167, 184.

7. Foucault, *L'herméneutique du sujet*, 17–18.

8. Ibid., 92. It is also—as Foucault knew—curiously related to Benjamin's formulation of "messianic time."

9. Foucault, *L'herméneutique du sujet*, 204.

10. Ibid., 205.

11. Ibid., 452.

12. Foucault, "La prose d'Actéon," *DE*, 1:330.

13. Foucault, *Le gouvernement de soi*, 4–5.

14. Ibid., 8.

15. Foucault, *Histoire de la sexualité*, 1:101. (Compare Huffer, *Mad for Foucault*, 238.) *Blason* also appears in this book on 165, where it is used to describe the bourgeois notion of sex as a counterpart to the feudal notion of blood. Elsewhere, in an interview, Foucault talks about male S&M communities as carrying out a degenitalization of erotic acts under the *blason* of masculinity. See Foucault, "Le gay savoir," 61–62; compare *Les mots et les choses*, 317, where it applies to conduct in general.

16. Foucault, *Le gouvernement de soi*, 9. I stretch the sense of the English "instituted" a bit in order to preserve Foucault's pun.

17. Ibid., 13.

18. Ibid., 14 (where the images are repeated), 22. I stretch the English "actuality" toward its most temporal meanings to preserve some of Foucault's resonances.

19. Ibid., 6, 41.

20. Ibid.

21. Ibid., 42.

22. Ibid., 7–8n (emphasis added).

23. Ibid., 344, 91n (for the quotation).

24. For example, ibid., 44, 46, 47.

25. Ibid., 322–323 (Pericles and Socrates); 313–314 (the "birth" of this "daughter").

26. Ibid., 49, 54, 61, 66–67.

27. Ibid., 77.

28. Ibid., 113 (Dumézil), 114 (for both quotations).

29. Ibid., 117, 119 (compare 127–128), 140.

30. Nietzsche, *Dionysos-Dithyramben*, "Klage der Ariadne," in *Sämtliche Werke*, 6:398, line 56 ; 401, lines 9–25. All ellipses are in the original.

31. Foucault, "Theatrum philosophicum," *DE*, 2:96. For other references, "Ariane s'est pendue," *DE*, 1:767–768; "Un si cruel savoir," 1:226–228.

32. Foucault, "Le vrai sexe." "Much criticized," I say, thinking not least of the famous section in Butler, *Gender Trouble*, 119–135, which attends to reports of Foucault's laughter while missing most of his textual ironies.

33. I take the "if" seriously. I don't presume that Foucault writes for all readers or that every reader interested in his topics will want to read his texts. There are good reasons for choosing not to spend reading time on Foucault. Still I would insist—this is my reader's piety—that a judgment not to read Foucault differs from a judgment on Foucault after reading, even if both are rejections.

34. For example, Foucault, *Le gouvernement de soi*, 243, 249.

35. Foucault, *Le courage de la vérité*, 3, 35.

36. Ibid., 64–65.

37. Ibid., 68, 88, 112; compare Nietzsche, *Fröhliche Wissenschaft*, no. 340, in *Sämtliche Werke*, 3:569–570. For a more detailed reading of Foucault on Socrates in the *Phaedo*, see Nehamas, *The Art of Living*, perhaps especially 157–161.

38. Foucault, *Le courage de la vérité*, 111.

39. Ibid., 142; compare 148–152, discussed previously.

40. Ibid., 159.

41. Ibid., 174. See also Tanke, *Foucault's Philosophy of Art*, 177–184.

42. Foucault, *Le courage de la vérité*, 160.

43. For the "transvaluation," see ibid., 233; for the ugly reflection, 209–210, 214, 248; for the limit, 210.

44. Ibid., 233 (public), 237 (poverty), 236 (dramatization), 169 (theater), 274 (for the animal inversion of convention).

45. Diogenes Laertius, *Vitae philosophorum* 6.96 (Marcovich, 1:437–439).

46. Foucault, *Le courage de la vérité*, 219–220, after Diogenes Laertius.

47. In his close reading of Foucault's argument here, McGushin is right to emphasize the ideal of a true and unconcealed life (*Foucault's Askêsis*, 151–153). My point in stressing its character as imitation or representation is only to note that the public presentation of bodily truths requires performance in view of the prevailing social taboos.

48. Tanke speaks of the "complicated intertwining of the discursive and the visible" in the Cynic's life (*Foucault's Philosophy of Art*, 188). He rightly connects it to Foucault's long engagement with painting. But that intertwining is much more immediately theatrical—as is Foucault's language about it.

49. Nietzsche, *Also sprach Zarathustra* 2, in *Sämtliche Werke*, 4:105–106; Foucault, *Le courage de la vérité*, 178.

50. Foucault, *Le courage de la vérité*, 307–308.

51. Ibid., 309, 310.

52. Foucault, *Histoire de la sexualité*, 2:15.

CONCLUSION: EMBODIED WRITING *OR* AMONG THE MOURNERS

1. Miller, *Passion of Michel Foucault*, 26–29, passim. The best reply to Miller's biographical plots on Foucault remains Halperin, *Saint Foucault*, 126–185.

2. The three texts are, respectively, Guibert, *À l'ami*, "Les secrets d'un homme," and *Le mausolée*.

3. Guibert, *À l'ami*, 15. The pseudonym has a number of associations. One is to the novelist Robert Musil. Elsewhere Guibert notes that Musil's wife destroyed the pages of his journals that concerned their intimate relations (*Le mausolée*, 302).

4. Guibert, *À l'ami*, 21.

5. Ibid., 25.

6. Ibid., 32.

7. Ibid.

8. Ibid., 97–98.

9. Ibid., 101–102.

10. Macey, *Lives*, 4, 10.

11. Ibid., 472.

12. Voeltzel, *Vingt ans*, 156–157.

13. Ibid., 159. On the circumstances of the book's composition, see Voeltzel, "Souvenirs de voyage," 57–58.

14. Foucault, *Le beau danger*, 40, 57–58.

15. Lindon, *Ce qu'aimer veut dire*, 46, 49.

16. Ibid., 188.

17. Ibid., 152.

18. Foucault, *Le beau danger*, 56.

Two cautions may help the reader make good use of this bibliography. (1) Only works cited in the notes have been included here. This is by no means a comprehensive or even well-balanced bibliography of writings by or about Foucault. (2) Since I have made my own translations throughout, it is also not a guide to translations of Foucault into English or any other language. Readers who are looking for help in navigating the ever-changing bibliography associated with Foucault should look elsewhere—and to regularly updated databases rather than printed pages.

Here, as in the notes, the abbreviation *DE* stands for Foucault, *Dits et écrits*. Full bibliographic information for this title is supplied in the list.

Acéphale: Religion, sociologie, philosophie. Preface by Michel Camus. Paris: Jean-Michel Place, 1995.

Agamben, Giorgio. *Che cos'è un dispositivo?* Rome: Nottetempo, 2006.

Arnaud, Alain. *Pierre Klossowski.* Paris: Seuil, 1990.

Artaud, Antonin. *Le théâtre et son double.* In *Oeuvres complètes*, 4:9–171. Paris: NRF / Gallimard, 1964.

Bachelard, Gaston. *La psychanalyse du feu.* Paris: Gallimard, 1949.

Barthes, Roland. *Oeuvres complètes.* Edited by Eric Marty. Rev. ed. Paris: Seuil, 2002.

Bataille, Georges. *Oeuvres complètes.* Paris: Gallimard, 1970–1988.

Baudelaire, Charles. *Écrits sur l'art.* Edited by Francis Moulinat. Paris: Le Livre de Poche / Librairie Générale de la France, 1992.

Beer, Dan. *Michel Foucault: Form and Power.* Oxford: Legenda / EHRC, University of Oxford, 2002.

Bellon, Guillaume. "'Je crois au temps . . . ': Daniel Défert légataire des manuscrits de Michel Foucault." *Revue recto/verso*, no. 1: *Genèses contemporaines* (June 2007). Available at http://www.revuerectoverso.com/spip.php?article29.

Benjamin, Walter. *Charles Baudelaire: Ein Lyriker im Zeitalter des Hochkapitalismus: Zwei Fragmente*. Edited by Rolf Tiedemann. Frankfurt: Suhrkamp, 1969. French edition: *Charles Baudelaire, un poète lyrique à l'apogée du capitalisme*. Translated by Jean Lacoste. Paris: Payot, 1982.

———. *Die Passagen-Werk*. Edited by Rolf Tiedemann. Frankfurt: Suhrkamp, 1983.

Bernauer, James W. *Michel Foucault's Force of Flight: Toward an Ethics for Thought*. Atlantic Highlands, NJ: Humanities Press International, 1990.

———. "Michel Foucault's Philosophy of Religion: An Introduction to the Non-Fascist Life." In *Michel Foucault and Theology: The Politics of Religious Experience*, ed. James Bernauer and Jeremy Carrette, 77–97. Aldershot, UK: Ashgate, 2004.

Blanchot, Maurice. *Celui qui ne m'accompagnait pas*. Paris: Gallimard, 1953.

———. *Chroniques littéraires du* Journal des débats: *Avril 1941–août 1944*. Edited by Christophe Bident. Paris: Gallimard, 2007.

———. *Comment la littérature est-elle possible?* Paris: José Corti, 1942.

———. *Michel Foucault tel que je l'imagine*. [Saint-Clément-de-Rivière]: Fata Morgana, 1986.

Bordeleau, Erik. *Foucault anonymat*. Quebec: Le Quartanier, 2012.

Brooks, Peter. *The Empty Space: Theatre—Deadly, Holy, Rough, Immediate*. New York : Touchstone / Simon and Schuster, 1996.

Brotchie, Alastair. *Alfred Jarry: A Pataphysical Life*. Cambridge, MA: MIT Press, 2011.

Brown, Peter. *Augustine of Hippo: A Biography*. Berkeley: University of California Press, 1967.

———. *Genèse de l'antiquité tardive*. Preface by Paul Veyne. Translated by Aline Rousselle. Paris: Gallimard, 1983.

———. *The Making of Late Antiquity*. Cambridge, MA: Harvard University Press, 1978.

Bruns, Gerald. "Foucault's Modernism." In *The Cambridge Companion to Foucault*, 2nd ed., ed. Gary Gutting, 348–378. Cambridge: Cambridge University Press, 2003.

Burckhardt, Jakob. *Die Kultur der Renaissance in Italien*. Edited by Horst Günther. Frankfurt: Deutscher Klassiker, 1989.

Butler, Judith. *Gender Trouble: Feminism and the Subversion of Identity*. 10th anniversary ed. New York: Routledge, 1999.

Carrette, Jeremy R. *Foucault and Religion: Spiritual Corporality and Political Spirituality*. London: Routledge, 2000.

Certeau, Michel de. *La possession de Loudun*. Edited by Luce Giard. Paris: Gallimard, 2005.

Char, René. *Oeuvres complètes*. Bibliothèque de la Pléiade. Paris: Gallimard, 1983.

Chevallier, Philippe. *Michel Foucault et le christianisme*. Lyon: ENS Éditions, 2011.

Clark, Elizabeth A. "Foucault, the Fathers and Sex." In *Michel Foucault and Theology: The Politics of Religious Experience*, ed. James Bernauer and Jeremy Carrette, 39–56. Aldershot, UK: Ashgate, 2004.

Daniel, Jean. *La blessure*. Paris: B. Grasset, 1992.

Davidson, Arnold I. "Archaeology, Genealogy, Ethics." In *Foucault: A Critical Reader*, ed. David Couzens Hoy, 220–233. Oxford: B. Blackwell, 1986.

De Villiers, Nicholas. *Opacity and the Closet: Queer Tactics in Foucault, Barthes, and Warhol*. Minneapolis: University of Minnesota Press, 2012.

Defert, Daniel. "Chronologie." In Foucault, *DE*, 1:13–64.

Derrida, Jacques. "Cogito et histoire de la folie." In *L'écriture et la différence*, 51–97. Paris: Seuil, 1967.

Diderot, Denis. *Les bijoux indiscrets*. In *Oeuvres complètes*, ed. Jean Macary, Aram Vartanian, and Jean-Louis Leutrat, 3:1–290. Paris: Hermann, 1978.

Dinshaw, Carolyn. *Getting Medieval: Sexualities and Communities, Pre- and Postmodern*. Durham, NC: Duke University Press, 1999.

Diogenes Laertius. *Vitae philosophorum*. Vol. 1, *Libri I–X*. Edited by Miroslav Marcovich. Stuttgart: B. Teubner, 1999.

Downing, Lisa. *The Cambridge Introduction to Foucault*. Cambridge: Cambridge University Press, 2008.

Dreyfus, Hubert L., and Paul Rabinow. *Michel Foucault: Beyond Structuralism and Hermeneutics*. Chicago: University of Chicago Press, 1982.

Dufresne, Roger. "Pour introduire la lecture française de Freud: Notes bibliographiques sur les traductions françaises de Freud." *Interprétation* [Montreal] 5, no. 1 (January–March 1971): 41–97.

Elden, Stuart. "The Constitution of the Normal: Monsters and Masturbation at the Collège de France." *boundary2* 28, no. 1 (2001): 91–105.

Ewald, François. "Au Collège de France." Interview with Philippe Artières. *Les cahiers de L'Herne* 95: *Michel Foucault* (2011): 47–52.

Farge, Arlette. "Un récit violent." In *Michel Foucault: Lire l'oeuvre*, ed. Luce Giard, 189–195. Grenoble: Jérôme Millon, 2012.

Foucault, Michel. "About the Beginning of the Hermeneutics of the Subject." In Foucault, *Religion and Culture*, 158–181.

———. [Afterword]. In Flaubert, *Die Versuchung des Heiligen Antonius*, 217–251. Frankfurt: Insel, 1964. Citations from *DE*, 1:293–325.

———. *Les anormaux: Cours au Collège de France, 1974–1975*. Edited by Valerio Marchetti and Antoinetta Salomoni under the direction of François Ewald and Alessandro Fontana. Paris: Gallimard / Seuil, 1999.

———. *Archéologie de savoir*. Paris: Gallimard, 1969.

———. "Ariane s'est pendue." *Le nouvel observateur*, no. 229 (March 31–April 6, 1969): 36–37. Citations from *DE*, 1:767–771.

———. *Le beau danger: Entretiens avec Claude Bonnefoy*. Edited by Philipe Artières. Paris: Éditions EHESS, 2011.

———. "Choix sexuel, acte sexuel" [Sexual choice, sexual act]. Interview with

J. O'Higgins. *Salmagundi*, nos. 58–59: *Homosexuality: Sacrilege, Vision, Politics* (Autumn–Winter 1982): 10–24. Citations from *DE*, 4:320–335.

———. *Le courage de la vérité: Le gouvernement de soi et des autres II: Cours au Collège de France, 1983–1984*. Edited by Frédéric Gros under the direction of François Ewald and Alessandro Fontana. Paris: Gallimard / Seuil, 2009.

———. "De l'amitié comme mode de vie." Interview with René de Ceccaty, Jean Danet, and Jean Le Bitoux. *Gai pied*, no. 25 (April 1981): 38–39. Citations from *DE*, 4:163–167.

———. "De l'archéologie à la dynastique" [Archeologie Kara dynastique he]. Interview with S. Hasumi. *Umi* 5, no. 3 (March 1973): 182–206. Citations from *DE*, 2:405–416.

———. "Des espaces autres." *Architecture, mouvement, continuité*, no. 5 (October 1984): 46–49. Citations from *DE*, 4:752–762.

———. *Dits et écrits*. Edited by Jacques Lagrange under the direction of Daniel Defert and François Ewald. Paris: Gallimard, 1994.

———. *Du gouvernement des vivants: Cours au Collège de France, 1979–1980*. Edited by Michel Senellart under the direction of François Ewald and Alessandro Fontana. Paris: EHESS, Gallimard, and Seuil, 2012.

———. "L'écriture de soi." *Corps écrit*, no. 5: *L'autoportrait* (February 1983): 3–23. Citations from *DE*, 4:415–430.

———. "Entretien avec Michel Foucault" [Conversazione con Michel Foucault]. Interview with D. Trombadori. *Il contributo* 4, no. 1 (January–March 1980): 23–84. Citations from *DE*, 4:41–95.

———. "La fête de l'écriture." Interview with Jacques Almira and Jean Le Marchand. *Le quotidien de Paris*, no. 328 (April 25, 1975): 13. Citations from *DE*, 2:731–734.

———. *Folie et déraison: Histoire de la folie à l'âge classique*. Paris: Plon, 1961.

———. "La folie, l'absence d'oeuvre." *La table ronde*, no. 196: *Situation de la psychiatrie* (May 1964): 11–21. Citations from *DE*, 1:412–420.

———. "Folie, littérature, société" [Kyôki, bungaku, shakai]. Interview with T. Shimizu and M. Watanabe. *Bungei*, no. 12 (December 1970): 266–285. Citations from *DE*, 2:104–128.

———. "Le gay savoir." Interview with Jean Le Bitoux. In Bitoux, *Entretiens sur la question gay*, 45–72. [Béziers]: H and O Éditions, 2005.

———. *Le gouvernement de soi et des autres: Cours au Collège de France, 1982–1983*. Edited by Frédérique Gros under the direction of François Ewald and Alessandro Fontana. Paris: Gallimard / Seuil, 2008.

———. *L'herméneutique du sujet: Cours au Collège de France, 1981–1982*. Edited by Frédéric Gros under the direction of François Ewald and Alessandro Fontana. Paris: Gallimard / Seuil, 2001.

———. *Histoire de la folie à l'âge classique*. 2nd ed. Paris: Gallimard, 1972.

———. *Histoire de la sexualité*. Vol. 1, *La volonté de savoir*. Paris: Gallimard, 1976.

———. *Histoire de la sexualité*. Vol. 2, *L'usage des plaisirs*. Paris: Gallimard, 1984.

———. *Histoire de la sexualité*. Vol. 3, *Le souci de soi*. Paris: Gallimard, 1984.

———. *"Il faut défendre la société"*: *Cours au Collège de France, 1976*. Edited by Mauro Bertani and Antoinetta Salomoni under the direction of François Ewald and Alessandro Fontana. Paris: Gallimard / Seuil, 1997.

———. "Introduction." In Ludwig Binswanger, *Le rêve et l'existence*, 9–128. Paris: Desclé de Brouwer, 1954. Citations from *DE*, 1:65–119.

———. "Le jeu de Michel Foucault." Interview with Dominique Colas, Alain Grosrichard, and others. *Ornicar? Bulletin périodique du Champ freudien*, no. 10 (July 1977): 62–93. Citations from *DE*, 3:298–329.

———. "Le langage à l'infini." *Tel quel*, no. 15 (Autumn 1963): 44–53. Citations from *DE*, 1:250–261.

———. *Language, Counter-Memory, Practice: Selected Essays and Interviews*. Edited by Donald F. Bouchard. Ithaca, NY: Cornell University Press, 1977.

———. *Leçons sur la volonté de savoir: Cours au Collège de France, 1970–1971*. Edited by François Ewald, Alessandro Fontana, and Daniel Defert. Paris: Gallimard / Seuil, 2011.

———. "Luttes autour des prisons." *Esprit*, no. 11 (November 1979): 102–111. Citations from *DE*, 3:806–818.

———. *Mal faire, dire vrai: Fonction de l'aveu en justice. Cours de Louvain, 1981*. Edited by Fabienne Brion and Bernard E. Harcourt. Louvain: Presses universitaires de Louvain, 2012.

———. "Michel Foucault et le zen: Un sejour dans un temple zen" [Michel Foucault to zen: Zendera taizai-ki]. Edited by C. Polac. *Umi*, no. 197 (August–September 1978): 1–6. Citations from *DE*, 3:618–624.

———. *Les mots et les choses*. Paris: Gallimard, 1966.

———. *Naissance de la clinique: Une archéologie du regard médical*. Rev. ed. Paris: Press universitaires de France, 1972.

———. "Nietzsche, la généalogie, l'histoire." In *Hommage à Jean Hyppolite*, ed. S. Bachelard et al., 145–172. Paris: Presses universitaires de France, 1971. Citations from *DE*, 2:136–156.

———. "Non au sexe roi." Interview with Bernard-Henri Levy. *Le nouvel observateur*, no. 644 (March 12–21, 1977): 92–130. Citations from *DE*, 3:256–259.

———. "Le 'non' du père." *Critique*, no. 178 (March 1962): 195–209. Citations from *DE*, 1:189–203.

———. "*Omnes et singulatim*: Towards a Criticism of 'Political Reason.'" In *The Tanner Lectures on Human Values*, 2:225–254. Salt Lake City: University of Utah Press, 1981.

———. *L'ordre du discours*. Paris: Gallimard, 1971.

———. "La pensée du dehors." *Critique*, no. 229 (June 1966): 523–546. Citations from *DE*, 1:518–539.

———. "La pensée, l'émotion." In *Photographies de 1958 à 1982*, by Duane Michals, iii–vii. Paris: Musée d'Art moderne de la ville de Paris, 1982. Citations from *DE*, 4:243–250.

———. "Le philosophe masqué." Interview with Christian Delacampagne. *Le monde*, no. 10,945 (April 6, 1980): *Le monde—dimanche*, i, xvii. Reprinted in *Entretiens avec Le monde*, I: *Philosophies*, 27–30. Paris: Le Découverte / Le Monde, 1984. Citations from *DE*, 4:104–110.

———. "Philosophie et psychologie." Interview with Alain Badiou. *Dossiers pédagogiques de la radio-télévision scolaire* (February 27, 1965): 65–71. Citations from *DE*, 1:438–448.

———. *Le pouvoir psychiatrique: Cours au Collège de France, 1973–1974*. Edited by Jacques Lagrange under the direction of François Ewald and Alessandro Fontana. Paris: Gallimard / Seuil, 2003.

———. "Preface." In *Anti-Oedipus: Capitalism and Schizophrenia*, by Gilles Deleuze and Félix Guattari, xi–xiv. New York: Viking, 1977. Citations from *DE*, 3:133–136.

———. "Préface." In *My Secret Life* [excerpts], 1–3. Translated by Christian Charnaux, Nicole Gobbi, Nathalie Heinich, and Marco Lessana. Paris: Les formes du secret, 1977. Citations from *DE*, 3:131–132.

———. "Préface à la transgression." *Critique*, nos. 195–196: *Hommage à G. Bataille* (August–September 1963): 751–769. Citations from *DE*, 1:233–250.

———. "Les problèmes de la culture: Un débat Foucault-Preti" [I problemi della cultura. Un dibattito Foucault-Petri]. Interview with G. Preti, ed. M. Dzieduszycki, and trans. A. Ghizzardi. *Il bimestre*, nos. 22–23 (September–December 1972): 1–4. Citations from *DE*, 2:369–380.

———. "La prose d'Actéon." *Nouvelle revue française*, no. 135 (March 1964): 444–459. Citations from *DE*, 1:326–337.

———. "La psychologie de 1850 à 1950." In *Histoire de la philosophie européene*, vol. 2, *Tableau de la philosophie contemporaine*, ed. Alfred Weber and Denis Huisman, 591–606. Paris: Fischbacher, 1957. Citations from *DE* 1:120–137.

———. "Qu'est-ce que les Lumières? " In *DE*, 4:562–578. An English version appeared first as "What Is Enlightenment?," in *The Foucault Reader*, ed. P. Rabinow, 32–50. New York: Pantheon, 1984.

———. "Qui êtes-vous, professor Foucault?" [Che cos'é Lei Professore Foucault?]. Interview with P. Caruso. In *Conversazioni con Claude Lévi-Strauss, Michel Foucault, Jacques Lacan*, 91–131. Milan: Mursia, 1969. Citations from *DE*, 1:601–620.

———. "Les rapports de pouvoir passent à l'intérieur des corps." Interview with Lucette Finas. *Le quinzaine littéraire*, no. 247 (January 1–15, 1977): 4–6. Citations from *DE*, 3:228–236.

———. "La recherche scientifique et la psychologie." In *Des chercheurs français s'interrogent: Orientation et organisation du travail scientifique en France*, ed. Jean-Édouard Morère, 173–201. Toulouse: Privat, 1957. Citations from *DE*, 1:137–158.

———. *Religion and Culture*. Edited by Jeremy R. Carrette. New York: Routledge, 1999.

———. "Réponse à une question." *Esprit*, no. 371 (May 1968): 850–874. Citations from *DE*, 1:673–695.

———. "Le retour de la morale." Interview with Gilles Barbedette and André Scala. *Les nouvelles littéraires*, no. 2937 (June 28–July 5, 1984): 36–41. Citations from *DE*, 4:696–707.

———. "La scène de la philosophie" [Tetsugaku no butai]. Interview with Moriaki Watanabe. *Sekai*, no. 394 (July 1978): 312–332. Citations from *DE*, 3:571–595.

———. *Sécurité, territoire, population: Cours au Collège de France, 1977–1978*. Edited by Michel Senellart under the direction of François Ewald and Alessandro Fontana. Paris: Gallimard / Seuil, 2004.

———. "Sexual Choice, Sexual Act." Interview with J. O'Higgins. *Salmagundi*, nos. 58–59 (Autumn–Winter 1982): 10–24. Citations from *DE*, 4:320–335.

———. "Sexualité et pouvoir." In *DE*, 3:552–570.

———. "Sexuality and Solitude." In Foucault, *Religion and Culture*, 182–187. Citations from *DE*, 4:168–178.

———. "Le souci de la vérité." Interview with François Ewald. *Magazine littéraire*, no. 207 (May 1984): 18–23. Citations from *DE*, 4:668–678.

———. "Le style de l'histoire." Interview with Arlette Farge and others. *Le matin*, no. 2168 (February 21, 1984): 20–21. Citations from *DE*, 4:649–655.

———. "Le sujet et le livre." Transcription by Frédéric Gros of an unpublished manuscript from April 1966. *Les cahiers de L'Herne* 95: *Michel Foucault* (2011): 70–91.

———. "Sur l'archéologie des sciences: Réponse au Cercle d'épistémologie." *Cahiers pour l'analyse*, no. 9: *Généalogie des sciences* (Summer 1968): 9–40. Citations from *DE*, 1:696–731.

———. "Sur les façons d'écrire l'histoire." Interview with Raymond Bellour. *Les lettres françaises*, no. 1187 (June 15–21, 1967): 6–9. Citations from *DE*, 1:585–600.

———. *Surveiller et punir: Naissance de la prison*. Paris: Gallimard, 1975.

———. *Technologies of the Self: A Seminar with Michel Foucault*. Edited by Luther H. Martin, Huck Gutman, and Patrick H. Hutton. Amherst: University of Massachusetts Press, 1988.

———. "Theatrum philosophicum." *Critique*, no. 282 (November 1970): 885–908. Citations from *DE*, 2:75–99.

———. "Le triomphe social du plaisir sexuel: Une conversation avec Michel Foucault." Interview with Gilles Barbedette. In *DE*, 4: 308–314. The interview was conducted in French but first appeared in English as "The Social Triumph of the Sexual Will," *Christopher Street* 6, no. 4 (May 1982): 36–41.

———. "Un si cruel savoir." *Critique*, no. 182 (July 1962): 597–611. Citations from *DE*, 1:215–228.

———. "Le vrai sexe." *Arcadie*, no. 323 (November 1980): 617–625. Citations from *DE*, 4:115–123. This is a somewhat fuller version of the text that appeared as the introduction to the English edition: *Herculine Barbin: Being the Recently Discovered Memoirs of a Nineteenth Century French Hermaphrodite*. New York: Pantheon Books, 1980.

Gheerbrant, Alain, and Léon Aichelbaum. *K éditeur*. Cognac: Le Temps qu'il fait, 1991.

Gracq, Julien. *Oeuvres complètes*. Paris: Gallimard, 1995.

———. *The Opposing Shore*. Translated by Richard Howard. New York: Columbia University Press, 1986.

Guibert, Hervé. *À l'ami qui ne m'a pas sauvé la vie*. Paris: Gallimard, 1990.

———. *Le mausolée des amants: Journal, 1976–1991*. Paris: Gallimard, 2001.

———. "Les secrets d'un homme." In *Mauve le vierge*, 101–111. Paris: Gallimard, 1986.

Hadot, Pierre. *Exercises spirituels et philosophie antique*. Preface by Arnold I. Davidson. Rev. ed. Paris: Albin Michel, 2002.

Hall, Stuart, ed. *Representation: Cultural Representations and Signifying Practices*. London: Sage Publications for the Open University, 1977.

Halperin, David M. *How to Do the History of Homosexuality*. Chicago: University of Chicago Press, 2002.

———. "Michel Foucault, Jean Le Bitoux, and the Gay Science Lost and Found: An Introduction." *Critical Inquiry* 37, no. 3 (Spring 2011): 371–380.

———. *Saint Foucault: Towards a Gay Hagiography*. New York: Oxford University Press, 1995.

Hart, Kevin. *The Dark Gaze: Maurice Blanchot and the Sacred*. Chicago: University of Chicago Press, 2004.

Henri-Lévy, Bernard. *Les aventures de la liberté: Une histoire subjective des intellectuels*. Paris: Bernard Grasset, 1991.

Hollier, Denis. *Le Collège de sociologie, 1937–1939*. Paris: Gallimard, 1995.

Huffer, Lynne. *Mad for Foucault: Rethinking the Foundations of Queer Theory*. New York: Columbia University Press, 2010.

James, Henry. "The Death of the Lion." In *Complete Stories: 1892–1898*, ed. David Bromwich and John Hollander, 356–392. New York: Library of America, 1996.

Jarry, Alfred. *Oeuvres complètes*. Edited by Michel Arrivé. Paris: Gallimard, 1972.

Jerome. *Epistule*. Edited by Isidor Hilberg. 2nd ed. Corpus Scriptorum Ecclesiasticorum Latinorum, vols. 54–56. Vienna: Verlag der Österreichischen Akademie der Wissenschaften, 1996.

Kelly, Van. "Passages beyond Resistance: René Char's *Seules demeurent* and Its Harmonies in Semprun and Foucault." *SubStance* 32, no. 3 (issue no. 102) (2003): 109–131.

Kierkegaard, Søren. *Søren Kierkegaard's Journals and Papers*. Edited by H. V. Hong and E. H. Hong, with Gregor Malantschuk. Bloomington: Indiana University Press, 1967–1978.

Klossowski, Pierre. *Le bain de Diane*. Paris: J.-J. Pauvert, 1956. Reprint, Paris: Gallimard, 1980. Illustration cited from the J.-J. Pauvert edition. Text citations from the Gallimard edition.

———. *Origines cultuelles et mythiques d'un certain comportement des dames romaines*. Ste-Croix-de-Quintillargues, France: Fata Morgana, 1968.

————. *Pierre Klossowski*. Preface by Nicole d'Huart. Gand: Ludion, 1996.

————. "Sade et Fourier." In *Les derniers travaux de Gulliver, suivi de Sade et Fourier*, 31–77. Montpellier, France: Fata Morgana, 1974.

————. *Sade, mon prochain*. Paris: Seuil, 1947.

————. *Un si funeste désir*. Paris: Gallimard, 1963.

Kojève, Alexandre. *Introduction à la lecture de Hegel*. Edited by Raymond Queneau. Paris: Gallimard, 1947.

Lawrence, D. H. "*A propos* of Lady Chatterley's Lover." In *Lady Chatterley's Lover; A Propos of Lady Chatterley's Lover*, ed. Michael Squires, 303–335. Cambridge: Cambridge University Press, 1993.

Lidell, Henry George, and Robert Scott. *Greek-English Lexicon, with a Revised Supplement*. Revised by Henry Stuart Jones with Roderick McKenzie. Oxford: Clarendon Press, 1996.

Lindon, Mathieu. *Ce qu'aimer veut dire*. Paris: POL, 2011.

————. "Rue de Vaugirard." Interview with Philippe Artières. *Les cahiers de L'Herne* 95: *Michel Foucault* (2011): 65–68.

Macey, David. *The Lives of Michel Foucault: A Biography*. New York: Pantheon Books, 1993.

Mains, Geoff. *Urban Aboriginals: A Celebration of Leathersexuality*. Preface by Mark Thompson. 20th anniversary ed. Los Angeles: Daedalus Publishing, 2002.

Mauriac, Claude. *Mauriac et fils*. Temps Immobile, 9. Paris: B. Grasset, 1986.

McGushin, Edward F. *Foucault's Askêsis: An Introduction to the Philosophical Life*. Evanston, IL: Northwestern University Press, 2007.

Megill, Allan. *Prophets of Extremity: Nietzsche, Heidegger, Foucault, Derrida*. Berkeley: University of California Press, 1987.

Migne, Jacques-Paul, ed. *Patrologiae cursus completa . . . Series Graeca*. Paris: Migne, 1857–1866.

Miller, James. *The Passion of Michel Foucault*. New York: Simon and Schuster, 1993.

Natanson, Thadée. "Estampes d'Outamaro et de Hiroshigé." *Revue blanche*, n.s., 4, no. 1 (1893): 139–145.

Nehamas, Alexander. *The Art of Living*. Sather Classical Lectures 61. Berkeley: University of California Press, 1998.

Nietzsche, Friedrich. *Le gai savoir*. Translated by Pierre Klossowski. Paris: Club Français du Livre, 1956.

————. *Sämtliche Werke: Kritische Studienausgabe*. Edited by Giorgio Colli and Mazzino Montinari. 2nd ed. Munich: DTV, 1988.

Norton, Rictor. *The Myth of the Modern Homosexual: Queer History and the Search for Cultural Unity*. London: Cassell, 1997.

O'Leary, Timothy. *Foucault and Fiction: The Experience Book*. London: Continuum, 2009.

————. *Foucault and the Art of Ethics*. London: Continuum, 2002.

Paglia, Camille. *Vamps and Tramps*. New York: Vintage Books, 1994.

Pinguet, Maurice. "Les années d'apprentissage." *Le débat*, no. 41 (1986): 122–131.

Privitera, Walter. *Problems of Style: Michel Foucault's Epistemology.* Translated by Jean Keller. Albany: SUNY Press, 1995.

Quinodoz, Jean-Michel. "How Translations of Freud's Writings Have Influenced French Psychoanalytic Thinking." *International Journal of Psychoanalysis* 91, no. 4 (August 2010): 695–716.

Rabinow, Paul. "Foucault's Untimely Struggle: Toward a Form of Spirituality." *Theory, Culture & Society* 26, no. 6 (2009): 25–44.

Rajchman, John. *Michel Foucault: The Freedom of Philosophy.* New York: Columbia University Press, 1985.

Richlin, Amy. "Foucault's *History of Sexuality*: A Useful Theory for Women?" In *Rethinking Sexuality: Foucault and Classical Antiquity*, ed. David H. J. Larmour, Paul Allen Miller, and Charles Platters, 138–170. Princeton, NJ: Princeton University Press, 1997.

Sluga, Hans. "Foucault à Berkeley: L'auteur et le discours." Translated by Jean-François Roberts. *Critique*, nos. 471–472 (August–September 1986): 840–856.

Sontag, Susan. *Against Interpretation.* New York: Farrar, Straus and Giroux, 1966.

Surya, Michel. *Georges Bataille: An Intellectual Biography.* London: Verso, 2002.

Sweedler, Milo. *The Dismembered Community: Bataille, Blanchot, Leiris and the Remains of Laure.* Newark: University of Delaware Press, 2009.

Tanke, Joseph J. *Foucault's Philosophy of Art: A Genealogy of Modernity.* London: Continuum, 2009.

Voeltzel, Thierry. "Souvenirs de voyage." Interview with Philippe Artières. In *Les cahiers de L'Herne* 95: *Michel Foucault* (2011): 57–62.

———. *Vingt ans et après.* Edited by Mireille Davidovici. Paris: Bernard Grasset, 1978.

White, Hayden. *The Content of the Form: Narrative Discourse and Historical Representation.* Baltimore: Johns Hopkins University Press, 1987.

Wittman, Carl. "Refugees from Amerika: A Gay Manifesto." *San Francisco Free Press*, December 22, 1969–January 7, 1970, 3–5.

Abbé C (Bataille), 24
abnormals/abnormalities: bodily
    resistance to discipline of, 85, 87–91;
    Christian confession's contribution to
    regulation of, 85–91; Christian pastoral
    practice adopted for discipline of, 85,
    86–87, 104–8; demonic possessions
    at Loudun in relation to, 87–90, 164;
    Foucault's lecture series on, 65–67;
    instinct as crucial category of, 74–75;
    "problem of sexuality" and, 85–86, 91,
    144; psychiatric reports on, 65–66, 67;
    reproduction as matrix for, 85; speech
    used to define sexual, 85, 86. *See also*
    Norm/normalizing; perversions;
    sexual morality
Abnormals (Foucault), 101, 113, 134, 164
"About the Beginning of the Hermeneutic
    of the Self" (Foucault), 170
accusation: Nietzsche's against Socrates,
    187; Creusa's rape and, 181–83; origin
    of truth telling in accusation of rape,
    183–84; truth-telling form of, 181
Acéphale (periodical): linking Bataille
    and Klossowski, 25; "Note about the
    Founding of a College of Sociology"
    in, 25–26
act of knowing, 173

"Âge cassant" (Char), 163
AIDS: Foucault's death due to, 193;
    stigma of, 198
Alcibiades, 156, 173
Alcibiades (Plato), 186, 187
alèthurgie, 133
alethurgy: counter-examples absorbed
    by notion of, 135; distinction between
    technical expertise for governing and,
    134; *exomologêsis* as ritual of, 135, 136–
    37, 138, 139, 141; Foucault using "the
    ritual" of, 180; liturgy of truth and, 133,
    135; verification of truth element of, 135
anatomo-politics of the body and power,
    113
ancient erotics: Christian spiritual direc-
    tion evolving from, 180; Foucault's
    examination of, 180–86; male-male,
    181. *See also* erotic stylization
anonymity, 153
anonymous speaker, 6–7, 145
Anthony the Great (saint), 139
antiquity. *See* Greco-Roman antiquity
aphrodisia, 145
Apollo: "Ariadne's Lament" as cry
    against, 182–83; Foucault's reading of
    Ion on, 181–86; oracle speaking truth in
    name of , 181

Apollon sonore (Dumézil), 181–82
Archeology of Knowledge (Foucault), 10, 37
"Ariadne's Lament" (Nietzsche), 182–83
Ariès, Phillipe, 152–53
Aristotle, 109
ars erotica: "ars theoretica, ars politica" and, 112; Foucault's language and, 111–12; *scientia sexualis* and, 124, 145–46, 150. *See also* stylization
art: antiquity's erotic problematization and, 154; style compared to, 154; *technê* and, 111–12, 154; Western philosophy on meaning of, 154. *See also ars erotica*, stylization
Artaud, Antonin: against a stable "I," 34; canon of "mad" writers includes, 14; cry in, 36, 190; Foucault eventually counts as exemplar, 38–39, 190; "suffering of flesh" in, 37–38
Artemidorus Daldianus, 160
"arts of existence," 150
asceticism, 190–91
Asclepius, 169, 173, 187
Ashbee, Harold Spence, 96
Athanasius (saint), 139
Athena, 181, 182
Augustine (saint), 166
Austin, J. L., 139
authors: aiming to produce the last book ever, 200; anonymity and, 6–7, 145; fandom and, 2–4; James's plea for closeting, 3; Kant on public and, 177, 178; Masked Philosopher on writing and, 5–7; reader's desire for body of, 2, 193; shared authorial processes in Sade, Fourier, and Loyola, 58. *See also* reading; writing

Bachelard, Gaston, 110
Baltard, Victor, 55
Balzac-type novel (in Blanchot), 36
Barthes, Roland, 58, 111
Bataille, Georges: *Acéphale* as collaboration of Klossowski and, 25; Foucault treats alongside Klossowski and Blanchot, 14–15, 33; Foucault's "Preface to Transgression" on, 15,

19–24, 27; Foucault's teacher of writing, 1; language to describe truth, 134; Nietzsche and, 14; prefaces to his own works, 20; relocation of the sacred registered by, 24–25; reversed eye in, 22. *See also* "Preface to Transgression" (Foucault)
Bataille titles: *Abbé C*, 24; *Bleu du ciel*, 23; *Inner Experience*, 21; *Madame Edwarda*, 20; *Story of the Eye*, 24
Bath of Diana (Klossowski): contradictory female-divine of, 31–32; refracting Christian terms, 30–31; restaging Ovid's version, 27; surveying Klossowski's corpus through, 27–32
Baudelaire, Charles: Benjamin's studies of, 154–55; dandy in, 155–57; modern Cynicism of, 188; modernity described by, 156–57; "Painter of Modern Life" by, 155
Benedict's *Rule*, 132
Benjamin, Walter: Baudelaire's dandy in, 155–57; Fourier's influence on, 58; "On Some Motifs in Baudelaire" by, 155; "Paris of the Second Empire in Baudelaire" by, 155; studies of Baudelaire by, 154–56
Bentham, Jeremy: Panopticon in, 54–55, 57–61, 164; penal reform proposed by, 57–58
Beyond Good and Evil (Nietzsche), 7, 73, 183
Binswanger, Ludwig, 153
"biopolitics," 113
biopower: analysis using security, territory, population, 127; anatomo-politics and cultivation of the species, 113; biomechanical and mechanical metaphors for, 75–77, 113; "normal" and the "pathological" as categories of, 117; prescription for writing in, 185; role of sexuality in, 114–15; three functions of sex within, 113–14
Birth of the Clinic (Foucault): *Discipline and Punish* and, 42–44; epochs of bodily description in, 42; gaze in, 42; Guibert's "Secrets of a Man" as retelling of, 198

Blanchot, Maurice: comparing Foucault to himself, 38; contestation in, 22; distinguishing two sorts of novels, 36–37; "experience of the outside" in, 34-35; Foucault linking to Bataille and Klossowski, 14–15, 33; Foucault's teacher of writing, 1; language described by, 33; "I speak" in, 34, 35–36. *See also* "Experience of the Outside" (Foucault)

blason, 176

Bleu du ciel (Bataille), 23

bodies: anatomo-politics and the cultivation of the species, 113; authorization to write about other, 184–85; *Birth of the Clinic's* on descriptions of, 42; Blanchot on novels and, 36; Christianity's archives overwrite, 197; control of ideas for submission of, 50; difference between speech and, 185; different forms of power associated with, 3–4; *Discipline and Punish* on bodily responses under duress, 42, 44; Eucharistic body of Christ, 55; Fabiola's public penance and, 136–37, 138, 139, 141, 142; flesh as instrument of Christian power, 88; Foucault on mortal body as event, 200; Foucault's interest in theatrical, 37-38, 140-41; Foucault's interest in truth manifested by, 135; Foucault's portrayal of convulsive, 183–84; Foucault's proposed "history of," 114; Foucault on transformation of subjected, 3–4, 38–39, 45, 138–39, 199; governmentality as applicable to living, 129; Guibert's *To the Friend* on death as experienced by, 194–96; historical reassignment of crime to money from, 48; *History of Madness* about sounds of missing, 13; hope for ethical transformation in scandalous, 199; instability and multiple forms of language about, 44; James's "Death of the Lion" on the author's, 2–3, 4; "living body of philosophy," 149; medical language on, 42–44; "micro-physics" of, 45;

Panopticon's control over, 54, 57–58, 61; paradoxes of Greek pedagogies for, 174; *quadrillage* and, 48, 49, 164; religious speeches and rituals for, 10; resistance to discipline through, 85, 87–91; soul as prison of, 45; space of enacted transformation in, 138–39; spirituality and emphasis on, 172–73; stylization of, 146; symbolic relationship between sin and, 142. *See also* "convulsive flesh," cry/cries; embodied lives; "flesh"

Brown, Peter, 152, 153

Burckhardt, Johann Ludwig, 154-55

Canguilhem, Georges, 110

canon law: Foucault on multiplication of perversions in, 104–8; Zacchia's summary of madness and, 84. *See also* Christian moralities/ethics

Carthage, 155

Catholic Church: Counter-Reformation of the, 84, 119, 132; Eucharistic body of Christ in the, 55; Foucault's fascination with topics related to, 197; Foucault's upbringing in the, 196; Jesus's crucifixion (*supplice*) as presented by, 46–47; liturgical calendars and practice of the, 57; modern forms of mysticism of, 87; Vatican II reform of, 132. *See also* Christian churches; Christian confessional practices

Catiline, 156

Certeau, Michel de: Foucault's reading of, 87–88; *Possession of Loudun* by, 87–91; tragicomedy of the Loudun possessions in, 90

Char, René, 48, 163

chastity of elephants, 166

chrêsis aphrodisiôn, 154

Christian Brothers, 196

Christian churches: five counter-conducts driving ecclesiastical history into modernity, 139–40; tensions within, 139. *See also* Catholic Church

Christian codes: contrasting dandyism with, 156; Foucault on multiplication of perversions by, 104–8; marriage chastity in, 158; Zacchia's summary of madness and, 84. *See also* Christian moralities/ethics

Christian confessional lessons: on bodies as site for resistance to discipline, 85, 87–91; on contribution of pastoral practice to modern disciplinarity, 85, 86–87; on sex and speech, 85–86

Christian confessional practices: Counter-Reformation, 84; for declaring an act of sin, 136; *exagoreusis* form of, 135–36, 137, 138, 139; *exomologêsis* form of, 135, 136–37, 138, 139, 141; Fabiola's public penance, 136–37, 138, 139, 141, 142; Foucault's lectures on truth telling and, 132–39, 179–80; proliferation of sexual sin in, 117; reform after the Council of Trent, 84, 104; "speech act" of, 139; three lessons applied to abnormality from, 85–91; truth telling and different versions of, 132–39, 179–80, 181; *veridiction* of, 135. *See also* Catholic Church; Christian speech; confession; rituals

Christianity: continuities between antiquity and, 166–67; contribution to modern forensic psychiatry by, 85; counter-conducts within, 131; Cynicism and, 188; dandyism contrasted with codes of, 156; differences between Israelite notions and, 129–30; doubling and verbalization rooted in, 137–38; epistemological and ontological poles of, 140, 190–91; ethical codes found within, 4; "flesh" as form of power in, 88; Foucault on risks of historiography of, 83–84; Foucault's preoccupation with, 8–10; Foucault on its principles for reading religious signs, 175–76; Gospel of Luke's manger scene, 83–84; governmentality and obedience in, 130–31; *History of Sexuality 2* on changes to sexuality made by, 160–67; history of sexuality and role of, 103–5; Jesus's crucifixion and, 46–47; Judaism's relationship to, 177; judgment after death

in, 196; judicial torture performed at sites of, 46; justifying torture, 46; Klossowski's juxtaposition of pagan theophany with, 30–31; overwriting bodies through records of rituals, 197; *parrhesia* in, 190; pastoral practices as forms of control, 85–86, 104–8; penal reform adopting practices from, 51–52, 57; personifications of, 84–87; religion of backsliders, 136; self-sacrifice in, 138, 140; sexuality arising from space cleared by, 113; understanding Foucault's writings about, 120–22. *See also* religion

Christian moralities/ethics: chastity of elephants as example in, 166; continuities between antiquity and, 166–67; contrasts between sexuality and earlier, 104–5; Cynics as alternative to, 190; distinguished by mechanisms of power, 125. *See also* canon law; Christian codes; moral problematization; religious moralities

Christian mysticism: Blanchot's writing contrasted with, 35; French association of spirituality with, 172; modern forms of Catholic, 87; modern survival of, 190–91

Christian pastoral power: characterizations in context of history of sexuality, 125, 126–27; comparing practices of Greco-Roman antiquity and, 125–26; Counter-Reformation and, 84, 119; "flesh" as form of, 88; four characteristics of, 129; homosexuality in modern sexuality and, 107; influential codes of religious ethics and, 4; prelude to governmentality, 126–32; shepherd in, 125; styles of, 130; tracing the shape of, 129–30. *See also* power

Christian pastoral practices: adopted for discipline of abnormalities, 85, 86–87; crises of, 118–32; modern subjectivity arising from, 122–23; pastoral care for sex before modern versions of, 119–24; project of sexuality and, 104–8; spiritual exercises and, 171

Christian speech: confession as "speech act," 139; contrasted with sexuality, 105; modern triumph over bodily act by, 140. *See also* Christian confessional practices

Christian spiritual direction: ancient pedagogy and, 108; understood as form of truth telling, 180, 186

Christmas story: Foucault's parody of the, 83; Gospel of Luke's manger scene, 83–84

circular memory, 102

citizen speech, 182

civil law: contemporary expansion of, 127; homosexuality and sodomy in, 105–8; medicalized characters under, 105-06; space between medicine and, 107

codes: canon law, 84, 104–8; Christian ethical, 4; Christian pastoral practices, 85, 86–87, 104–8; contemporary expansion of, 127; dandyism and Christian, 156; ethics-oriented moralities and moralities of, 150–51; Foucault's fondness for writing about, 111; *History of Sexuality* and, 104–8, 111; included in history of morality, 150; moral problematization in absence of, 149–52; shift across European codes from boys to women to children, 161; style of life beyond, 153–54; *S/Z* (Barthes) on breaking text into different, 111

Collège de France: Foucault's appointment to, 63; Foucault's lectures series at, 63, 98; free academic space of, 64. *See also* Foucault lectures (Collège de France)

College of Sociology: founding of, 25–26; split over theoretical disagreements, 26

comic power: Certeau on oscillation between fear and, 91; expert opinion and, 67; Gracq on official formulas and, 79; *King Ubu* undoing conventions of embodiment through, 69–71, 72, 90

Communist Party (France), 196

confession: Creusa's transit from cry to, 181–83, 185, 191; *exomologêsis* form of,

135, 136–37, 138, 139, 141; "speech act" of, 139, 181; truth telling and different versions of, 132–39, 179–80, 181. *See also* Christian confessional practices

connaissance and *savoir*, 177–78

contestation (in Blanchot), 22

convulsive flesh: Creusa and, 183; Fabiola's public penance and her, 136–37, 138, 139, 141, 142; female gendering of, 183–84; Foucault's piety when writing about, 199; philosophical theater as space for, 190; resistance through, 86, 87–91; stylized for Christian paradox of permanent change, 142; *supplice* of, 89–90; Ursuline nuns performing, 87–89, 164. *See also* bodies; "flesh"

Council of Trent, 84, 104

counter-conducts (in Christianity), 131

Counter-Reformation, 84, 119, 132

Crates (philosopher), 189

Crébillon, Claude Prosper Jolyot de, 70

Creusa (in *Ion*): convulsing body of, 183; Cynic's transmutation of, 189–90; rape brought to speech by, 181–83, 185, 191; transit from cry to confession by, 185, 191

crime: Fourierist view of petty, 59; historical move from bodies to money, 48; prisons meant to control by redescribing, 56; public torture punishment for, 41, 44, 46, 49; rape as, 181–86. *See also* Delinquent; penal reform; violence

Critique (journal), 15

Critique of Pure Reason (Kant), 109

crucifixion as *supplice*, 46–47

cry/cries: "Ariadne's Lament" narrating, 182–83; authorization for writing about others', 184–85; Creusa's, 182, 189–90, 191; Cynicism written as, 191–92; elements of a ritual, 182; transit to speech from, 185, 191. *See also* bodies

culture: madness excluded in order to constitute modern, 16–17; Reason and Madness as distinguished by, 15–16

Cynics/Cynicism: alternative to Christian morality, 190; another form of truth

telling, 186–90; associated with *bios*, 191; contrast between Platonist and, 191; description of bodily behaviors of, 188–89; gender expectations inverted by, 189; King Ubu's connection to, 189; modern legacy of, 188, 191
Cyprian (saint), 132

Damiens, Robert-François, 41, 44, 46, 49
dandyism: Benjamin's study of Baudelaire and his, 155–57; characteristics of, 156 Christian codes and, 156
Davenport, Guy, 1
death: Christianity on judgment following, 196; Guibert's *To the Friend* on, 194–96; of Michel Foucault, 193
death of God: language following the Nietzschean, 33; liberating language to speak its empty non-self, 35; "Preface to Transgression" on sexuality's link to, 21, 23–24. *See also* Nietzsche
"Death of the Lion" (James), 2–3
Defert, Daniel, 121, 199
Delacampagne, Christian, 4–5
Delinquent: correlation between power and, 55–56; individual in detention as, 105–6; template for forming individuals, 56. *See also* crime; *homo criminalis*
Delphic oracle, 181
democracy: citizen speech of, 182; *Ion* on passage from political truth telling to, 185–86; philosophy made possible by, 182
demonic possession: Certeau's description of, 87, 88–91; early modern phenomenon of, 87; Loudon convent as site of, 87–90, 164; Surin's exchange with Jeanne des Anges during her, 90; witchcraft contrasted with, 87
démonstration, 76
Derrida, Jacques, 19
Desire–Knowledge contrast, 70
Diderot, Denis, 97–99
Diogenes Laertius, 123
Diogenes's bird calls, 189, 190
Dionysus, 29
Dionysus Dithyrambs (Nietzsche), 182

disciplinary society, 59
discipline: Bentham's Panopticon and, 54–55, 57–61; bodies as site for resistance to, 85, 87–91; Delinquent and, 55–56, 105–6; measured within a specific space, 53; normalizing function of, 53–54; without *oripeaux*, 134. *See also* punishment
Discipline and Punish (Foucault): allegory of city in, 51; "austere institutions," 116; *Birth of the Clinic* and, 42–44; church practice of making liturgical calendars in, 57; correlating power and Delinquent as subject, 55–56, 105–6; correlative history of modern soul and new power to judge as topic of, 102–3; doubling the subject of law as *homo criminalis* in, 137–38; *exagoreusis* connected with language of, 135–36, 137, 138, 139; Foucault's four "general rules" for study of, 45; Fourierists and utopian communities cited by, 57–62; history of mutations of punishment narrated by, 47–52, 102–3; I here interrupt footnote ending, 61–62, 65, 103; modern prison reform's treatment of body and soul in, 44–47; opening with the public torture of Damiens, 41, 44, 46, 49; Parisian reformatory rules excerpted in, 41–42; process of historiography in, 128–29; punishment as sign in, 50–52; punishment without *oripeaux* in, 134; scholarly narcissism parodied by, 61; spatial analogies of power in, 164; story of displacement of bodies told by, 54, 57–58, 61; studying failed utopias, 58; *supplice* analyzed by, 46–47, 48, 50, 65; three stages of punishment and penal reform in, 47–52. *See also* Foucault titles; penal reform
discontinuities: experienced by *History of Sexuality* readers, 143–45; Foucault's interest in moral, 151; mutations of power producing, 148
dispositif: *Discipline and Punish* using military meaning of, 48–49; not included in *History of Sexuality* 2 and 3, 164

divinity: contradictory female-divine, 31–32; Nietzschean mask associated with presentations of, 7; simulacrum as opposite of, 28–29

Dominicans, 27

Dostoyevsky, Fyodor, 15

doubling: claim of a Christian origin for verbalization and, 137–38; complexities of in Christian confessional practice, 138–39; instrument of both control and undoing, 138; marriage and "double sexual monopoly" as form of, 158; modern soul as new form of power and, 164; positing a perversion behind certain sexual acts through, 106; subject of law as *homo criminalis* created by, 137. *See also* Foucault's writing

dramatourgia, 133

dream interpretation, 160

Dumézil, Georges, 10, 169–70, 181–82, 187

Durkheim, Émile, 10

"earnestness," 147

Égarement (Crébillon), 70

embodied lives: challenge of writing responsibly about, 4; Foucault's warning on writing about, 3; Nietzsche as tragedian of, 181. *See also* bodies

en pointillé, 94

epimeleia, 187

epistemological Christianity, 140, 190

erotic stylization, 158–60. *See also* ancient erotics

ethics-oriented moralities, 150–51

Eucharistic body of Christ, 55

Euripides, 181–86

"eventual reader," 6

exagoreusis, 135–36, 137, 138, 139

exomologêsis: as alethurgy of bodily ritual, 136, 141; Fabiola's public penance as dramatization of, 136–37, 138, 139, 141, 142; form of confession and, 135, 138; wordless enactment of, 139

exorcisms, 87–88

experience: three "theoretical shifts" required to attend to, 176–79

"Experience of the Outside" (Foucault):

Blanchot's "I speak" in, 34, 35–36; culmination of Foucault's essays on models for writing about the divine, 33–34; warning that Blanchot's writing is not a negative theology, 35. *See also* Blanchot, Maurice

expert opinions: capacity for provoking laughter, 67; Foucault's lectures as seeming to reinforce his own, 77; function of in psychiatry of delinquency, 106; "homosexual" personified by, 66; normalizing psychiatric power of, 71–72; psychiatric profile (1955) in murder trial, 65–66, 67; psychiatric profile (1974) in blackmail trial, 65, 66–67; scientific authority brought into courtrooms by, 67; three features of, 67; "Ubu-esque," 67

"expiation," 53

Fabiola's public penance, 136–37, 138, 139, 141, 142

fantasies: city-as-allegory, 51; of penal reform power without *oripeaux*, 134; translated by the dandy into action, 155–56

fascism, 25

fiction: Foucault's "fictional use" of archival material, 80; politics of, 81; "problem of," 81

First Analytics (Aristotle), 109

"flesh": deployed as instrument by Christian power, 88; Fabiola's public penance through, 136–37, 138, 139, 141, 142; posited as source of sin, 125; space of enacted transformation in, 3–4, 38–39, 45, 138–39; speaking the self in relation to, 126. *See also* bodies; "convulsive flesh"

footnotes: *Discipline and Punish* and "I here interrupt," 61–62, 65, 103; *History of Madness* on poetic rule from Char, 18; *History of Sexuality 1* on promised volumes, 101; *History of Sexuality 2* on certain arts of existence, 154. *See also* Foucault's writing

forensic psychiatry: Christian pastorate's contribution to, 85; "normal" and "pathological" as categories of, 117; *scientia sexualis* animated by, 108, 116. *See also* medical power

"Formal Partition" (Char), 18

forms: comic, 69; constituting the subject through, 178; distinguishing in knowledge between content and, 178; Foucault's essays as experiments in, 15, 32; Foucault's study of history in pursuit of, 170–76; learned by Foucault from music, 1; Reason and, 18; theatrical, 37; truth telling and form of life, 187–88. *See also* power forms

"Foucauldian" genre, 144

Foucault lectures: "About the Beginning of the Hermeneutic of the Self," 170; Catholic University of Louvain, 123; differences between his Collège de France lectures and other, 123; erotic presented in, 179–80; Foucault on the themes used in his, 176; Foucault on "the ritual of the alethurgy" in his, 180; *omnes et singulatim* as title at Stanford, 125; on Kant at Berkeley, 156–57; "On Other Spaces,"165; Proustian style of last lecture series, 179; Tanner Lectures at Stanford, 122; Tokyo University, 122, 124, 125–26, 145–46; University of Vermont, 123, 133; various locations of, 133

Foucault lectures (Collège de France): *Abnormals*, 101, 113, 134, 164; Christian pastoral power and governmentality in, 126–32; Christian personifications and history of confession in, 84–87; differences between his other lectures and those at the Collège, 123; erotic presented in, 179–80; Foucault on the themes used in, 176; Foucault on "the ritual of the alethurgy" in, 180; Foucault's authorial voice during, 64; Foucault's reflections on his situation at, 64–65; "Hermeneutic of the Subject," 170–78; limitations of the published versions of, 63–64; "On the Government of the Living," 122, 132–

39; performing academic power, 82; reinforcing Foucault's expert speech, 77; "Security, Territory, Population," 126–32; *supplice* as analogy for, 65. *See also* Collège de France

Foucault, Michel: antireligious leanings of, 196–97; Blanchot's comparison between himself and, 38; born into Catholic family, 196; brief membership in Communist Party of, 196; claim about his remarks on "death of the author," 4; Collège de France appointment of, 63; contradictions of standard versions of history by, 81, 123–24; controversy over Guibert's *To the Friend* and, 194–96; death from AIDS, 193; describing himself as "negative theoretician," 121; describing mortal body as event, 200; education of, 196–97; examination of Christian texts after *History of Sexuality 1*, 119–24, 132; examining charge of misogyny against, 184–85; "Greco-Latin trip" taken by, 170; inner circle at memorial of, 197, 199; "Masked Philosopher" as teasing figure for, 4–7; pleasure produced from reading, 3; reader of ancient philosophy, 169–70; Richlin's criticism of, 143; "seconds of satisfaction" at completion of writing by, 200; unrestrained curiosity of, 169, 197

Foucault's writing: against gender expectations, 184; Catholic topics in, 197; charge of misogyny and, 184–85; comparing Gracq's novel and power epics of, 80; contradictions of standard history by, 81, 123–24; deliberate variation of metaphors in, 74; engaged in *ethopoiêsis*, 199; footnote convention in, 61–62, 65, 103; Foucault's reflections on his situation element of, 64–65; games played by, 148–49, 159; genre of, 144; importance of theater in, 140–42; interest in religion and Christianity in, 8–10; "literary period" of, 13–14; Nietzsche's influence on, 1, 9, 98; piety when writing about convulsing bodies, 199;

present philosophy linked to its past by, 148; resistance to father's profession by, 198; "seconds of satisfaction" when completing, 200; speaking as the Masked Philosopher about writing, 5–7; transformation of subjected bodies in, 3–4, 38–39, 45, 138–39, 199; trying to understand Christianity through, 120–22; types of topics in, 37, 197; which he calls the "living body of philosophy," 192. *See also* doubling; footnotes; metaphors; writing

Foucault titles: *Archeology of Knowledge*, 10, 37; *Birth of the Clinic*, 42–44, 198; "Experience of the Outside," 33; *History of Madness*, 13–19, 33, 36–37, 59, 60, 84, 164, 199; *History of Sexuality 3*, 120, 144–52, 160, 162–64, 200; *History of Sexuality 4: Confessions of the Flesh*, 120; *Order of Things*, 10; "Preface to Transgression," 15, 19–24, 27; "Prose of Actaeon," 27–33. *See also Discipline and Punish*; *History of Sexuality 1*; *History of Sexuality 2*

Fourier, Charles, 1, 57, 58

Fourierist utopias, 57–62

Freud, Sigmund: anonymous author of *My Secret Life* compared to, 97; *History of Sexuality 1* appearance of, 144; instinct as understood by, 73–74; "pansexualism" of, 115

Fronto, Marcus Cornelius, 139

games, 148–49, 159

Garden of Eden, 29

gay liberation, 107, 108

Gay Science (Nietzsche), 28, 73

gay style of life, 153

gaze and gazer: *Birth of the Clinic* on, 42; Panopticon and, 54

gender: authorization to write about resisting bodies and, 184–85; Halperin's analysis of deviance from, 107; rape as violence linked to, 181–86; spatial segregation of, 158. *See also* sex

gender expectations: Cynic life inverting, 189; Foucault's writing against, 184

geometrico-logical metaphors, 76

God: absence of, 22; confused with Devil as twin, 28; death of, 21, 22–24, 33, 35

gods/goddesses: *The Bath of Diana* (Klossowski) and myths about, 27–32; Euripides's *Ion* on the, 181–86, 191; oracle of Delphi's "oblique" truth in name of, 181; Socrates's dying request to sacrifice to, 169, 173, 187

Gogh, Vincent van, 14

Good Shepherd. *See* Shepherd

governmentality: art of governing, 128; Christian obedience and, 130–31; Christian pastoral power as prelude to, 126–32; Foucault's history of, 128; Kant on relationships between government and self, 176; levels of application to living bodies, 129; pastoral mutations from Jewish origin to European, 131–32; security, territory, and population as contexts of, 127–32

Gracq, Julien (Louis Poirier): comparing Foucault's language to competing images of power in, 80; distance between official formulas and material realities described by, 79; *Rivage des Syrtes* by, 77–81

Greco-Roman antiquity: comparing Christian pastoral power to that of, 125–26; continuities between Christianity and, 166–67; Foucault's examination of sexuality from, 122; Foucault's "hypotheses" on roots of *scientia sexualis* and, 124–26; Foucault's Tokyo lecture on, 131–32; heterotopia in, 166; Klossowski's *Bath of Diana* taken from, 27–32; modern stylization based on template from, 157; stylization of male-male erotics during, 158–60, 181

Greek philosophy: conception of time in, 175; continuity of spiritual exercises to Ignatius of Loyola from, 171–72; contrast between *parrhesia* and, 180–81; contrast between spirituality and, 171; Foucault's study of, 169–70; Greek erotic metaphors used to describe,

159; paradox of teaching self-care in, 174; pedagogies for decentering the received self in, 173–74. *See also* Western philosophy

Greenblatt, Stephen, 155

Gregory the Great (saint), 132

Gregory of Nyssa (saint), 188

Guibert, Hervé: blurring memoir and fiction, 194; controversy over *To the Friend* by, 194–96, 200; in inner circle of mourners at Foucault's funeral, 197, 199; "The Secrets of a Man" by, 198

Hadot, Pierre, 148, 171–72

Halperin, David, 107

Hegel, Georg Wilhelm Friedrich: *Phenomenology of Spirit* by, 73; Sadean speech opposing moral law demanded by, 34

"Hermeneutic of the Subject" (Foucault), 170–78

heterotopia: Cynicism's "other life" as, 191; distinguished from utopia, 165–66; five characteristics of a, 166; pre-Christian antiquity as, 166–67. *See also* society

hidden battle (metaphor), 60

Hipparchia (philosopher), 189

historiography: Foucault on representations of power in, 82–83; Foucault on risks of hyperbolic personification and, 83–84; Foucault's *History of Madness* and *Discipline and Punish* as shifting assumptions of, 128–29; Foucault's parody of scientific, 83; personification and, 81–84

history: "biopolitics" driving, 113; five counter-conducts pushing ecclesiastical history into modernity, 129–30; Foucault's contradictions of standard versions of, 81, 123–24; Foucault's pursuit of a form for, 170–76; Foucault's "rupture" in style after *History of Sexuality 1* and, 147; French *histoire* both story and, 98; space of, 16–17; storytelling connected to, 98

"history of bodies," 114

History of Madness (Foucault): about the sounds of missing bodies, 13; Char's language in, 19; cultural distinction of Reason and Madness in, 15–18; Derrida's criticism of original preface to, 19; fitting into Blanchot's distinctions of novels, 36–37; footnote on poetic rule from Char, 18; "Formal Partition" and, 18; informed by analysis of disciplinary society, 59; murmuring language of, 33, 60; *partage* as ritual in, 48; Pascal and Dostoyevsky in original preface of, 15; procedure of historiography in, 128–29; on rise of modern category of insanity and its institution, 13–14; spatial analogies of power used in, 164; Zacchia's summary of church law cited by, 84. *See also* madness

History of Sexuality 1 (Foucault): attempt to find language for pre-Christian sexuality, 30; canon law, Christian pastoral practice, and civil law in conception of, 104–8; effects on reader intended by, 108–111; *en pointillé* argument of, 94; five part circular structure of, 101–2; Foucault's examination of Christian texts after writing, 119–24; *Indiscreet Jewels* in, 97–99; interpenetration of present and past in, 102; ironic beginning of, 93–94, 120; "*Longtemps*" copied from Proust in, 96, 102; misunderstood by readers, 93–95; personification of "homosexual" analyzed by, 66; plans for further study of sexuality after, 99–103; pleasure's meaning in, 118; reader frustration by, 145–47; repetition and memory return in, 102; reversing assumptions of gay liberation, 107; "Security, Territory, Population" in relation to, 126–27; sexuality arising from two axes of biopower, 113; style as notion in, 153; subtitles of, 95, 99; three "hypotheses" emerging from, 124–26; title misleading, 98; tracing genealogy of sexuality, 119; will to sexual knowledge as motivating, 99. *See also* Foucault titles; sexuality

History of Sexuality 1 and power analytics: imaginative sediment of earlier forms of power, 109–10; meaning of "analytics" in relation to earlier sources, 109–11; in place of a theory of power, 108–11, 115; power and resistance as dependent on coding, 111; relation of "analytics" to theory and art, 111–12.

History of Sexuality 2 (Foucault): antiquity's moral problematization of sexual activity linked to art, 154; beginning of, 144, 145, 147–49; Char quotation on back cover of, 163–64; compared to volume 1 of series, 120, 144; differences in sexuality attributable to Christianity, 160–63; footnote on certain arts of existence in, 154; later morality present throughout as contrasting future, 162; genealogy of stylization in, 152–57; Lindon's recollection on Foucault's reaction to finishing, 200; male-male sexuality within, 146, 181; moral problematization as question for, 149–52; Platonic valorization at end of, 160; problematization of sexuality and advent of Christianity in, 160–67; problematization of sexuality in antiquity, 157–60; readers' unmet expectations of, 145–47; salience of stylization of male-male sexuality in, 146; subjects of desire across history and, 147–49. *See also* Foucault titles

History of Sexuality 3 (Foucault): Artemidorus and dream interpretation in, 160; ; Char quotation on back cover of, 163–64; compared to volume 1 of series, 120, 144; Foucault's reflections on, 151–52; future morality present throughout, 162; Lindon's recollection of Foucault's finishing, 200; moral problematization and, 149–52; reader frustration and unmet expectations of, 145–47.

History of Sexuality 4: Confessions of the Flesh (Foucault), 120

Hölderlin, Friedrich, 14, 34

homo criminalis, 137–38. *See also* Delinquent

homosexuality: distinction between identities and acts of, 105–8; Foucault's parallel passages on sodomites and, 106–7; "homosexual" personified, 66; liberating language about, 103. *See also* male-male relations

homosexual life style, 153

homosexuals: contrasting the sodomite and, 105–7, 117; personifying homosexuality, 66

Huxley, Aldous, 87

identities: Delinquent, 55–56, 105–6; distinction between homoerotic acts and sexual, 105–8; Foucault's writing mistakenly associated with politics of, 93

Ignatius of Loyola, 171

"I here interrupt" (footnote in *Discipline and Punish*), 61–62, 65, 105

Indiscreet Jewels (Diderot), 97–99

Inner Experience (Bataille), 21

insanity. *See* madness (or insanity)

instinct: crucial psychiatric category, 74–75; Freud's use of, 73–74

Ion (Euripides): characters and plot of, 181; Creusa's rape, accusation, and confession in, 181–83, 185, 191; Dumézil's analysis of, 182; four types of truth telling in, 181–86; showing passage to democracy, 185–86

irony: ancient philosophic teaching and, 147–48; *History of Sexuality* and, 93–94, 120; misread as literal, 93

"I speak" (and Blanchot), 34, 35–36

Israelite notions: comparing Christian and, 129–30; Hebrew solidarity, 130; pastoral transformation of into modern governmentality, 131–32

James, Henry: "Death of the Lion," 2–3, 4; reading the works of, 1

Jarry, Alfred: interest of the Loudun exorcisms to, 90; *King Ubu* by, 68–71, 90, 134–35

Jeanne des Anges, 90

Jerome (saint), 136
Jesus's crucifixion, 46–47
John Chrysostom (saint), 139
Judaism-Christianity relationship, 177
judicial torture: *Discipline and Punish* opening with Damiens', 41, 44, 46; liturgical Christianity justifying, 46–47
Julius Caesar, 156
"juridical subject" (*sujet juridique*), 45

Kant, Immanuel: author's relation to public in, 177, 178; *Critique of Pure Reason* by, 109; Foucault using essay by as *blason*, 176; Foucault's Berkeley lecture (1983) on, 156; Foucault's study of, 176–78; his interest in addressing the reader, 7; his notion of moral law rejected by Sade, 34
Kierkegaard, Søren, 25
King Ubu (Jarry): caricature undoes conventions of embodied power in, 69–71, 72; comic-book violence and slang in, 68–69; compared of Cynics and , 189; likened to tale of the emperor's new clothes, 68; possessions at Loudun compared to, 90; stagecraft of, 68–71, 134–35; Ubu and power without trappings, 134–35
Klossowski, Pierre: *Acéphale* as collaboration of Bataille and, 25; associated with Bataille and Blanchot by Foucault, 14–15, 33; *Bath of Diana* by, 27–32; Foucault's "Prose of Actaeon" on, 27–33; Foucault's teacher of writing, 1; *Gay Science* translated by, 28; reader of Nietzsche, 14; religious biography of, 26–27. *See also* "Prose of Actaeon"
knowledge: Bachelard on imaginative error versus scientific, 110; distinguishing between content and form of, 178; divided into *connaissance* and *savoir*, 177–78; *History of Sexuality* offering knowledge about our, 108–11; language and administrative, 98; self-care and metaphysical, 191; truth attained by act of, 173; will to sexual, 98–99. *See also* power-knowledge

Knowledge–Desire contrast, 70
Kojève, Alexandre, 73

Laches (Plato), 186, 187
languages: *ars erotica*, 111–12; Bataille's circular, 22, 23; Blanchot's description of, 33; Blanchot's "I speak," 34, 35–36; capturing power through multiple, 71, 72–73; failure of, 22–23; Foucault's essays on condition of, 14–15, 33; four operations required for fabricating, 58; Gracq's description of power using competing, 80; instability of references to the body in, 44; medical, 42–43, 105–6; murmuring and, 33, 60; penalties as, 50; sacred as outside of, 36; sexuality produced by, 103. *See also* metaphors; power language; space of language; speech
Lautréamont-type novels, 36
Lawrence, D. H., 115, 144
Laws (Plato), 158
Legman, Harold, 96
leitourgia, 133
liberation: ancient ritual for freeing slave, 174; *History of Sexuality 1* mocking, 173; Seneca on emancipation of self, 174
Lindon, Matthieu, 199, 200
literature: connection between madness and, 14; Foucault on the "problem of fiction," 81; Foucault's alleged "literary period," 13–14; language and "subject" of, 34; veering from fear to laughter, 91. *See also* novels
liturgical calendars, 57
Logos (as reason), 34
"Logothetes" (Barthes), 58
Longtemps, 96, 102
Louis XV, King of France, 41
Luke (gospel), 83–84
Lupus, Marius, 132

Madame Edwarda (Bataille), 20
madness (or insanity): connection between literature and, 14; excluded in order to constitute modern culture, 15–18; lost language of Reason and,

17–18; Zacchia's summary of church law related to, 84. *See also History of Madness*

Making of Late Antiquity (Brown), 152

male-male relations: contrasted with marriage, 159; Foucault's chronological scheme and, 152; *History of Sexuality 2* on sexual acts within, 146, 181; sexual austerity of, 152; sodomy, 105–7, 112–16; stylization in ancient, 158–59. *See also* homosexuality; sexual activities

Marcus Aurelius, 139

Marcus, Stephen, 95

marriage: contrasted with male-male relationships, 159; "double sexual monopoly" of, 158; marital problematization of antiquity precursor to Christian chastity in, 158

"Masked Philosopher" (interview), 4–7

mask (image): Foucault's use of, 5–7; Nietzsche's association of divinity with, 7

master-slave relation (in Hegel), 73, 76

matador's eye (in Bataille), 24

Mecca, 51

mechanical and biomechanical metaphors, 75–77, 113

medical language: change in, 42; contrast between juridical definition of sodomy and, 105–6; space variously conceived in, 42–43

medical power: abnormalities treated by, 91; language and space of, 42–43; perversions emerging between law and, 107; sexual abnormalities defined by, 85–86, 91. *See also* forensic psychiatry

memory return, 102

metaphors: *démonstration*, 76; *dispositif*, 49; Foucault's deliberate variation of, 74, 76–77; Foucault's personifications of power and, 74–77; geometrico-logical, 76; hidden battle, 60; mechanical and biomechanical analogies and, 75–77, 113; *opérateur*, 76; philosophy and Greek erotic, 159; power described by contradictory, 81; *pulluler*, 76; Shepherd, 125, 129–30, 132;

vecteur, 76. *See also* Foucault's writings; languages

Mettray (penal colony), 57

"micro-physics" (of body), 45

misogyny, 184–85

modernity: Baudelaire on antiquity and, 157; Christian pastorate as prelude to governmentality in, 126–32; Cynicism in, 188, 191; ecclesiastical counter-conducts that drive towards, 139–40; Foucault on Baudelaire's notion of, 156–57; Foucault on pastoral care for sex before, 119–24; marks triumph of epistemological over ontological Christianity, 140; medical power of forensic psychiatry in, 85, 108, 116–17; philosophy as discourse about, 177. *See also* penal reform

Le monde–dimanche (Foucault interview), 4–7

Montaigne, Michel de, 192

morality: codes and behaviors in history of, 150; Foucault on kinds of, 150–51; Foucault's interest in continuity of, 151

moral problematization: "arts of existence" and, 150; distinguished from prohibition, 149; moral subjectivation and, 150–52. *See also* Christian moralities/ethics; sexual problematization

murmuring, 33, 60

music: ancient sense of care and, 187; Foucault's learning form from, 1

My Secret Life, 96–97, 99

mysticism. *See* Christian mysticism

Natural History (Pliny), 166

Nerval, Gérard de, 14

Nicomachean Ethics (Aristotle), 109

Nietzschean images: "masked philosopher" and anonymous author, 5–7; masks associated with representations of divinity, 7; present pictured between past and future, 163; time that resists representation, 174; Zarathustra, 22, 24, 28

Nietzsche, Friedrich: Bataille and Klossowski as readers of, 14; Burckhardt as teacher of, 154–55; conception of power in, 73; Foucault's model for writing, 1, 9, 98; his charge against Socrates, 187; his judgment on Euripides, 181; his preference for reading ancient philosophers, 123–24; in Foucault's canon of "mad" writers, 14; language after dialectic and, 22; Masked Philosopher's allusions to, 5–7; "transvaluation of all values" in, 190; unmasking of religion by, 25. See also death of God

Nietzsche's titles: "Ariadne's Lament," 182–83; Beyond Good and Evil, 7, 73, 183; Dionysus Dithyrambs, 182; Gay Science, 28, 73; Will to Power, 73; Zarathustra, 73, 102, 182, 190

Norm/normalizing: disciplinary function of, 53–54; Foucault's interest in sexuality as, 102; psychiatric opinion as, 71–72. See also abnormals/abnormalities

novels: Balzac-type, 36; Blanchot's image of bodies of words in, 36; Égarement (Crébillon), 70; Foucault on the "problem of fiction," 81; Foucault's last lecture series and Proust's, 179; History of Madness and Blanchot's distinction of, 36–37; Indiscreet Jewels (Diderot), 97–99; Lautréamont-type, 36; Pauliska (Reveroni), 70; Rivage des Syrtes (Gracq), 77–81. See also literature

obedience, 130–31. See also resistance
omnes et singulatim (in Stanford lectures), 125
"On the Government of the Living" (Foucault), 123, 132–39
"On Other Spaces" (Foucault), 165
"On Some Motifs in Baudelaire" (Benjamin), 155
ontological (or bodily) Christianity, 140, 190–91
opérateur, 76
oracle at Delphi, 181, 182
Order of Things (Foucault), 10
Organon (Aristotle), 109
oripeaux (of power): Christian forms of,

141; "earnestness" as clever version of, 147; Foucault's on nature of, 134; Foucault's representations of, 142
"Other" (in Christian rhetoric), 167
"other life" (Cynicism), 191–92
Other Victorians (Marcus), 95
"outside": Foucault on Blanchot's experience of, 34–35; Sade and, 34

pagan antiquity. See Greco-Roman antiquity
"Painter of Modern Life" (Baudelaire), 155
Panopticon: discipline and, 54–55; exposes the body to the gaze, 54; Foucault's spatial analogies to power and, 164; perfect control over bodies within, 57–58, 61; utopian association with, 57–61
"Paris of the Second Empire in Baudelaire" (Benjamin), 155
parrhesia: current forms of, 186; description of, 180; examples of in Euripides's Ion, 181–86; Foucault's lecture series on, 179-187
partage, 16, 18, 48
Pascal, Blaise, 15
pastoral practices. See Christian pastoral practices
Pastoral Rule (Gregory the Great), 132
Paul (apostle), 166
Pauliska (Reveroni), 70
penal reform: arising from brute exercises of power, 113; Discipline and Punish on stages of, 47–52; failures of so many schemes for, 56; fantasizing a power without oripeaux, 134; Fourierist attacks on "false," 59; Panopticon as model of, 54–55, 57–61; Parisian prison rules (1838), 41–42; religious practices adopted by, 51–52, 57; supplice provoking several movements of, 48, 54; treatment of body and soul under, 44–47, 61–62; utopian association with Panopticon and, 57–61. See also crime; Discipline and Punish (Foucault); modernity
penance. See public penance

Penderecki, Krzysztof, 87
perception and writing, 5–6
"Père Angélique" (in Bataille), 20
personifications: Christian, 84–87;
    Foucault on risks of hyperbolic, 83–84;
    Foucault's succession of, 74–77; histori-
    ography and, 81–84; "homosexual," 66;
    temptation to personify power, 82
personnage, 6, 55, 105, 160
perversions: doubling sexual acts with,
    106; emergence between law and medi-
    cine of, 107; Foucault on multiplication
    of, 104–8. *See also* abnormals/abnor-
    malities; sexual problematization
phalange, 57
La phalange (Fourierist newspaper), 57
Phenomenology of Spirit (Hegel), 73
Philosophy. *See* Greek philosophy;
    Western philosophy
Piranesi, Giovanni Battista, 1
Plato: *Alcibiades* by, 186, 187; Foucault on
    erotics of, 159–60; Hellenistic self-trans-
    formation and, 174; *History of Sexuality*
    2 on Platonic valorization of love, 159–
    60, 162; *Laches* by, 186, 187; *Laws* by,
    158; narration of Socrates's death, 187;
    Statesman by, 131
Platonists, 191
pleasures: Foucault on meaning of, 118;
    moving to "care of self" from "use of,"
    161; reading Foucault as, 3; stylistics
    (*stylistique*) of, 154
Pliny, 166
population: biopower and, 127; govern-
    mentality and, 127–32
Possession of Loudun (Certeau), 87–91
power: changing its scripts for resistance,
    91; dangers of writing about, 3–4;
    Discipline and Punish on mutations
    of, 47–52, 102–3; expert opinion and,
    67; Foucault's disinterest in theory of,
    127; *History of Sexuality* 1 and analyt-
    ics of, 108–11; *King Ubu*'s caricature
    and conventions of, 69–71, 72, 90;
    justification of judicial punishment,
    45–46; Nietzsche's description of, 73;
    Panopticon automating, 54; religious

ethics and, 4; sexuality and, 103, 112-
    15; spatialization of subjects by, 164;
    understood as relation and art, 111–15;
    vivid stories told by strong, 47. *See also*
    Christian pastoral power
power forms: anatomo-politics and spe-
    cies body, 113; comic, 67, 69–71, 72, 79,
    90, 91; correlated with objects and sub-
    jects, 45–46, 55–56, 102–03, 112; "flesh"
    as form of Christian, 88; Foucault's
    lectures and academic, 82; imagined,
    109–10; master-slave relation, 73, 76;
    medical and psychiatric, 42–43, 85–86,
    91, 107, 108, 116–17. *See also* forms
power imagined: anachronistic represen-
    tations in, 73, 82, 110; effects of igno-
    rance on, 72; power's concealments
    and, 82–83, 147; three errors in, 72
power-knowledge: biopower and, 113;
    correlated with produced objects,
    45–46, 86; concealing itself, 82; self as
    artifact of, 148; sexuality produced by,
    103. *See also* knowledge
power language(s): description by mul-
    tiple, 71–74; Foucault lectures on
    inherited images of, 71–74; Foucault's
    succession of metaphors and personifi-
    cations, 74–77; Gracq's *Rivage des Syrtes*
    on, 77–81; metaphors clashing in, 81;
    oripeaux of, 134, 141, 142, 147; *quadrillage*
    and relationship of bodies to, 48, 49,
    164; spatial and temporal analogies for,
    164; temptation of personification in, 82.
    See also languages; space of language
"Preface to Transgression" (Foucault):
    Bataille's language and images in,
    19–21, 22, 23; "blasted stump" in, 21,
    25; contradiction of limited transgres-
    sion in, 22, 23; failure of language
    in, 22–23; resemblance to "Prose of
    Actaeon," 27; sexuality linked to death
    of God by, 21; structure of, 21–24. *See*
    also Bataille, Georges
"Prose of Actaeon" (Foucault): approach
    to Klossowski's corpus, 27–32;
    Christian conversion in, 30; con-
    tradictory female-divine in, 31–32;

Nietzsche in, 28-29; resemblance to "Preface to Transgression," 27; rules for Klossowski's characters summarized by, 29–30; translating Klossowski into another genre, 32–33. *See also* Klossowski, Pierre

Proust, Marcel: Foucault's last lectures likened to, 179; guide for Foucault's writing, 98–99; *History of Sexuality 4's* editorial state likened to manuscripts of, 121; *Longtemps* in, 96, 102; modern discourses of sexuality and, 96–97

psyché, 191

psychiatric opinions. *See* expert opinions

psychiatry of delinquency, 106

"psychic energy," 74

Psychoanalysis of Fire (Bachelard), 110

public penance: Fabiola's, 136–37, 138, 139, 141, 142; later requirements for, 138–39; theatrical, 141

pulluler, 76

punishment: Delinquent and, 54–56; *Discipline and Punish* on changes in, 47–52; judicial justifications for, 45–46; signs and, 50–52; torture as, 41, 44, 46–47, 49; without *oripeaux*, 134. *See also* discipline

quadrillage, 48, 49, 164

queer theory, 93

Quaestiones medico-legales (Zacchia), 84

quinte, 194

rape: "Ariadne's Lament" as, 182–83; *Ion* and, 181–86; truth telling in accusation of, 183–84

reader(s): author's body and, 193; "eventual," 6; Foucault's discontinuities and, 143–45; *History of Sexuality 1* and unmet expectations of, 145–46; Kant on author and, 177, 178; mistaking ironic for literal, 93; physical traces left by, 3-4. *See also* authors

Reason: distinction between Madness and, 15–18; division and forms of, 18; lost language of Madness and, 17–18. *See also* Western rationality

religion: Foucault's interest in, 8–10; interpretation of signs by, 175–76; Nietzschean mask and, 7; Nietzsche's unmasking of, 25; penal reform as reformation of, 54–56; personifications of, 84–87; speech about bodies in, 10. *See also* Christianity; sacred

religious camp, 141, 142

religious moralities: effect of modern norm on, 54; ethical codes defining, 4; rhetoric of survives in antireligious speech, 104. *See also* Christian moralities/ethics

religious signs, 175–76

Renaissance Self-Fashioning (Greenblatt), 155

repression: history of sex as beginning with, 108; power not merely, 72; Victorian era, 95, 98–99

resistance: authorization to write about others', 184–85; bodies as site for, 85, 87–91; "convulsive flesh" as effect of, 86, 87–91; dependent on coding, 111; Foucault's writing as, 198; "getting outside" as image for, 164; power's adaptations to, 91; violence done to women and, 183–84. *See also* obedience

Reveroni Saint-Cyr, Jacques-Antoine de, 70

reversed eye: Bataille's image of, 23; speechlessness and, 22

rhetoric: "Other" in Christian, 167; *parrhesia* and, 180–86, 190

Richlin, Amy, 143

ritual(s): Acéphale and, 21; ancient gesture of manumission, 174; Christianity's records of, 197; cry and, 182; *exomologêsis* as bodily alethurgical, 135–36, 137, 138, 139, 141; Fabiola's public penance as bodily, 136–37, 138, 139, 142; Foucault's lectures as alethurgical, 180; *partage* as, 48; sacrifice as, 25, 47, 158; Seneca's emancipation of self as, 174; *supplice* and, 46–47; truth telling as, 134. *See also* Christian confessional practices

Rivage des Syrtes (Gracq), 77–81

Rule (Benedict), 132

Russell, Ken, 87

sacred: absence of, 14, 20-21, 118; Bataille and relocation of, 24–25; Bataille's spaces and, 20, 22; canon of "mad" writers and pursuit of, 14; history of term, 9–10; madness and, 14; outside language, 36. *See also* religion

"sacred sociology," 25, 26

sacrifice: modern self without Christian paradox of, 140; rituals related to, 25, 47, 158; self-sacrifice in Christianity, 138, 140; Socrates's dying words on, 169, 173, 187

Sade, Fourier, and Loyola (Barthes), 58

Sade, Marquis de: "experience of the outside" in, 34; hatred of virginity by, 31; juxtaposition of philosophy and erotic episodes by, 22

Sales, Francis de, 166

Salmagundi (periodical), 153

savoir: connaissance and, 177–78; understood as artisanal or compositional, 178

scientia sexualis: ancient erotic stylization and, 150; *ars erotica* and, 124, 145–46, 150; Christian "repression" in fact inaugurates, 115–16; description of, 98; development of the discursive practice of, 103; forensic psychiatry as animating, 108, 116; Foucault on development of, 124–26; Foucault on escaping from, 116–18; Freud's "pansexualism" as form of, 115; gay liberation trapped within, 108; late pagan teaching as basis of, 124–26; Lawrence and triumph of, 115; sexuality as correlate of, 103. *See also* sex

scientific knowledge: Bachelard on, 110; power of medical versions of, 42–43, 85–86, 91, 107

Second Analytics (Aristotle), 109

"Secrets of a Man" (Guibert), 198

security: biopower and, 127; governmentality and, 127–32

self: ancient practices for decentering, 173–74; asceticism as suspicion of, 190;

Christian roots of hermeneutics of, 138; curiosity and detachment from, 148; dandy and making of, 155–57; epistemological Christian self and modern, 140; etho-poetic writing as shaping, 149; *exomologêsis* and, 135–36, 137, 138, 139, 141, 142; flesh and speaking of, 126; hermeneutics of text and of, 139; Kant on government and, 176; "pragmatics" of, 178; truth obligations and technologies of, 135

self-care: ancient development of, 173; Cynics' truth telling and, 191; metaphysical knowledge and, 191; move from "use of pleasures" to, 161; paradoxes of ancient, 174. *See also epimeleia*

self-fashioning: dandyism as, 155–56; historical relation in, 157; moral domain for, 150; space for, 157; temporal element of, 163; theater and, 190

Seneca, 174

Septimius Severus, 133

sex: *ars erotica*, 111–12, 145–46; "austere monarchy" of, 116; authorization for writing and, 184–85; Christian confession and definition of abnormal, 85, 86; claim of sinning against, 104; correlate and mask of modern power, 113–14; doubled as perversions, 106; modern attributes of, 94; passed from religion to medicine, 91; premodern pastoral care for, 119–24; reproduction as matrix for abnormal, 85; sexuality contrasted with, 98. *See also* gender; *scientia sexualis*

sexual activities: Diderot on narration of, 97–98, 116, 118, 189, 198–99; dreams of, 160; Foucault not writing history of, 97–98, 144; homosexual defined in relation to, 107. *See also* male-male relations; sexual problematization

sexual austerity, 150, 152, 162

sexuality: abnormality characterized in relation to, 85–86; Christianity in history of, 103–5; correlate of modern power, 103; death of God and rise of, 21, 23–24; discontinuity in notion of,

145; Foucault's "hypotheses" for history of, 124–26; *History of Sexuality 1* on genealogy of, 119; modern power's invention of and uses for, 112-114; normalization and, 102; obligation to confess one's, 86; pastoral power and history of, 125, 126–27; "problem of," 85–86; will to knowledge and history of, 108. *See also History of Sexuality 1*

sexual morality: codes, behaviors, and ethics in, 150–51; continuity and discontinuity of, 151; perversions multiplied in, 104–08; stylization in contrast of ancient and Christian, 152. *See also* abnormals/abnormalities

sexual problematization: abnormalities and, 85–86, 91, 144; historical shifts from boys to women to children in European, 161; *History of Sexuality 2* on, 157–67; stylization of ancient homoerotic relations and, 150, 158–60. *See also* moral problematization; perversions; sexual activities

sexual reproduction, 85

Shepherd: as Christian metaphor, 125, 132; transfer of the flock's sins onto the, 129–30

simulacrum (Klossowski), 28–29

sin(s): confessional proliferation of sexual, 117; *exagoreusis* as verbalization of, 135–36, 137, 138, 139; Fabiola's, 136–37, 138, 139, 141, 142; "flesh" as source of, 125; symbolic relationship between the body and, 142; transferred from flock to shepherd, 129–30. *See also* transgression

society: allegorized as city, 51; context for contrasting utopia and heterotopia, 165–67; Foucault's decoding of Fourier's, 60; Foucault's writings informed by disciplinary, 59; imaginary utopian, 57–62, 165–67; responding to a ritual cry, 182. *See also* heterotopia

Socrates: death of, 187; last words of, 169, 173, 187; Nietzsche's accusation against, 187; transformation of subject by, 173

sodomite: homosexual contrasted with, 105–7, 117; recalled in expert opinion, 66

solidarity, 130

Sontag, Susan, 141

soul: ancient exercises for body and, 148; body displaced by modern, 45, 56, 106; direction of, 132, 139; *Discipline and Punish* as history of the modern, 45–46, 102–3; mapping faculties of, 164; modern pastoral power and, 88; philosophy as hospital for, 173; Platonism identified with, 191; prison of the body, 45

space: bodies analyzed in, 48, 52–53; body as, 36; Collège de France as academic, 64; cultural, 29; discipline bounded by, 53; discursive, 72; empty, 16, 20, 21, 24, 33, 35; erotic, 159, 181; "flesh" as, 138–39; gender segregation and, 158; historical, 16–17; judicial, 67; medical conceptions of, 42–43; metaphors for power and, 60, 76, 159, 164–65; middle, 28, 91, 107, 150, 157; mirror, 28; "On Other Spaces," 165–66; sacred, 22; self-fashioning and, 157; sexuality arising from empty cultural, 113; sexuality in domestic, 158; social, 166; textual, 61, 162; theatrical, 32, 38, 69, 198; virtual, 30. *See also dispositif*; heterotopia; *quadrillage*

space of language: appearing when speaking subject disappears, 34–35; Blanchot and, 34; lost language of Reason and Madness, 17–18. *See also* languages; power language

species body, 113

speech: Blanchot on, 33; Christian control of sex in, 85–86, 88–89, 120; Christian varieties of, 46, 94, 104; citizen, 182; confession as "speech act," 139, 181; cry and, 183-185, 191; expert, 66–67; Foucault imitating Christian, 9; free, 95; "I" and, 35; King Ubu's, 70–71; legibility of bodies and, 185; *logos* to *bios*, 187; loss of, 22, 29, 136–37, 198–99; mad, 13–14; origins and boundaries of, 179, 189; pastoral, 90–91; psychiatric opinion as nonjudicial, 71–72; religious rhetoric persisting in liberatory, 104; revolutionary, 107; ritual and bodily, 10, 112; unreported, 44; utopian, 57. *See also* languages

spiritual direction: ancient and Christian, 180; truth telling in, 180, 186

spiritual exercises, 171–72

Spiritual Exercises (Ignatius of Loyola), 171

spirituality: contrast between philosophy and, 171; mysticism and, 172; shifting meanings of, 172; transformation of embodied subjects and, 172–73

Stanford University, 122, 125

Statesman (Plato), 131

Stesilaus (in *Laches*), 187

Story of the Eye (Bataille), 24

style de vie, 153–54

style(s): anonymity as, 153; art compared to, 154; beyond codes, 153–54; changing over time, 162–63; *chrêsis aphrodisiôn*, 154; "earnestness," 147; expressed through image, 153; Foucault's "rupture" in, 147; mutating circulation of, 158; Platonic dialogues as dramatizations of, 153, 159–60; searching to find a place for homosexual life through, 153; *style de vie*, 153

stylistics (*stylistique*): *History of Sexuality 3* and sense of, 152; of pleasure, 154

stylization: across activities, 154; aesthetics and, 154; ancient male-male relations and, 158–60; Ariès on "stylistics of existence," 152–53; art criticism as origin of term for, 154; central to contrast with Christianity, 152; changing over time, 162–63; compared to game, 159; distinguished from moral law, 151–52, 161; erotic, 158–60; genealogy of, 152–57; modernity and ancient template of, 157; philosophy and erotic, 159; space of ancient erotic, 150. *See also* ars erotica

stylize (*stylizer*), 152

possibility of new, 164–65; subjects of sexuality produced by, 146; spirituality and, 172–73

subject: conditions for forming moral, 187; correlated with power, 55–56, 102–03, 112; desiring, 147–49; *ethopoiêsis* and, 199; forms for constituting, 178; Foucault's writing and transformations of, 3–4, 38–39, 45; "games of truth" and, 191; gaze and gazer as, 42, 54; "Hermeneutic of the Subject," 170–78; internal spatialization of, 164; Socratic conversion of, 173; space of language and speaking, 34–35; spirituality and transformation of, 172–73; truth and, 171

subjectivation: auto-subjectivation and trans-, 174; "liberation" as, 147; moral, 150-51

supplice: "convulsive flesh" and, 89–90; *Discipline and Punish* on, 46–47, 48, 50, 65; Foucault's lectures compared to, 65; Jesus's crucifixion as, 46–47; liturgy of, 50; penal reform movements provoked by, 48, 54

Surin, Jean-Joseph, 90

"Suzerain" (Char), 18

S/Z (Barthes), 111

Tanner Lectures, 122, 125

technê, 111–12, 154

territory: biopower and, 127; governmentality and, 127–32

theatrical body, 38

theatricalization: Foucault and Sontag on, 141; Fabiola's public penance as, 136–37, 138, 139, 142; Foucault staging of sickness, madness, and crime as, 140–41; Nietzsche's transient event, 140–41; power's *oripeaux* and, 134, 141, 142

theories: analytics in place of, 108–11, 115; modern meaning compared to Greek, 111-12; Foucault's disinterest in pursuing unified, 121, 127; queer, 93

"theoretical shifts" (in Foucault), 176–79

time: analogies to power and, 164; bodily, 1, 3, 195, 197, 199; Nietzschean, 174; "On Other Spaces" and, 165–66; philosophical conceptions of, 175

To the Friend Who Did Not Save My Life (Guibert): blurring memoir and fiction, 194; death of "Muzil" in, 194–96; Lindon's reaction to, 200

torture: *Discipline and Punish* opening with, 41, 44, 46, 49; liturgical Christianity justifying, 46–47; *supplice* form of, 46–47

"Transcendental Analytic" (Kant), 109

transfiguration, 163

transformation: Christian paradox of permanent, 136, 142; Christianity and historical, 180; conceived as intensity rather than sequence, 175–76; flesh as space of, 138–39; Foucault on subjected bodies and, 3–4, 38–39, 45, 138–39, 199; hope of scandalous bodies for ethical, 199; religious images and, 104; Socrates on, 173; spirituality and, 172–73

transgression: contradiction of limited, 22, 23; relationship to sexuality, 23; ritual of empty, 22. *See also* sin

"transvaluation of all values," 190

Tree of Redemption, 29

truth: access to, 171, 173; obligations in relation to technologies of the self, 135; oracle of "oblique" god and, 181; two modes of relation between subject and, 171

truth telling: alethurgy as liturgy of, 133, 134; conditions of subjectivation, 187; confession and, 132-39, 179-80; Creusa's accusation and origin of, 183; Cynics and, 186–91; Euripides's *Ion* and types of, 181–87; *exagoreusis*, 135–36, 137, 138, 139; *exomologêsis*, 135–36, 137, 138, 139, 141, 142; Foucault's interest in how bodies manifest, 135; oracular, 181, 182; relation between form of life and, 187–88; rituals of, 134; spiritual direction and, 180, 186

Ubu. *See King Ubu* (Jarry)

Ubu power: conventions of embodied power and, 69–71, 72; disregarding impressions, 134–35

University of Tokyo, 122, 124, 125–26, 145–46

University of Vermont, 123, 133

Ursulines, 87–90, 164

utopia: contrasted with heterotopia, 165–67; utopian communities, 57–62

Van Gogh, Vincent, 14

Vatican II, 132

vecteur, 76

veridiction, 135

Veyne, Paul, 131–32, 187

Victorian era: *History of Sexuality* on, 95, 98–99; *My Secret Life* and, 96–97; "we others" as new Victorians, 95

violence: Damiens's torture and writing of, 41, 44, 46, 49; liturgical Christianity justifying, 46–47; rape and writing of, 181–86. *See also* crime

virginity, 31, 166

vocable, 163, 164

Voeltzel, Thierry, 197, 199

Watanabe Moriaki, 140

Western philosophy: access to truth through, 171; contrast between spirituality and, 171; dandy and, 156; definition of, 171; discourse of modernity in, 177; "living body of," 148–49, 192; present linked to past of, 148; Socrates's last words as founding, 169, 173. *See also* Greek philosophy

Western rationality: alternatives to modern development of, 170; Logos and birth of, 34

Whiting, John, 87

Wilde, Oscar, 141

Will to Knowledge (as subtitle for *History of Madness*), 95

Will to Power (Nietzsche), 73

witchcraft, 87

writing: authorial mask and, 5–7; authorization for, 184–85; bodily act of, 3, 191–92; compared to medical diagnosis, 198; Cynics' cry and, 191–92; dictated by sex of author, 185; embodied lives and, 3–4; etho-poetic, 149, 199; last book as goal

of, 200; risk necessary in, 185; "seconds of satisfaction" at completion of, 200; self-writing, 139; verbalization of self and, 139. *See also* authors; Foucault's writing
Wycliff, John, 132

Yourcenar, Marguerite, 1

Zacchia, Paolo, 84
Zarathustra, 22, 24, 28, 37
Zarathustra (Nietzsche), 73, 102, 182, 190
Zeller, Florian, 123